FATHER OF THE YEAR

FATHER
OF THE
YEAR

Bill Rundle: All-American Jekyll and Hyde

GLENN PUIT

BERKLEY BOOKS, NEW YORK

THE BERKLEY PUBLISHING GROUP
Published by the Penguin Group
Penguin Group (USA) Inc.
375 Hudson Street, New York, New York 10014, USA
Penguin Group (Canada), 90 Eglinton Avenue East, Suite 700, Toronto, Ontario M4P 2Y3, Canada
(a division of Pearson Penguin Canada Inc.)
Penguin Books Ltd., 80 Strand, London WC2R 0RL, England
Penguin Group Ireland, 25 St. Stephen's Green, Dublin 2, Ireland (a division of Penguin Books Ltd.)
Penguin Group (Australia), 250 Camberwell Road, Camberwell, Victoria 3124, Australia
(a division of Pearson Australia Group Pty. Ltd.)
Penguin Books India Pvt. Ltd., 11 Community Centre, Panchsheel Park, New Delhi—110 017, India
Penguin Group (NZ), 67 Apollo Drive, Rosedale, North Shore 0632, New Zealand
(a division of Pearson New Zealand Ltd.)
Penguin Books (South Africa) (Pty.) Ltd., 24 Sturdee Avenue, Rosebank, Johannesburg 2196,
South Africa

Penguin Books Ltd., Registered Offices: 80 Strand, London WC2R 0RL, England

The publisher does not have any control over and does not assume any responsibility for author or
third-party websites or their content.

FATHER OF THE YEAR

A Berkley Book / published by arrangement with the author

PRINTING HISTORY
Berkley mass-market edition / May 2009

ISBN: 978-0-425-22866-1

BERKLEY®
Berkley Books are published by The Berkley Publishing Group,
a division of Penguin Group (USA) Inc.,
375 Hudson Street, New York, New York 10014.
BERKLEY® is a registered trademark of The Berkley Publishing Group.
The "B" design is a trademark of The Berkley Publishing Group.

PRINTED IN THE UNITED STATES OF AMERICA

10 9 8 7 6 5 4 3 2 1

Most Berkley Books are available at special quantity discounts for bulk purchases for sales, promo-
tions, premiums, fund-raising, or educational use. Special books, or book excerpts, can also be
created to fit specific needs.

For details, write: Special Markets, The Berkley Publishing Group, 375 Hudson Street, New York,
New York 10014.

This book is dedicated to the memory of Layne Staley

CONTENTS

CONTENTS

INTRODUCTION

I first came into contact with Bill Rundle and his murder case in 2002 as a reporter for the *Las Vegas Review-Journal* newspaper. I spent fourteen years in the news business and covering crime for Nevada's largest newspaper. While the experience made me jaded about violent criminals, I must admit I was fascinated with Rundle during his murder trial. He did not seem like other hardened, violent criminals. He sniffled in a tissue in front of a jury. He appeared kind and courteous. It bothered me to think of him that way, though, because I knew what Rundle was: a notorious con man and cold-blooded killer, suspected of two murders, a man against whom the authorities were seeking the death penalty.

I concluded later that this was what Bill Rundle does. It's his MO. He cons people into liking him. He could con you even when you *knew* he was a killer. He wants everyone around him, including a jury, to think of him as just some average guy who somehow, some way, ended up in the middle of a horrific murder case, due to fate and circumstances beyond his control.

I met with Bill Rundle in 2006, and interviewed him extensively. It was one of the most interesting interviews I've ever conducted, because Rundle didn't hold back. He talked extensively about the death of his wife, Shirley; and the disappearance of his mother, Willa; and his life as a con man. He told one hell of a story, and when I was done with the interview, I'd confirmed my initial suspicions of Rundle: He's an extremely rare person. He has an ability to lie and deceive that is far beyond your average con man's. The man is a cold-blooded killer, and yet his social skills are so advanced that he can look you in the face and make you feel like he's an okay guy.

The facts of this book were gathered through interviews and public record materials, including trial transcripts, grand jury transcripts, police reports, and police actions. There were some people involved in this case who declined my requests for an interview. I respect their decision to do so. In those instances, as allowed for under the First Amendment and Nevada's open records laws, I used their comments to law enforcement and in trial proceedings to provide an account of their experiences with Rundle.

You'll note as well that this book is dedicated to the memory of Layne Staley, whose incredible musical talents changed my life. If you are struggling with addictions or severe setbacks in life, stay strong and keep the faith in yourself. I know you can make it. If you would like more information on how you can help people struggling with heroin addiction, please visit www.laynestaleyfund.com.

Finally, I want to thank you for reading my books.

Glenn

1 . . . VANISHED

For we wrestle not against flesh and blood, but against
principalities, against powers, against the rulers of the
darkness of this world, against spiritual wickedness.

—Ephesians 6:12

On August 19, 2002, part-time Las Vegas housekeeper
Janet Bertrand was pet-sitting at the home of a friend,
Mary Truedsdale*, in southwest Las Vegas, when Bertrand
noticed something unusual across the road on Poppywood
Drive.

The large, stucco home belonged to Bill and Shirley
Rundle, and the couple's garage door was open.

Bertrand is a pretty woman who, in addition to house-
keeping, at times brought in an income pet-sitting and
watching homes for those on vacation from the Las Vegas
neighborhood near Tropicana Avenue and Buffalo Drive.
It's a nice area, just down the road from big-money homes
in the exclusive, gated community of Spanish Trails. The
neighborhood on Poppywood Drive is one of big stucco
structures, desert-and-grass landscaping, scattered skimpy
trees in the front yards, sport utility vehicles in the

* Denotes pseudonym

driveways, and the brown mountains of the Mojave Desert in the distance.

Bertrand had previously worked at the Rundles' home across the street, and when she saw the garage door open, she sensed there might be something wrong.

The Rundles *never* left their garage door open.

"It just didn't look right," Janet said. "They never leave the garage door open, even when they go to the mailbox."

Bertrand knew that the Rundles were former casino workers: Bill Rundle had been a security guard at the downtown Union Plaza casino and later at the King 8 casino, then a small-time gaming joint off Interstate 15, and Shirley Rundle had worked at the Union Plaza, the Stardust, the Hacienda, and the Luxor. The Rundles told neighbors they'd retired from the casino business and started a PostNet postal business in the upscale Las Vegas shopping center on West Charleston Boulevard.

They seemed like a normal couple.

The Rundles' huge, new, three-thousand-square-foot house was a short drive down Tropicana Avenue to the Orleans casino, some low-rent weeklies, and second-rate gaming properties leading to the big names of the Strip—the MGM, the Luxor, and the Mandalay Bay to the southeast. It was a nice neighborhood in a big city, and it attracted some very decent people. David and Mary Truedsdale had moved into their house across the street around the same time as the Rundles in 1996.

Bill Rundle, fifty-seven, was a big, gray-haired man who could have easily passed for a typical Vegas retiree. He was tall, with a long but deep face, a modest roll around his waist, and he often wore shorts and a short-sleeve shirt on his aging but still large six-foot-four frame. He also wore very thick, rather dorky glasses on his sagging face, and often a baseball cap.

Bill Rundle had a good personality. He was funny, witty, and easy to talk to, although when Rundle was at home, he spent most of his time sitting in his living room in a creased leather chair watching sports on television and worshipping his gambling tickets.

Bill's wife, Shirley Rundle, was a sixty-three-year-old Filipino immigrant who was, by all accounts, sweet, pretty, and very nice. She had jet-black hair and was five feet four inches tall. She was a dignified woman, and those who knew her said her nature was as soft as a butterfly's flight. She wore colorful clothes, and she, too, wore big glasses.

Shirley Rundle kept a meticulous house. The kitchen in the home on Poppywood Drive was spotless. The furniture in the residence was high-end and dust-free. There were never any clothes or magazines strewn about. There was nice art on the wall, and there were throw rugs in the living room. Shirley had a specific place for each and every one of those throw rugs.

Janet Bertrand was particularly fond of Shirley Rundle, whom she considered to be a very kindhearted soul. And she knew that the Rundles had endured a terrible tragedy nearly two decades earlier when Bill Rundle's little boy from a prior marriage, Richie Rundle, had been killed by a drunk driver. Since that day, the Rundles had kept a shrine to the dead child in an upstairs room of their home.

"A glass cabinet with a lot of memorabilia and certificates and stuff," Bertrand said of the shrine to the child.

Neighbors and friends unfailingly described Shirley Rundle as a quality individual, a soft, loving woman who cared very deeply for her family. She was from a very large family in the Philippines, and she loved each of her brothers and sisters dearly. She regularly kept in touch with her relatives in the Philippines by phone even though she was more than 7,300 miles away from them. She cooked a Filipino dinner for one of her neighbors on a special occasion.

Shirley Rundle also had a beautiful daughter, Magda Belen, who lived nearby in Las Vegas. Magda, like her mother, is a very attractive woman with shining black hair,

and she and her husband, Rodel—a chef in Las Vegas—
helped manage the Rundles' postal store. The Belens also
gave the Rundles a remarkable gift from God in the form
of a precious little granddaughter named Gretchen.

The Rundles adored the ten-year-old child.

It seemed to neighbors, from a distance, that the Rundles
were normal grandparents with a successful, happy marriage. The couple's white Buick sedan was adorned with
the personalized license plate HONYBUN, and "honeybun" was what the husband and wife called each other.

"That's from the first time we went to California," Rundle would tell people. "When I drove Shirley to California
to take my son Richie to Disneyland, we stopped in Baker,
California, and saw [a restaurant mascot] called Bun Boy."
The mascot had struck Shirley as funny and charming, and
she'd started calling Bill her "bun boy." The name quickly
evolved into "honeybun."

Neighbors thought the Rundles were in love.

"Everything that we saw indicated that they got along
extremely well and they were a loving couple," Mary Truedsdale recalled. "They were devoted . . . They loved to travel
together." The Rundles even brought souvenirs home for
their neighbors from their vacations.

When the Rundles weren't traveling, neighbors saw the
couple "almost every day," Truedsdale said. "At least my
husband did, at the mailbox. And, uh . . . [we saw them] frequently at church and at events that we had on the block."

Truedsdale's husband, David, noted that the Rundles
seemed to spend a lot of time together.

"I can't remember when they'd [go] anywhere separately," he said. "They always went [places] together. Rarely
would he have gone somewhere in the car by himself."

The Rundles even went to the mailbox together.

"They're devoted," David Truedsdale said.

But about two months before the garage door was left
open, something unusual did happen on Poppywood Drive.

The Truedsdales said they had a strange encounter with Bill Rundle. David ran into Bill Rundle at their neighborhood's collection of mailboxes, and during the encounter, Rundle blurted out a startling revelation.

"It was almost like he was reluctant to say it, but he wanted to say something," Truedsdale recalled. "So it was brief, and kind of abrupt. He said, basically, there are some Filipinos who . . . asked [him] for a large sum of money."

David Truedsdale was shocked. He and his wife had moved to the neighborhood because it was nice and safe, and now his neighbor was telling him about some sort of extortion operation out of Southeast Asia?

Mary Truedsdale recalled what her husband told her about his strange conversation with Bill Rundle. "He mentioned to my husband that he was concerned because there was a car that kept parking down the street . . . [They were being] pressured by some Filipinos that Shirley had reached out to help," Mary Truedsdale said. "They thought they were rich because they owned a PostNet with their kids, and they were demanding that they loan them money. [It was] in the thousands."

David Truedsdale knew Shirley Rundle was from the Philippines, too, and he was a little bit alarmed.

"[Rundle said,] 'They come over here from the Philippines and they see we live in a two-story house and we've got a store, and they think we're millionaires,'" David Truedsdale quoted Bill Rundle as saying about the extortionists. "He said, 'They've asked us for a large sum of money, and I told them, "We don't have that kind of money." They started demanding money.'"

"He says, 'I think they're stalking us . . . I think they're watching the house, watching where we go and what we do,'" Truedsdale said. "He didn't even tell me what kind of car, and I didn't ask," the neighbor added. "I was reluctant to, you know, pry."

A few days later, he talked to Bill Rundle again over the

phone, and during the conversation, Rundle said he was looking out his window for possible assailants. He seemed very paranoid about the extortionists who wanted his money.

"[Rundle] said, 'Right now, I'm looking out of the upstairs here with my binoculars because I think they're stalking us,'" Truedsdale said. "'I think they're watching the house. Watching where we go and what we do.'"

David Truedsdale was becoming extremely concerned. He asked Bill Rundle if there was anything he could do to help, but Bill Rundle said there wasn't.

Shirley Rundle's daughter, Magda Belen, is a professional, intelligent woman with flowing black hair, a pretty face, and a soft-spoken, kind nature clearly inherited from her mother. In August 2002, Belen was a young mother herself, and she appreciated the loving relationship she had with her own mother. The mother and daughter were the best of friends who spoke to each other almost every day on the phone, and they felt very lucky to be able to live so close to each other in Las Vegas.

"She was actually my mother, my friend, and my sister," Belen told *Dateline NBC*. "I don't have any brothers and sisters, so she's everything to me."

The Rundles and the Belens made for a very loving and trusting family, and at the center of the family structure was the Belens' daughter, Gretchen, an intelligent and sweet girl like her mother and grandmother. In 2002, Gretchen was the most cherished part of the Rundles' lives.

The Rundles never hesitated in telling friends how special a child Gretchen was, and they spent as many hours as possible with their granddaughter. The proud grandparents kept two rooms for her at their home, and took her on vacations to Disneyland.

On August 19, 2002, Shirley told her daughter she would pick up Gretchen at the Rundles' PostNet store on West Charleston. She planned to take her granddaughter shopping for school clothes and then to the movies.

To Magda Belen's surprise, however, Bill and Shirley Rundle were no-shows for their scheduled pickup of Gretchen that afternoon. Magda worried about her mother and stepfather when they failed to appear, since she knew in her heart that Shirley Rundle would have called if she was not going to pick up her granddaughter as scheduled.

"It was not like them," Magda Belen said. "I know them too well. Every time they would promise my daughter something, they would make it a point to talk to her and see her."

The last time Magda had seen the Rundles was at the PostNet store on August 17, two days earlier. There hadn't been anything unusual about the meeting, and the last conversation she'd had with them hadn't revealed anything abnormal. Shortly after their no-show, however, Magda and Rodel Belen asked Gretchen to call her grandparents at their home and on their cell phones. There was no answer to the calls.

"We still kept trying and trying to contact them," Magda Belen said. "The whole day, no call, no show. So I just told my daughter, 'Maybe they went someplace to do something very important.' So I told her that we're going to try again the very next day."

The Belens returned home and worried throughout the night. The next morning, Magda Belen got out of bed and called her mother again.

No answer.

Something is definitely wrong! Where in the heck are they? she wondered.

Rodel was at the PostNet store around noontime when he got a phone call from Janet Bertrand. Bertrand knew the Belens because of her prior stints cleaning for the Rundles, and she knew that the Belens were the Rundles' closest relatives in Las Vegas. She decided to call the Belens to let them know that the garage door had now been open for a second day in a row.

Rodel Belen immediately called his wife.

There is something wrong! This is not like them!

Magda was now very worried, and she asked her husband to go over to her mother's home to see if he could learn anything about the Rundles' whereabouts. Rodel Belen drove to the Rundles' home, where the garage door was indeed open. The Buick sedan with the HONYBUN license plate was missing, and when Rodel walked into the garage, he found something very curious. On a door leading from the garage to the interior of the home was a handwritten, unsigned note in black ink. The note read:

Alarm is set! Be home 09-06. Emergency trip to the Philippines.

Rodel Belen thought the note was strange.

"The first thing that came to mind [was that I was] hoping they're in good condition and that there's really not a big problem back in the Philippines," Rodel Belen said. "[I assumed] that they had to go real quick. Since it's my wife's family, I went over to her and asked her to call the Philippines to find out what was the emergency."

Rodel Belen brought the note home to show his wife, and Magda Belen inspected it. The contents of the note seemed preposterous. Magda was very close to her mother, and Shirley would never go to the Philippines without calling her.

Something is terribly wrong! Please, God, let them be okay!

"I was actually really worried because I'm thinking,

'Okay, this is not like them,'" Magda Belen said. "There is no way they would leave the country without letting me know."

Magda drove quickly to her parents' home and saw for herself that the garage door was open and her mother's car with the HONYBUN tag was gone.

"We actually checked [the house] and went around in the backyard to see if there [was] anything suspicious," Magda Belen said. "There was nothing. We were hoping to at least, you know, to be able to peek through the windows, but all the blinds, the curtains, were all closed. [That's when] we called the cops."

Three Las Vegas police officers in tan uniforms arrived at the home of Bill and Shirley Rundle and greeted Magda Belen on the evening of August 20. The officers and neighbors realized immediately that Belen was very upset and that she sensed something was amiss because her mother would never leave suddenly for a family emergency without telling her about the trip.

"I recall the daughter and the son-in-law, and the little granddaughter, I believe, showed up a little later in the evening," neighbor Mary Truedsdale said. "I went over to see them and talk with them, and comfort them."

Officer William Ronald Webb Jr. was one of the three officers to respond to the scene and he spoke with Magda Belen. He and the other officers got as much information as possible about the Rundles from Belen. He wrote down Bill and Shirley Rundle's height and weight, and he learned that the older couple hadn't been seen for three days. The officers were shown the note on the interior garage door, but Webb and his fellow officers didn't quite know what to make of its contents.

Alarm is set! Be home 09-06. Emergency trip to the Philippines.

"Basically, she [Magda Belen] told me the circumstances," Webb said. "She said that she had the right to go inside the house, but she didn't have access to the key right now, and a locksmith was called out."

A locksmith opened the interior garage door, and the officers went inside.

"We just checked every room and every closet and under the beds, and we were checking [for] people in need of medical [attention] or anything of that sort," Webb said. "We left what's called a red card. It's a contact card with information that we had entered the residence and we'd conducted a welfare check."

Belen waited anxiously outside for the officers during their search, but she learned nothing new about the fate of her mother and stepfather.

"They came out after they checked the inside of the house, and then they told me there was nothing suspicious inside," Magda Belen said. "Everything [was] in order."

The officers invited the Belens to go inside the home.

"I went inside with my daughter and husband . . . [and] we looked around," Magda Belen said. "We started downstairs and upstairs, and then looked around again downstairs and everything looked in order, so I didn't think anything [was] wrong."

Officer Webb used to work patrol at Las Vegas's McCarran International Airport, the nation's seventh largest airport; given the contents of the note found on the Rundles' garage door, he called his colleagues at the airport to see if there was any record of the Rundles having been there.

"I had them check the parking lots for the [Rundles'] vehicle to see if maybe they did go to the airport and catch a flight," Webb said. "No vehicle at the airport. No ticket purchases."

Webb ran the white Buick sedan license tag HONYBUN through a police records check, but got no hits. The officers urged Magda Belen to consider filing a missing persons report on her mother and stepfather. Belen agreed. Even though nothing unusual was found in the Rundles' home, she was still sick from worrying. She knew something was wrong. She called her mother's relatives in the Philippines when she got home, just to make sure her mother wasn't there, but no one had heard from Shirley Rundle.

"No one knew anything," Magda Belen said. "No emergency in the Philippines."

Magda Belen called the six major airlines that fly routes to the Philippines, and determined that her mother and stepfather had not purchased any tickets. She could not take the worry any longer. On August 21 she went to the Las Vegas Police Department's Missing Persons Detail on West Charleston Boulevard and reported Bill and Shirley Rundle missing.

She wrote a narrative for detectives about the events of the last forty-eight hours. The following are excerpts from her missing persons report:

> *My mom and step dad's housekeeper said she saw their garage door open and noticed it's open for two days. She called our [PostNet] store and told my husband, so I had him and my daughter go to their house. They found the garage door open and found a note on the door in the garage stating "Alarm is set! Be home 09-06. Emergency [trip to the] Philippines!" My husband brought the note to me. I told him there's no way either one of them will leave a note saying the alarm is set nor their date back home . . . If there's any emergency trip, they call me and let me know.*
>
> *I called our relatives in the Philippines and they said there's no emergency. My mom will only go there if any of her brothers or sisters is in trouble. I talked to my aunts in the Philippines and they talked to the rest of the relatives. One aunt said she talked to my mom*

*last Saturday, 8-17-02, which was the last day I saw
her. I called ADT alarm company and the operator
said their alarm is temporarily out of service. I went
back to their house with my husband and daughter and
I called the police. After waiting for about one and a
half hours outside their house, three policemen came.
They called the locksmith to open their door at the garage, they got it open and the alarm was NOT SET AT
ALL! Policemen checked but didn't find anything suspicious. They left a pink form on their kitchen counter
and advised me to wait until Thursday to file this report. I told the officers that I . . . will [file the report].*

The missing persons report fell on the desk of Detectives Thomas Marin and Gary Sayre. The two detectives
are strapping old-school cops who see hundreds of missing
persons cases every year, and they make no assumptions
on them; every case is different, with different facts, and
those facts dictate their actions. The detectives met with
Magda Belen the next day and learned all the details they
could about how the Rundles had vanished. The authorities
did a little investigating and learned that, as of August 22,
the Rundles had several bank accounts at Bank of America
in Las Vegas. One money market account belonging to Bill
and Shirley Rundle had had several recent large withdrawals, and the account was drained. The Rundles also had
another account, a savings account, containing $1,629.
Three weeks earlier, on July 30, $1,300 in cash had been
withdrawn from that account.

The detectives noticed in the Rundles' bank records
that Bill Rundle had also held a joint bank account with his
mother, Willa Rundle, who was listed as being eighty-
seven years old. Bank records showed that Willa Rundle's
$1,200 Social Security check was deposited into the ac-
count on the first of every month. A check of transactions
in the account showed $18,300 in cash had been recently

withdrawn from the account shared by Bill and Willa Rundle, over a time span of twenty-three days.

Clearly, this was valuable evidence. The withdrawals
raised the very real possibility the Rundles might have
cashed out of Vegas and split, like thousands of people
have done over the years. The cycle has repeated itself
time and again. People flee the city out of either frustration
or dismay over the lack of second and third chances they'd
searched so desperately for there.

The detectives interviewed the Rundles' neighbors, and
they learned of the reported extortion plot from David
Truedsdale, but they also received information from the
same witness that seemed to contradict the idea that the
Rundles had left for the Philippines.

"You know, everything points to the fact that they
weren't about to go anywhere," David Truedsdale told the
police. "And as to a trip to the Philippines, I was standing
by the mailbox with him one day, and we were talking with
the mailman, and [Bill] said, 'Uh, we're not going back to
the Philippines for a long time. It's getting very dangerous
over there.' He said, 'I'm not going back there for a long
time.'"

Truedsdale told police his theory: that the Rundles "got
so scared of these people [attempting to extort them] that
they ran off to hide and didn't have time to tell anybody.
But you'd think they'd call the kids."

Another witness, Steven Williams, forty-one, gave Detective Gary Sayre some background information about
the Rundles' business and Bill Rundle's love of televised
sports.

"I used to work as a supervisor at the OfficeMax on
Charleston and Fort Apache, and their PostNet is right in
that shopping center," Williams said. Williams's wife was
also from the Philippines, so he had a lot in common with
the Rundles. "I would walk over and send my packages
through them to my wife, and buy phone cards. [Shirley]

was Filipino, and she had the best rate for phone cards so I [could] call my wife."

Williams used to play semipro baseball and football in Canada, and he and Bill Rundle loved to discuss sports.

"Bill's an athletic freak. He loves athletics. And, because we developed a relationship in talking about sports, I even showed him my highlight tapes from college."

He portrayed Bill as a man who, at times, could seem distant.

"Sometimes it was just the way he'd talk and his demeanor. He was humble, and we'd just be talking stats and who's going to make the play-offs and everything, and then he'd just turn toward the laptop and . . . he wouldn't say nothing."

Williams said the Rundles had an "immaculate" house that gave the impression of wealth. "He's got a beautiful house," Williams said. "He's got this big-screen TV, two dishes so we can watch multiple games."

Steven Williams noticed a change in Bill Rundle, however, when the topic of his dead son, Richie, came up.

"I got close to Bill because of the portrait he showed me of his eleven-year-old son [who was killed]," Williams said. "I couldn't believe that happened, and . . . that's terrible for somebody to go through." And even though the men had a relaxed relationship, Rundle clearly still had trouble talking about Richie. "He praised his eleven-year-old, he [had] pictures of him around the house, and [he] showed me his drawings, and stuff like that. [Bill] was just embarrassed to talk about him. You talk about depression. That's when he would sort of go in[to] a funk."

Williams was baffled as to what could have happened to the Rundles. Sayre told the witness that the police were at a loss to explain their whereabouts.

"Basically, they've disappeared," Sayre said. "We haven't a clue as to what happened to them. The house was open. They are gone. Their daughter doesn't know where they are. There's been no contact."

The detectives needed more information, but Magda Belen knew something was wrong. She begged Detective Marin to meet her back at her parents' house because she wanted to go back inside and look around again. This time, she wanted to perform a very detailed examination of the home on Poppywood.

"He [Detective Marin] asked me if I had full access to the house first," Magda Belen said. "He said he needs a search warrant to do that. I told him I used to have a key, but I don't have that anymore."

Marin agreed to meet Belen at the house anyway, but he knew he could not go into the Rundle home without good reason.

"[She] stated she wanted to go back inside her parents' residence, but [that she] had secured the doors when the patrol officers were there," Marin said. "I told Belen I could not get into the residence without going through the legal process. [She then] asked me if I could meet her at her parents' residence, and I told her yes."

Marin planned to do interviews with the Rundles' neighbors. He knew driving to the home that this was not a standard missing persons case. Usually, an older couple just doesn't go missing like this, and the note about the trip to the Philippines was extremely curious. As the sun was about to set, Marin parked his car. Magda Belen was already trying to gain entry into the Rundles' home. She had friends with her—a woman named Christine Lopez, and Lopez's husband. The three had been able to open the door to the home, and Magda Belen invited Detective Marin inside.

"We looked around," Belen said. "We searched downstairs, and then we went upstairs, [and] when we went upstairs, we went in the closet, and I noticed the luggage was

missing. I pointed that out to Detective Marin. Detective
Marin told me [that] maybe they are on vacation, and he actually gave me his business card, and he said, 'Well, if you
find anything, then go ahead and contact me,'" Belen said.

Belen wanted Marin to stay. Marin, however, returned
to his car with a plan to interview more neighbors. After
Detective Marin left, Magda walked back into the home
with the intention of scrutinizing every single detail in the
residence. Slowly, as she walked through room after room,
she realized some things in the home weren't quite right. A
few items were missing. A cordless phone with caller ID, a
portable stereo, and Bill Rundle's laptop computer were all
gone.

"[I was looking for] my mother's address book because
I wanted to contact more people, and it was not there either,"
Belen recalled.

Now that she was inspecting the home with more diligence than before, Belen also noticed that some throw rugs
were out of place in the Rundles' living room. Her mother
never left the throw rugs out of place. Belen walked into
the living room and started to straighten out the rugs.

"My mother fixed her area rugs on the floor, and I noticed [that] they were all crooked," Belen said. She went to
adjust one.

"I had to bend over and fix it and pull it. When I was
trying to lift it up, I saw a stain. Like a dot. So I lifted the
whole thing up, and that's when I saw the blood."

Magda Belen nearly collapsed from the sight.

"I was in shock," she said. "I was crying, and my friend
had to pull me out of the family room. She had to take me
to the living room."

Marin was still in his car when Magda Belen emerged
with her friends. She was frantic. The detective noticed the
panicked look on her face.

"[She was] extremely excited and nervous and I could

see tears are in her eyes," Marin said. "She told me she saw a bloodstain on the carpet."

Marin rushed back into the home and saw the bloodstain, which was large and looked like someone had tried to cover it up with the throw rug.

"[It was located] in the family room, just underneath the chair," Marin said. "I made the request that Homicide be notified, and we called the crime scene analysts, additional support teams, and additional missing persons detectives."

2 ... DECEIVER

Bill Rundle was brought into this world in North Hollywood, California, on October 5, 1945, during a truly great American era.

World War II was just over. The dominant media publication was *Life* magazine. There were fewer than seven thousand television sets in the land, and velvet-voiced singers like Bing Crosby and Johnny Mercer ruled the airwaves with hits like "White Christmas" and "Accentuate the Positive" on the radio.

Bill Rundle was born the only child of two very loving and special parents: Richard and Willa Rundle. Richard Rundle was the general manager of a Cadillac dealership in posh, celebrity-laden Beverly Hills, and Willa Rundle, an immigrant from Austria, ran the Rundle roost at the family's North Hollywood home on Kraft Avenue.

Willa Rundle was a strong-willed woman, and the disciplinarian of the family. She had been born on March 28, 1915, in Austria.

"Her father and mother had money and somehow got

her to America in the late 1920s," Willa's son would later say. "They settled in Costa Mesa, California, and lived there for several years. Both of her parents died early in her life, and she was raised by her grandmother."

Willa later got a job at Republic Pictures in Studio City, California, where she worked as a secretary. She received her certificate of naturalization from the United States on March 24, 1944, and she was proud to be an American. She was a woman of small frame and large character who smoked cigarettes and tended to wear gaudy clothes; her tastes in jewelry included big earrings combined with her favorite Mickey Mouse watch. Willa could be quite sassy, according to those who knew her, and she wasn't afraid to tell you what she thought, whether it was good or bad.

But while Willa Rundle had a colorful personality and a fondness for Disney, she was all business in her daily life. Willa had a strong work ethic, and she believed all her hard work and personal sacrifice was an investment in the future of her son. She was a model of domestic efficiency in her home, where she cooked breakfast for her husband and son daily. She packed the lunches, washed and ironed the clothes, cleaned every day, and then produced a full dinner at the table every evening.

"My mom was a great mom," Bill Rundle said. "I never lacked for anything . . . I remember my mother forced me to take piano lessons, and I hated that. I wanted to play baseball and all the other sports, but I had to learn that damn piano. She wanted me to become the next Victor Borge or Liberace."

Richard Rundle, Bill's father, took great pride in providing for his family. The Rundles were definitely upper middle-class. They had a pool in the backyard of the home, and Richard drove a Cadillac. He smoked Pall Malls and Camel nonfilter cigarettes, pretty much from the moment he woke up until he went to bed at night. He was a clean-cut man of five feet ten inches tall, with receding hairline, and he made his living peddling Caddies underneath the sweet, glassy-blue skies of Beverly Hills.

"Presley, Marilyn Monroe, and Nat King Cole were in the dealership," Bill Rundle bragged. "Nat King Cole was a very good friend of my father. I worked there for two summers, and I got to see a lot of celebrities coming in and out."

Father and son were close, and shared a passion for sports. Richard and Bill Rundle were both hardcore fans, and there were plenty of sports to follow in Southern California. Richard Rundle took his son to as many professional sports events in the region as possible.

"My father was an exceptional man," Rundle said. "A kind, caring . . . great father. My relationship was good with both my parents. My parents had very few fights that I can remember. The only arguments they had were over my father's heavy drinking. My mother was not a bad or mean mom. She was always kind to me and my friends."

The younger Rundle was quite handsome as a young man, though he didn't particularly resemble either of his parents. "My dad was five feet ten inches, and my mom was five feet four inches," Rundle said. "I ended up six feet four inches tall, so everyone kept joking with me that I was adopted. I didn't fit."

His father regularly urged him to play sports, and Rundle took up basketball and baseball. He enjoyed both. As he blossomed from middle school to high school, his height kicked in. It was a huge advantage on the basketball courts of North Hollywood.

"At six feet four, I would play forward in the early sixties because there were not a lot of big strong kids. The athletic ability in the fifties and sixties was nowhere near where it is now, and we didn't have the equipment to better ourselves like they do now," Rundle said.

Bill Rundle's parents had high expectations for their son, but for some reason, he showed little interest in school.

He made his grades, barely, but he didn't excel. Instead, he focused on playing hoops, chasing girls, and hanging out at the beach or on the side of a pool. His unwillingness to focus on his schooling was an ongoing battle with his parents. Willa Rundle, in particular, wanted her son to apply himself.

But Rundle was lazy, which led to some terrible grades in high school. He was getting mostly Ds in his junior year at North Hollywood High, and he worried that his parents were going to find out.

"I was doing really poor in school even though I was a smart person," Rundle said. "I was basically ashamed of this report card, and I didn't want to show my mom and dad the grades I was getting."

He decided to forge his report card. A close friend helped Rundle carry out the plan.

"Forged the card, six subjects, all As and Bs, and I took it home," Rundle said. "My parents were happy. I took it back, my friend signed my dad's name to the real card, and I turned it back in to my teacher."

It was a bold betrayal of his parents, and Rundle felt guilty. Yet he also found the experience thrilling because although it scared him, he'd gotten away with it.

"I was terrified by it," Rundle said. "When I was a senior, I changed a little bit for the better, and I was getting Cs and Bs again. I realized I didn't want that to happen again. I didn't want to do something like that again."

Rundle somehow managed to stay on the North Hollywood baseball and basketball teams despite his laziness and poor grades, and he managed to graduate from North Hollywood High in 1963 with a diploma that noted Rundle "has been found worthy in character and citizenship."

He enrolled that year at Los Angeles Valley Junior College with a dream of playing baseball at the school, but by the end of just one semester, he'd failed on both the field and in the classroom. He was an average athlete who didn't work very hard at his baseball skills, and he was receiving a steady stream of Ds and Fs in all of his classes.

Rundle makes no excuses for his failure.

"Anything that was hard, where I'd have to study, I just figured the hell with this, and I dropped a class," Rundle said. "When I registered [for classes], I would sign up for like fifteen credits a year and finish six to nine credits. I didn't have the desire to take certain math courses or certain science courses. I could learn it, but I didn't want to."

Rundle dropped out of college in 1963, and faced the daunting task of telling his parents. Instead of breaking the news to Richard and Willa, however, Rundle once again started to lie. He crafted a façade: he told his parents he was doing well in school, when in fact he wasn't even in class. Instead, he spent his days hanging out on campus and playing intramural basketball at the college gym.

"When I dropped out of college, every day my parents thought I was still in school," Rundle said. "In college, there were no report cards. You get your grades, and that was it. I just hung around the gym every day playing basketball. I dropped out, [but] I stayed there."

Willa and Richard Rundle simply took their son's word that he was still attending college.

The deception continued for three full years.

"With my parents, it was funny," Rundle said. "They never asked me how I was doing. They didn't check on what I was doing. Everything I told them, they believed."

3 ... 1968 (GAMBLER)

You find all types at the racetrack. During the summer months, particularly in August at the more established Thoroughbred American tracks like Saratoga Springs in beautiful upstate New York, you can see ultrarich men dressed in suits and top hats, with their wives wearing long flowing dresses, looking as if they had walked to the track from the 1800s, to take in the ponies.

There is, of course, another side to the sport of kings, and it ain't as pretty. At a lot of other racetracks, you'll find plenty of chronically drunken gambling derelicts taking tokes off cigarettes as they piss away their last buck on a sport that offers truly terrible odds.

Bill Rundle liked the contradictions at the racetrack, and he liked gambling on the ponies. His love affair with horse racing started in the 1960s when, as a young man, a friend took him on a day-long jaunt to the Santa Anita track. Rundle was intoxicated by the excitement. He was hooked on the feel of betting on a horse and seeing the beautiful animal charging around the final turn. It made Rundle's heart race.

"I love the track," Rundle said. "Thoroughbreds. In 1965, I probably hit seventy of the seventy-five days at Santa Anita. That was a long drive from the San Fernando Valley, but I just loved it.

"You could go in there, you could walk around and talk to the jockeys at that time—Bill Shoemaker and Jerry Lambert," he said. "And, as soon as Santa Anita closed, Hollywood Park would open. I was not a hundred-dollar player because I didn't have money like that. But I just enjoyed it so much. "

Rundle liked studying the race sheets and picking the horses. It captivated him. Gambling on horses—and on all sports—was like a hit off a crack pipe for him. Once he got the taste, it was damned hard to stay away. If he had money in his pocket, he kept going back.

Rundle spent most of his time in the early to mid sixties gambling on horses and playing pickup basketball in college gymnasiums. The track and the basketball court were escapes for him. He had no job, he spent his days at the racetrack and playing sports, and all the while, he was lying to his parents about whether he was even in school.

"I was a gambler," Rundle said. "At times, I was real good at picking the horses, and I studied them hard. I got the racing form at night, and by the next morning, I'd have it all handicapped for the next day. I went to the track every day and basically pissed away my years from eighteen to twenty-one.

"[When I was at the track] I was hanging around some of the seediest individuals you'd ever want to meet in your life," Rundle said. Still, he claimed, "they were all good people. They weren't killers, but if you needed anything, they'd get it for you."

Rundle made friendships with several low-level con

men at the track. One was a professional forger and con named Eddie Franklin* who, during breaks between races, befriended Rundle and schooled him on the value of faking documents and how to do it. Rundle was a liar, but so far the only document he'd ever forged was his report card. What Franklin was telling him piqued his interest. If he could fake documents such as a bogus college diploma, it would help him further the lie he'd told to everyone: that he was in school and now close to graduating.

"I got a four-year diploma—a fake one," Rundle said. "San Fernando Valley State College which is now Cal State Northridge."

A copy of the diploma, according to police records, was awarded to William James Rundle, "who by diligent study has successfully completed the prescribed four-year course at Valley State College in the state of California, and by proficiency in scholarship has merited graduation and is hereby awarded this bachelor of arts in business."

The diploma was supposedly signed by Dr. Ralph Protor, president, of the college, on June 7, 1968, but in reality, it was a complete fake.

"When I said I finished at LA Valley College, I told everyone I had to go to a four-year college to get my degree," Rundle said. "I stepped on campus at San Fernando Valley State College probably forty times, all to watch basketball games. I never even enrolled there. I just told everyone I had enrolled and I [made] my own diploma. The [fake] diploma I had was better than the real one."

At times, Rundle thought about getting his act together. He thought about a real career in teaching and coaching at some school somewhere, but this was impossible without a degree or a work ethic.

"I could have gotten a job at the General Motors plant

* Denotes pseudonym

in Van Nuys, California," Rundle said. "I told my dad how much I disliked school, and my dad said he could get me a job there, but he also wanted me to graduate because he wanted a better life for me. "

Little did old man Rundle know that his son wasn't even in school.

In 1967, Rundle was swimming at an apartment complex pool in Southern California, wasting some more time away, when he met the woman who would soon become his first wife. Sarah Reitig* was a kind, very attractive, full-bodied Southern California girl with dark hair. She was young when she met Rundle—just eighteen—and she found the twenty-two-year-old young man with a somewhat dark tan handsome.

"I thought he was nice-looking, and he seemed like a nice person," Reitig said. "I was so young and very naïve."

Rundle told Reitig a lie right off the bat: He said he was in college. Within the first few moments of the conversation, there appeared to be some chemistry.

"She was pretty," Rundle said. "She was swimming, and I hit on her at the pool. Her parents hated me, and my parents weren't really crazy about her. She was Jewish. We were Christian. Five months later, we got married, and we didn't tell anybody.

"We kind of eloped at a justice of the peace in California," Rundle said. "I had no job, and she thought I was going to college. I lied."

"We started hanging out together, and then it was probably six weeks after we decided to get married during my split shift from work," Reitig said. "He was a couple of years older than me, and we secretly got married."

* Denotes pseudonym

At first, the couple kept quiet about their marriage. "Nobody knew—just the two of us," Rundle said. But eventually the secret got out, and the news didn't go over well.

"I couldn't keep it a secret any longer, and the crap hit the fan when everyone found out," Rundle said. "Our parents thought we were too young to be married, and my parents were angry."

"His father was very nice—a really nice person," Sarah Reitig said. But Rundle's mother was a different story. Reitig said Willa Rundle was furious. The first time she met Willa, Bill's protective mother made it perfectly clear she was angry with her son and Sarah.

"The first time I met Willa, I was told she was from Austria, and when we were leaving, she chased us down the street yelling at me," Reitig recalled. "She didn't like me. I think it was because I was Jewish and also because we ran away and got married secretly. My parents were not happy, either."

Rundle and his wife lived in a one-bedroom apartment in the Van Nuys area. For the first year of the marriage, Reitig worked at a telephone company and Rundle leeched off his wife's salary while he spent his time going to the track and playing hoops. Every morning, Rundle got up and told Reitig that he was heading off to class. In reality, he headed to the gym or snuck off to the racetrack with his wife's hard-earned money.

"I was going to the track every day, and my wife thought I was going to college," Rundle said.

In 1968, the couple moved to Las Vegas. They felt that Las Vegas might offer a fresh start, and Bill Rundle told his wife that he'd gotten a job working security for the Howard Hughes Corporation. In many respects, the city the Rundles arrived in in 1968 was far different from the Las Vegas of today. In 1968, there were only about 270,000 people living in the sun-baked Las Vegas Valley, and there

was always an element of mobsters, hookers, and low-level
hoods to be found on the famed Strip. Away from the
Strip, you literally could drive from one end of the Las
Vegas Valley to the other in just a few minutes, impossible
today in the city's gridlock traffic.

The city is very different nowadays. There is still a
locals' presence in Las Vegas, and many of the longtime
Vegas families hold powerful positions in gaming and
government. But the majority of Vegas residents today
are part of a new wave of Americans who moved to the
city from economically stagnant parts of the country over
the last two decades, in search of steady, consistent
work.

In 1968, though, Las Vegas was not yet the crazy big
city of never-ending suburbs and interconnecting freeways
that it is today. The city still had a small-town charm, and
its most valued resource—the casinos—were in the midst
of an ownership changeover from the mafia to Howard
Hughes, who was living as a recluse in hotels while his financial empire gobbled up Strip casinos. On the Strip,
there was no MGM Grand, Bellagio, Wynn, or Mandalay
Bay. There was instead the Aladdin, where Elvis Presley
married Priscilla in 1967, and a string of other properties
that illuminated the desert night. On one side of the Strip
were the Flamingo, the Sands, the Desert Inn, the Riviera,
the Thunderbird, and the Sahara. On the other side were
Circus Circus, the Stardust, the Silver Slipper, the Frontier,
the Castaways, Caesars, and Bill Rundle's favorite, the
Dunes.

Today, in an American megacity that loves to re-create
itself, many of these properties are only memories.

There is one thing about Vegas, however, that will always remain the same. It is still the best place in the world
to go to if you want to let loose and do the crazy things
you'd never do at home.

Bill Rundle gravitated almost immediately to the dark side of Las Vegas when he arrived in 1968. The twenty-three-year-old started hanging out at a nondescript pizza joint on the Strip about a quarter-mile from the Dunes. Rundle said the pizza joint was a gathering place for cab-drivers and some of the front-line laborers in the Vegas mafia racket.

"It was the hangout for shady people," Rundle said. "Shy-locks and loan sharks. It was a big hangout for cabdrivers and anyone who needed money, and I fell in with those people."

At the pizza shop, Rundle met a man he identified only as "Jasper." Jasper was running a criminal loan-sharking operation, and he put Rundle to work collecting money. Rundle was a big, muscular, healthy-looking young man who was willing to play tough guy to collect cash from those desperate enough to risk borrowing money from the mob, at ridiculous interest rates.

"Jasper would loan someone $500, and they would pay him back $25 a week in juice until the balance was paid in full," Rundle recalled. "They thrived on the fact that they [knew] the guy can't come up with the $500 at one time. They are paying $25 a week in interest for the rest of their lives. They can't come up with the $500, and the last pay-ment is $525. It's loan-sharking.

"Basically, I ran a few illegal things for him," Rundle said. "If you didn't pay them back, they wouldn't sue you. They'd probably just kill you. They were hard-core."

In retrospect, Rundle thinks he started hanging out with criminals like Jasper on the Strip partly because of a story his father had told him years earlier, about Vegas mobsters who had shown up at the Beverly Hills Cadillac dealership where old man Rundle worked and brought bundles of cash with them.

"[They] bought three Cadillacs from my dad in Beverly Hills," Rundle said, and they paid in cash, from "shoe boxes filled with one-hundred-dollar bills that had obviously been skimmed."

Rundle was curious about the financial profits to be had from crime. Now, in Vegas, he was starting to flirt with criminality himself by collecting for shylocks.

"It was an easy way to do things," Rundle said. "I was just looking for money to get by. I never did anything serious. A little collecting. I never harmed anyone. I just basically said, 'Hey, you owe him money, and you've got to pay.' I knew it was illegal, but it was so easy that I didn't really need to do anything else."

Jasper got Rundle a job at Nellis Cab Company, where Rundle did shuttle cab fares, but more often drove to the pizza parlor and then headed off to collect money for his "friends."

"No one knew I was doing this except the people I was hanging around with," Rundle said. "At times, I made decent money. At times I wouldn't make decent money."

When he wasn't collecting money for Jasper or driving cabs, Rundle was gambling on sports. He'd started his gambling career on the horses, but now he was gambling on his passions—basketball and baseball.

"I'd bet $10 to $20 on a baseball game, basketball game, or football game, depending on what the season was," Rundle said. "They didn't have cable TV back then, and it was all local television stations. Sports books weren't like they are now, where they have agreements with all the tracks for simulcasts. Back then, you couldn't see the games [you'd bet on] on television, so you would sit at the bar, drink, and watch as the ticker went by or wait until the next day and read the newspaper to find out the score.

"But let me tell you something—it was just like narcotics for me," Rundle said. "I spent a lot of time in the sports books."

While Rundle was spending his time getting drunk and gambling on sports, collecting for bad guys, or driving a cab, his wife was at home alone in the couple's one-bedroom apartment, and she knew nothing about what he was doing. She was kept completely in the dark. Rundle told Reitig he was working security for the Howard Hughes Corporation, and when he got home, he was verbally abusive to her.

"He was very controlling," Reitig said. "It was Bill's way, and that was the only way. I was so young and naïve. I thought whatever I'm supposed to do I'll do. Whatever he wanted.

"He had a real bad temper," she added. "Not yelling and screaming but acting out."

In 1968, Sarah Reitig got pregnant, and in December of that year, Rundle's first son, Justin*, was born in Vegas. Justin Rundle was, by all accounts, a wonderful, beautiful child, and the Rundles moved from the apartment to a two-bedroom rental home behind the Boulevard Mall in East Las Vegas.

Bill Rundle said he loved his son dearly, but Justin Rundle and Sarah Reitig would later question that. Rundle was rarely even around.

"I spent all my time in the sports books," Rundle said. "When I wasn't driving to get a few bucks on the meter and doing work for Jasper, I spent all my time in the race and sports books," or occasionally playing golf. Rundle was, over time, making more friends in organized crime, and his crime buddies liked to golf, so they would invite him along to play a round with them at Vegas's premier courses.

* Denotes pseudonym

"I played a lot of golf, and I loved it," Rundle said. "These guys got me into golf in '69-'70, and there were fourteen courses in the valley at the time. We played at the Desert Inn, the Tropicana, the Dunes, and I would go out with these guys and they would all pay, and the golf clubs would treat these guys like kings. It was basically the underworld, and they got whatever they wanted."

Rundle said, over time, his gangster buddies also wanted him to do some heavy lifting. They wanted him to be a full-fledged thug, but Rundle said he resisted, even though he knew he could've earned more money. He claimed that he didn't have the stomach for being violent.

"I was capable of earning a lot more, but I didn't want to do some of the stuff they wanted me to do," Rundle said. "They knew that I was closemouthed and that I didn't talk to anybody about anything they were doing, so I was okay, but they wanted me to become violent to make more money. They hurt some guys and did some terrible things, and I didn't want to do that."

Rundle recalled one dinner conversation where Jasper and his friends laughed about a guy going in front of a grand jury and testifying about someone in Jasper's close circle of friends.

"I didn't really know anything about it," Rundle said. "Two or three days later, over by Palos Verdes [in East Las Vegas], this guy and his wife were gunned down at night. This was 1970, and that stuff bothered me. I was hanging out with some bad people."

By 1970, Reitig had realized that Rundle was no ideal husband when she found out he'd lied about his job in Las Vegas.

"He told me he had gotten a job to do plain-clothed security for Howard Hughes Corporation," Reitig said. "One day I got a phone call, and it was from a cab company, and they asked for Bill Rundle. I said, 'Who is it and why do you want to get ahold of him? Why are you calling?' The person on the phone said, 'He works for us,' and that's when I knew he was lying. I'm just a very kind, good person, and I just trusted him with my life."

Rundle said that year his wife had what he described as a "kind of a mental breakdown."

"She became very paranoid and thought that some of my friends were going to kill her and stuff like that," Rundle said. "She didn't know what was really going on or what I was doing all day. She still doesn't to this day.

"So, her mother and father came up here in the middle of the night to Las Vegas with a moving van, packed all of her stuff up, took my son, and took her and moved back to Southern California," Rundle said.

Rundle was depressed over the development, and he started to drink heavily.

Bill Rundle had seemed to show little interest in his wife and child when they were in Las Vegas, but after a few months of hard drinking in Vegas by himself, he decided to chase after them and to try to make things right. He followed Sarah and Justin back to Southern California and Van Nuys with the idea that he would spend some time with them. Reitig reluctantly let Rundle back into her life, and the couple rented a home in Van Nuys. Rundle even went out and got a real job as a salesman with a third-tier insurance company. It was the first real job of his life, and Rundle didn't like what working felt like.

"I had to wear a suit and tie every day in Van Nuys, and they paid you $130 a week as a draw," Rundle said. "I was like, 'one thirty a week?' There were times when I [made] that in a day with what I was doing in Las Vegas for Jasper."

Nevertheless, the insurance job wasn't completely dissimilar to the one he'd had collecting for loan sharks.

"I didn't believe in life insurance," Rundle said. "They ran a scam called weekly premium. You would sell them to poor families, and they would buy one to two thousand dollars in burial insurance. That's all that it cost at that time to bury someone, and they would pay like two dollars and fifty cents a week.

"This company thrived on sending their agents out to collect this crap," Rundle said. "You would knock on the customer's door and hope they would have the ten dollars to pay for the entire month so you wouldn't have to keep driving your car back to them every week to collect two dollars and fifty cents a week. [Sometimes they couldn't even] pay two dollars and fifty cents, and some of them would cry on your shoulder, saying, 'I can't let my policy lapse,' and you would cover for them for a week. I felt so bad because they were in this type of financial shape. I just couldn't take it."

Bill Rundle met two coworkers at the insurance company who, like Rundle, loved to bet on the ponies. Joey Martin* and Frankie Schwartz† talked to Rundle about the horses every day, and pretty soon the trio started to make regular jaunts to the racetrack during work hours.

"We would go out to Santa Anita," Rundle said. "This was 1971, and we were going to the track every day. We used our own money—we didn't steal from the company or anything like that. I never stole a dime from the insurance company. Well, I guess I can't say that I never stole. I took a paycheck and didn't work. It was a different form of thievery."

Sarah Reitig, meanwhile, was again gravely disappointed in her husband. She'd given Rundle a second

---

* Denotes pseudonym

† Denotes pseudonym

chance, yet the couple argued frequently. At the same time, Willa Rundle was slowly warming up to her daughter-in-law, and she and Richard often gave Reitig help in raising Justin.

"She actually taught me how to cook," Reitig said. "She made the best snowball cookies. Willa, after she got over the initial shock [of the marriage], tried [to accept me]. But I knew where I stood with her. I took her son away."

The marriage between Reitig and Rundle was fatally flawed, however, and one day Bill Rundle just walked out on his wife and child. He simply vanished.

"I left her and got an apartment in Van Nuys," Rundle said. "I left her. I disappeared. She was just tired of it. She just wanted to take care of our son, and I would rather do nothing."

Reitig later told Las Vegas law enforcement that after she filed for divorce, she learned that Rundle had spent about $2,200 of her grandmother's $3,000 trust fund. And there was something else Reitig learned about her husband following the divorce: According to Las Vegas police, "toward the end of the marriage, [Rundle] was receiving his mail at another woman's house and hiding money from [Reitig]."

Reitig sued for divorce and got $40 a month in child support out of Rundle. More important, she and her son emerged with significant emotional scarring.

"He's my father," Justin Rundle would later tell Las Vegas authorities, but added, "You really couldn't call it a relationship."

Sarah Reitig and her son ended up moving to the same neighborhood in North Hollywood where Richard and Willa Rundle lived. And, according to Las Vegas law enforcement records, Bill Rundle's parents stayed relatively close to their son's first wife and their grandson.

"They lived right down the street," Justin Rundle said

of his paternal grandparents. "I spent a lot of time with them." The same could not be said of his father. "My father really wasn't—he wasn't the type of guy who was there."

4 . . . DARK HEART

I've got this terrible story to tell.

—Bill Rundle

Sherri Grayson* was from a good Catholic family in Southern California. In the early 1970s, she was working at a Bob's Big Boy restaurant in Van Nuys when a tall, handsome man and three of his friends walked into the fifties-themed burger joint.

Grayson was a young, innocent, and beautiful girl with blond hair and a great figure. The man strolling into the Bob's Big Boy was immediately attracted to her, and he introduced himself.

"I knew him as William Randau," Grayson told the author in a story for the *Las Vegas Review-Journal*. "I thought he was good-looking. He had dark hair . . . [and] he was the funniest guy in the world. That's what I fell for. He was funnier than hell."

The "William Randau" flirting with Grayson was Bill Rundle's alias. He had run out on his first wife and child,

* Denotes pseudonym

and the divorce from Reitig was pending. Now he was drawn to the gorgeous young Big Boy waitress seven years his junior. Rundle saw that Grayson had a very sweet, loving personality and, well, she was also very hot.

"I really liked her because she had long legs," Rundle said. "She was very, very nice, and she turned out to be the most wonderful person I've ever met in my entire life."

About a week after their meeting at Big Boy, Rundle saw Grayson sitting at a bus stop in Van Nuys. He pulled up to the bus stop in his old beater Chevy and offered her a ride home. She accepted the offer, and Rundle was quickly hooked on her.

"I had no ulterior motive except to give her a ride home," Rundle claimed. "I gave her a ride home, and then I started going into Bob's Big Boy every day."

Grayson and "William Randau" began dating. During their courtship, Rundle didn't mention that he was freshly divorced, or that he had fathered a little boy. Grayson introduced her new beau to her parents. Bob and Sheila Grayson* were strict Catholics whose big family also included Sherri Grayson's five brothers and sisters.

"She told me how strict her parents were," Rundle said. "I didn't tell her about my marriage. She told me her parents wouldn't like an older person, and that they would hate someone who had been divorced because they were a strong Catholic family, so I said, 'Gee, I like this girl a lot, and she's not going to go out with me because her parents are going to crap all over me when they find out that I was divorced.'"

But to Rundle's shock, Grayson's parents loved him. Rundle said when he first met them, he presented himself as "a nice, modest person."

"That was a flimflam," Rundle admitted. "But anyways,

* Denotes pseudonym

I took her out, and I told her parents we'd be home early—
we are just going to get a bite to eat—and I'd drop her back
off, and they liked me right away. So we had a great time
and laughed. I also told her, 'You've got to stop smoking.
You are nineteen years old, and that's terrible,' and that 'I
can't stand anyone who smokes. You've got to stop that.'
So she did. She stopped smoking, and her parents loved me
for that."

The Graysons figured that "Randau" must be a good
influence on their daughter. "Her father told me once, 'I
like you—you are a tremendous person,' " Rundle recalled.
Rundle became very close with the Graysons, and he liked
being a part of their family. He said he sat in the Graysons'
living room pretty much every night and drank beer and
watched television with his girlfriend's family, even though
"I was starting to have a terrible drinking problem. It was
getting brutal. I went to bars a lot, and I spent a lot of time
drinking beer."

Grayson's parents knew "William Randau" was a North
Hollywood boy, and they naturally asked Rundle about his
family. Rundle knew he couldn't admit that his parents
lived only a short drive away. If he did, the Graysons
would want to meet them, and his prior marriage and his
fatherhood would be exposed. Rundle made up a whopper
of a lie to explain to the Graysons why they couldn't meet
his parents.

"I told them my parents were wealthy and they were in
Europe traveling," Rundle said. "I told them, 'I never bring
friends over to their house.' "

Rundle told the Graysons that his parents were in the
mountains of Austria. It was a preposterous account, but
the Graysons bought it.

"It was stupid," Rundle said. "Ridiculous. It didn't make
sense, but they bought it completely. I was keeping my two
lives as separate as possible."

To prove that Willa and Richard Rundle were touring

Austria, Bill Rundle forged glowing letters from his parents to Sherri Grayson, postmarked from Austria. In the letters, the Rundles told Grayson how excited they were about her and how much they looked forward to meeting her.

"Then I started to fall in love with [Sherri] heavy, and I really liked her," Rundle said. "I wished I had met her way before my first wife."

Rundle came up with a plan. He contacted his old friend from the Santa Anita racetrack, forger Eddie Franklin, and the two met at a popular ocean-view restaurant in San Clemente called the Jolly Roger.

"I was totally honest because he was a hoodlum," Rundle said. "I told him I was there to get some fake ID. He asked, 'What do you need?' I said, 'I need a driver's license and a Social Security card.' I didn't need them to be real, but I needed them to be passable in case someone got into my wallet and looked at who I was."

In a couple of weeks, Franklin met Rundle again, and he produced picture IDs for "William Randau." With the IDs in hand, Rundle returned to Van Nuys and proposed to Sherri Grayson. Grayson, too, was head over heels in love, and she accepted the offer. Her family started planning a traditional Catholic wedding.

"The sad part is I wasn't after their money," Rundle said. "I wasn't after anything except for Sherri. I wanted to be with her. It was unbelievable how much I loved her and how much I wanted to be with her.

"So I proposed and everybody was happy," Rundle said. "But to marry into the Catholic religion, you have to attend classes and stuff like that, and so now I was going to these religious classes, and I basically had to become a Catholic. I'm going to these classes under a false name, and then they tell me they have to do an investigation into me."

Rundle met with a Van Nuys priest the next day. The

priest asked him questions pertaining to the background of William "Randau," and Rundle lied his way through it. Two days later, the priest died of a heart attack.

The wedding date for Bill "Randau" and Sherri Grayson was set for April 8, 1972, and Grayson's family went all out for the big day. They sent out invitations, they planned for the wedding at a Van Nuys area church, and they prepared for a smash reception and feast at the Grayson house. The Graysons were good people, and they wanted a special wedding day. As part of their preparations, they asked their future son-in-law for the mailing addresses of his parents and friends from North Hollywood who might want an invitation to the wedding.

Rundle was a nervous wreck. His parents didn't even know he was dating Sherri Grayson, much less engaged to her, and he was convinced that before he could marry her, someone was going to reveal him for the fraud that he was.

"They started to get the invitations together, and they wanted to know how many invitations I wanted, and of course, I wasn't going to send them out under a false name to all the people that I knew," Rundle said. "So I said my parents were still traveling in Europe and they weren't going to make it."

The Graysons also asked "William Randau" for a photo for the newspaper announcement of the marriage.

"I said, 'No, I'd just as soon not have a photograph,' and it still didn't ring a [warning] bell with them," Rundle said. "My dad read the paper every day, and he would have seen my picture in there next to 'Bill Randau marrying,' and so and so. There were so many red flags such as 'no friends,' and 'my family is still traveling.'"

Rundle invited just a couple of people to the wedding. He invited two gambling buddies—his best man was Joey

Martin, and he also invited Stevie Winchamp*, a good friend he knew from drinking beer at the Vegas pizza parlor. Both men knew Rundle was going to marry Sherri Grayson under a false name, and they went along with the cruel trick.

"They were totally in on it," Rundle said.

Martin stayed at Rundle's parents' house in North Hollywood the night before the wedding. Richard and Willa Rundle were already terribly distraught over their son's recent divorce from Sarah Reitig and what amounted to his abandonment of his own baby son. Rundle wasn't about to tell his parents that he was marrying again, under an alias, the next day.

"My mom and dad were married 58 years," Rundle said. "They were married that long, so how could I get a divorce in a few years? They didn't even know who Sherri was. They had no idea about anything I was doing, and so I told my parents I was moving to Albuquerque, New Mexico, with Joey Martin," Rundle said.

The next day, Rundle and Grayson had a beautiful wedding in Van Nuys, and Martin and Winchamp both offered remarks about their longtime friend "William Randau" at an exquisite reception at the Grayson home.

"[The Graysons] paid for it—thousands of dollars. Martin and Winchamp both spoke a few words about me, and I was sitting there, and I couldn't believe it," Rundle said. "I was like, 'God, these guys are as good as I am.' Martin played the whole role. Total cover."

The couple received hundreds of dollars' worth of gifts. Rundle's friend, Martin, gave them a spectacular thirty-one-inch television.

"At this time, that was an expensive TV," Rundle said. "Beautiful. I've never seen a set so nice in my life. He

* Denotes pseudonym

bought it for us as a wedding gift, and he never paid a dime because he had a false ID. He bought it under an alias and never paid a dime for it."

There was, however, a scare during the couple's wedding reception. Rundle said a woman at the reception named Amy Boyne* recognized him. Boyne knew him because Rundle had dated a friend of hers years ago. Fear temporarily paralyzed Rundle when she approached him. If he was found out now, in the middle of his wedding reception, he might be beaten to a pulp, or worse, by Grayson's brothers.

"She came over, we started talking, and she said, 'Didn't you used to go out with Traci Heminock?'" Rundle recalled. "And I said, 'Yeah I did.' And I had to try and think of something real quick, but she didn't remember my last name. She started showing me some pictures of Traci because they were really good friends."

Boyne didn't realize Rundle was marrying under a false name, and after the reception, the "Randau" couple headed off for their honeymoon to San Clemente. They also went to Reno and then stopped in Vegas, where Rundle rented an apartment at the old Leroy Continental apartments on Sierra Vista. It was the same complex where he'd rented an apartment at in Las Vegas with his first wife.

"I was just trying to keep it secret," Rundle said. "I had buried myself so badly at that time that I couldn't go back to being Bill Rundle, normal working person. It was too late. I had gotten in so deep.

"Unbelievable how easy identity theft is. If I had've gone into that business, I could have made a fortune. I'm not saying I would've done it, but it's easy. It's amazing how stupid the American public is. It's unbelievable. They are ignorant of what can happen, and they don't look out for themselves."

* Denotes pseudonym

After setting up at the Leroy Continental, Rundle got a job at the Metropolitan Insurance Company by making up an outlandish story: that he was co-owner of a Kentucky horse farm.

"I introduced myself to the manager, and he was a big horseman," Rundle said. "It was on East Sahara, and I talked to him about horses."

Rundle gave the insurance company a fake name of the horse farm, and he wrote down his friend Joey Martin as a reference. He paid for a phone line and hired an answering service to answer the phone for a week in the name of the horse farm, and almost immediately, the insurance office manager called Martin to talk about Rundle's horse farm in Kentucky.

Martin gave him a reference, and Rundle was hired as "William Randau."

"I'd been hired by the largest insurance company in the country under a name that didn't exist and under a Social Security number that was no good," Rundle said.

Rundle said he was increasingly interested at the time in publications from Paladin Press, which later published such literary classics as *Hit Man: A Technical Manual for Independent Contractors* and *How to Make a Silencer for a .22*. Rundle really enjoyed books about changing one's identity and disappearing in America. "It was the early seventies, and they published the *The Paper Trip*," Rundle said. "You can't do this now. This was to get legitimate false IDs. In the seventies, it was the Bible of getting a new identification. How to change your name and disappear. This is what Paladin Press was doing.

"You could go down to the hall of records and find infants who had died around the time you were born," Rundle said. "You could get their birth certificate. That birth certificate was now you. You applied for a Social Security number under that birth certificate. You applied for a driver's license because you had a legitimate birth certificate—

not a phony. Now you can't do it. Now when you are born
you get a Social Security number. You didn't have to do
that before. That was [forger Eddie Franklin] who put me
onto that because that was his business."

Rundle said he hated every waking moment of his insurance job at Metropolitan because of a demanding boss.
He eventually quit when his work hours conflicted with his
downtime, and he went back to work doing odd jobs for the
loan sharks at the pizza shack.

Sherri Grayson thought she'd married a dream of a man.
Her new husband got along great with her parents. He was
providing for her at their apartment at the Leroy Continental in Las Vegas, and he talked about having a child. Grayson was from a big family, and she wanted to start a family
of her own. She'd gotten a job at a Big Boy on Maryland
Parkway in Vegas, and this job, combined with her husband's salary at Metropolitan Life Insurance, could certainly support a child.

"I thought everything was great . . . He [Rundle] would
put on a suit every morning and head off to work," she said.

In 1973, Grayson got pregnant, and about four months
into the pregnancy, she and Rundle drove to her parents'
home in Van Nuys for a weekend getaway. The couple went
to bed that night, and when Grayson woke up the next morning, Rundle was gone. He didn't return all day, and she
started to panic.

"I thought he'd been in a car accident," she told the *Las
Vegas Review-Journal*. "I was devastated. I was calling
the hospitals and the morgue."

Grayson was terrified. She was young and pregnant,
and her husband was missing. When Rundle first disappeared, her family held out hope that perhaps he was simply
catching a breather from the pressures of a new marriage
and the prospect of having a baby. Every prospective father,

after all, freaks out when he first learns he is going to be a daddy. But the next day, something very curious happened: The mailman came to Sherri's parents' house in Van Nuys and delivered a certified letter to Bob and Sheila Grayson.

"It was addressed to my parents, not me," Grayson said. "It said, 'I [William Randau] am dying from cancer, and I'm going off to Europe to be with my parents [to] die.'"

Grayson's parents and siblings were shocked, and they smelled a rat. The contents of the letter seemed ridiculous. If "William Randau" really was sick with cancer, he wouldn't have disappeared like that. They started to suspect that Sherri had been lied to in the most heartless fashion, and they suspected Bill "Randau" had scammed his nineteen-year-old bride and then left her when she was four months pregnant.

Grayson wanted to believe that her husband would not do that to her. He had been so nice to her, and he'd said he wanted to have a child. This man who professed his love for her would not leave her alone and pregnant during their first year of marriage.

But the cold, hard truth of her abandonment became obvious in the following days. Grayson's brothers found a snapshot in some family album that showed Rundle's car in the background, and they had the photo blown up. The photo revealed a license plate, and the number came back registered to a Bill Rundle—not Bill "Randau." A search of the phone book turned up a string of families with the name Rundle in the immediate area, and one address belonged to Richard and Willa Rundle in North Hollywood. Grayson's father went to the home and knocked on the door and was greeted by Rundle's parents—the same parents who'd supposedly been touring Austria for the last year.

The Rundles said they hadn't been to Europe, and they told Mr. Grayson that their son couldn't be the William Randau married to his daughter. Their son was named

William Rundle, and he was living in Albuquerque, recovering from his first marriage to a woman named Sarah Reitig.

But when Bob Grayson told them the whole terrible story about his pregnant daughter, Richard and Willa Rundle became convinced that their son had scammed another woman.

"My father came home and presented pictures [to me] of Bill 'Randau's' first wife, and I said, 'Oh, my God,'" Grayson recalled. "That's when it first started hitting me. 'Who is this guy?'"

Even more alarming to Grayson was the realization that her bank account had been pilfered. Rundle had even gone to Bob's Big Boy and picked up her last paycheck without her knowing.

"My last check—$85," Grayson told the *Las Vegas Review-Journal*.

About five months later, Grayson gave birth to a beautiful little girl, and she made the extremely difficult decision to give the baby up for adoption. It was the most tortuous thing she'd ever had to do in her life.

She said she punished herself for years over the decision because of guilt.

Bill Rundle admits everything he did to Sherri Grayson. He admits he married her under a false name, got her pregnant, and then abandoned her. He said he couldn't take the idea of being married and having another child, and he bolted.

"I said to myself, 'I've got to get out of this,'" Rundle said. "Maybe I'll go see Eddie Franklin and get another identification under another name, and I'll move somewhere else in the country and start over again. Forget about the cons. Clean slate. No more cons. None.

"I drove back to Las Vegas, and left her there pregnant,"

Rundle said. "I drove back to Las Vegas, packed up all my stuff at the apartment, packed it into storage on Desert Inn Road, and I rented a downtown Las Vegas motel room at Eighth and Fremont Streets," Rundle said.

"At that time, rooms were like $20 a night, something like that, so I basically hid out for a week and never went back," Rundle said. "I felt so bad, and I knew one of her brothers was in law enforcement and that they would come looking for me because he and her [other] siblings loved their sister.

"Eventually, they [Grayson's brothers] came and went up and down Fremont Street looking for me," Rundle said. "I was scared to death. I feared the worst—that they would have me arrested for whatever, so I hid out for a whole week."

Rundle eventually placed a call to his old friend Joey Martin, and Martin told him the Graysons had been to Rundle's parents' house. Richard and Willa Rundle now knew their son had married another woman, this time under a fake name, and that he'd abandoned her while she was pregnant. They were beside themselves with anger and disappointment. Richard and Willa were already dealing with the aftermath of Rundle's failed first marriage, and they were trying to help care for Rundle's first son, Justin, when they learned of the Sherri Grayson debacle.

"My dad had a bad heart, and the worst I've ever felt in my life was when he found out what I had done to that girl," Rundle said.

"But he forgave me."

5 . . . MIRACLE

"But now he is dead, wherefore should I fast? I shall go to him, but he shall not return to me."

—2 Samuel 12:23

There are strippers, hookers, methamphetamine freaks, gangsters, dope slingers, cocaine addicts, and the reckless on the dark side. They come to Las Vegas for the next high, the next gambling spree, the next drunken binge, and the next sexual rush. The Devil's city is a cold and punishing place for those without discipline. Losing streaks, loneliness, and despair are on the faces of those who walk the city's streets. They rummage through Dumpsters or mill at the bus station. They sleep in piss-stained alleys and line up in droves at downtown homeless shelters. They beg in the shadows of billion-dollar mega resorts. Too many fucking drugs. Too much booze. Too much gambling. Their lives are worth nothing. Nothing at all.

Bill Rundle was a mean, coldhearted son of a bitch by the age of twenty-nine, and the tragedy of his life so far was that it hadn't had to be this way. Unlike a lot of criminals, Rundle had been given a pretty great shot at succeeding in life. He'd been born into a loving family, and showered with affection and care. Richard and Willa Rundle had tried to groom him for college and gave him every opportunity to succeed in North Hollywood. But Rundle preferred lying and gambling and chasing girls and drinking. Rundle had basically lied his way through life so far. He'd conned his parents about college, he'd lied to his first wife and fathered a child with her, and then he'd abandoned them. He conned his second wife into believing he was someone he was not, married her under a false name, and after getting her pregnant, abandoned her and their baby as well.

Most disturbing about Rundle's behavior was that he really didn't seem to care about the ramifications and all the pain and devastation his deviant behavior caused. As he approached the age of thirty, Bill Rundle wasn't just a failure: he'd blossomed into a real heartless motherfucker.

But then, in 1975, Bill Rundle became the beneficiary of a truly miraculous gift from God that left him humbled and thankful. He was given a beautiful miracle in the form of a child named Richie Rundle, and maybe, just maybe, he could make amends with God. Maybe God would someday forgive him for all his terrible past sins.

The year was 1974, and Bill Rundle had devastated the Grayson family with his vicious treatment of Sherri Grayson. He'd left her pregnant and alone and hid out for weeks in a seedy downtown Vegas stretch of hotels, drinking and gambling in the casinos, constantly scanning the downtown Vegas streets for any sign of Grayson's brothers. He feared he would one day see the angry faces of Grayson's brothers hunting him down like the dog he was, scared that he might be in for a real beating, or worse, if they found him.

As the days and weeks passed, Rundle started to realize that the storm cloud of deception he'd conjured up in Van

Nuys was dissipating. The Graysons, he figured, must have decided that they were going to have to forget about Rundle and move on if they were ever going to recover from the emotional damage he'd cast upon them. Rundle realized he couldn't hide out forever, and he was going to have to start over again. He again took a job driving cabs from casino to casino underneath a scorching Vegas summer sun. He spent a lot of his time drinking at a Vegas restaurant called Mirabelli's and another beer-swilling spot called the Flying Dutchman.

"I had two hundred bucks to my name, my clothes, and my stuff in storage," Rundle said. "I got a room at the Todd Motel, and I went to work at Checker Cab. I took my 'Randau' license and the Social Security number [documents] I had and put them in a safe deposit box I got. I got a post office box, too, so the phony stuff was not in my home . . . I separated those lives. Don't mix them up."

In 1974, a mutual friend introduced Rundle to the woman who would become his third wife. Amy Castor* was a very pretty single mother. She was only twenty, and she was raising a precious young daughter named Kelli.† The young mother was struggling to make ends meet in Vegas as a waitress at a Denny's near the Stardust on the Strip, and Rundle was starting to show an interest in her.

"She was very attractive," Rundle said. "Long blond hair. A good person, and for some reason she liked me a lot."

Rundle was also close friends with Castor's parents, Jake and Terri‡. Jake Castor worked as a cabdriver with Rundle, and Rundle regularly went bowling with the couple. The

* Denotes pseudonym

† Denotes pseudonym

‡ Denotes pseudonym

Castors, like the Graysons before them, came to like the tall, handsome man with dark hair and an outgoing personality. They had never heard of Bill "Randau," and the Castors had no objection to Rundle dating and eventually marrying their daughter.

"I hooked up with Amy, and we'd go out and drink and bowl and have a good time, and we took good care of Kelli," Rundle said. "I was driving cab, and this was five, six months after I left Sherri."

Amy Castor did not know any of the details of her husband's past with Grayson, although Rundle did tell her of his marriage to Reitig. The couple rented an apartment at Palos Verdes and Twain Avenues in Las Vegas in 1975.

The money from cabdriving and Castor's work at the restaurant was not great, and the couple struggled. Rundle figured he'd go back to see his friend Eddie Franklin at the Jolly Roger in San Clemente to try to come up with some less-than-legal solution for bringing in some more cash, and Franklin suggested ripping off finance companies on small-time loans. The loans Franklin talked about were the predecessors to what are now known as payday loans.

"He told me to go to a finance company, use [my] false ID, set up a voice mail thing in Las Vegas where they'll answer the phone and verify you are employed," Rundle said. Bill Rundle again used the fake Thoroughbred farm as a front, and once the finance companies called the voice mail, he'd get a payment the next day.

"Eddie told me, 'They don't check, and they don't want to check,'" Rundle said. "'They want to give you this money.' I did that probably ten times with the finance companies and then with credit cards."

The scam was not a big-time operation because Rundle could get only a few thousand dollars at a time from the finance companies. Even though he got the cash loans under a false name, he claimed he paid the loans back over time to maintain flush lines of credit on the bogus accounts. The loans were a help, Rundle said, in supporting his new family in their Vegas apartment.

Within a few months of the marriage, Castor was pregnant.

The beautiful, glorious miracle in Rundle's life officially arrived on May 20, 1975. He was a tiny, fragile infant, and the couple named the baby after Rundle's father, Richard. Neither the younger Rundle nor his new wife had any clue at the time just how special little Richie Rundle would turn out to be.

In fact, eleven years later, the entire city of Las Vegas would realize that little Richie Rundle really was a glorious gift from God.

There was something special about Richie Rundle from the moment he was born. He was small and fragile and innocent. The newborn's magic melted the hard heart of his father, and Bill Rundle said seeing his little son Richie cry in front of him in 1975 in a Las Vegas hospital sparked a personal transformation. He said he decided he was going to be a real father to little Richie and not the phantom of a man who'd left his first son, Justin, along with his mother in Southern California or the man who'd abandoned Sherri Grayson pregnant and alone just a few miles down the road.

Rundle knew, of course, that there was no going back after what he'd already done, and only time would tell if he could truly experience a transformation. According to records with the Clark County, Nevada, District Attorney's Office, his third wife, Amy Castor, would allege that around the time Richie was born, Rundle drank a lot and was emotionally abusive to her.

Rundle disputed this, claiming he set out to live a better

life after Richie's birth. He decided he was going to take care of Richie, and he also promised himself that he was going to stop scamming people.

"I had a son," Rundle said. "I had screwed my [previous marriages] up. I told myself, 'I'm not going to do this again,' and I promised I was going to take good care of Richie and [my stepdaughter] Kelli.'"

If Rundle was going to turn his life around and try to make amends, however, he had to start by repairing a forever-scarred relationship with his parents. Rundle said the elder Richard and Willa Rundle were at their wits' end over their son's pattern of deviant behavior. Learning that their son had mistreated so many women and abandoned two children was a life-altering shock for the Rundles. All of Bill Rundle's uncles and aunts also knew of the notorious trail he'd left through Southern California, and Bill Rundle was officially a family embarrassment. He'd tarnished the Rundle name.

Richard and Willa Rundle were two stable, hardworking people with ethics and morals, and they had not raised their son to turn out this way. This is evidenced by the role the aging couple played in the life of their son's first child, Justin. According to Las Vegas police records, the elder Richard and Willa Rundle stayed in touch with Justin, and they each took a very active role in their grandson's life even after Bill Rundle abandoned him.

"I had a relationship with [my father's] mother and father—Richard and Willa Rundle," Justin Rundle told Las Vegas authorities. "They were very instructional in my upbringing as a little boy."

Bill Rundle, in interviews with the author, was guarded and vague about his relationship with his mother. He spoke fondly of Willa, called her a good person, and described his relationship with her as very good. But he has little to say about her beyond that.

In fact, the elder Richard and Willa Rundle had considered giving up on their son when they found out about his treatment of Grayson. Willa Rundle, in particular, was mortified at her son's behavior, and she let him know as much. In the mid to late 1970s, Willa was getting into her early sixties, and she knew how hard it was to raise a child with two parents, let alone one. To see her son out lying and cheating and walking away from his responsibilities sickened her.

But when Richie Rundle was born in Las Vegas in 1975 and named after Bill Rundle's father, Rundle promised himself that this time it was going to be different. This time, he was going to be a real father to his child, and he was also going to be a good son to his parents. Rundle said he wanted to make things right with his future life, and this meant telling the elder Richard and Willa Rundle about the birth of their grandson.

"I called my parents, told them everything that happened, and that was a hard day for me to have to face them," Rundle said." I told my dad that Richie was born, that he had another grandson, and that this time I wasn't going to let him down. I wasn't going to screw around. I was going to take care of Richie and make him proud of me. He said, 'Okay, you have to prove that to us,' and I said, 'Okay, fine.'"

Rundle claims both his parents forgave him for his lies and the pain he'd caused the women in his life. The idea that Rundle's parents completely forgave him for his treatment of Sherri Grayson and Sarah Reitig seems hard to believe, given what Rundle had done, but later actions by Richard and Willa Rundle would seem to prove it was, in fact, true—the elder Richard and Willa Rundle forgave their son yet again.

After the birth of little Richie, Bill Rundle and Amy Castor settled into their apartment. There was some degree of normalcy to the marriage early on. Rundle drove cabs, and Castor took care of Richie and Kelli while working as a waitress to try to support this life they'd chosen in Vegas.

"I'd drive home, and we'd sit and have dinner like a family," Rundle said.

Rundle and Castor realized early on that Richie was a special child. He was a beautiful baby at birth, and as every parent knows, a child's magic only gets better as time passes. Richie certainly did not disappoint in this regard. He was a small, blond-haired boy who was intelligent, sweet, and compassionate.

"A wonderful boy," Rundle said.

But within a year of Richie's birth, it became apparent that something was not right. He seemed very small and delicate, and over time, he stayed small, which worried his parents. And then, at the age of two, Richie started to cry constantly and get sick often. His mother and father were alarmed and concerned, and they were convinced something was seriously wrong with little Richie.

"Richie started running fevers," Rundle said. "He's two years old, and he's sick, so Amy took him to the pediatrician. They did some tests on him and they found out he had diabetes."

Only parents of a diabetic child know what a life-altering experience this is, and the Rundles seemed ill-equipped for handling Richie's disease. Richie was diagnosed as a Type 1 diabetic, and required daily shots of insulin. Rundle and Castor were warned that if Richie didn't get his shots, it could be lethal. Diabetes is a vicious predator for those who don't stay on top of their insulin intake.

Thankfully, though, diabetes is not a death sentence. If insulin injections are properly managed and a diabetic gets a good diet and exercise, then diabetics diagnosed at the youngest of ages can live healthy lives. The shock of his son's condition officially hit home for Rundle when he was told the boy was going to need shots daily, and if Rundle was going to follow through on his promise of turning his life around, he was going to have to look out for little Richie and make sure he got his insulin injections.

"He was insulin-dependent," Rundle said. "I was crushed. My son was two years old and sick. He was just learning to walk, just learning to talk, and he was going to have to take insulin shots for the rest of his life, so I learned how to give shots. We learned, and we practiced on oranges and learned how to give them, but he was very hard to stabilize. A two-year-old, and he was sick all of the time. We had to go to the hospital repeatedly. It was terrible."

Rundle and Castor faced frequent trips to the hospital over the next year for Richie. The boy was struggling with his diabetic condition, and it just seemed Richie wasn't doing well, no matter how meticulously the injections were managed. He was often ill, and Bill Rundle wondered whether God was punishing him by making this beautiful child he loved so dearly so very ill and fragile.

"The pediatrician that we first went to was a jerk," Rundle said. "He said, 'Did you know that one out of every two children who get diabetes at this age die before they reach the age of eighteen?' Instead of giving me encouragement, he's giving me all the negative stuff, and I didn't want to hear that.

"I said, 'I'm not going to give in,'" Rundle recalled. "I'm going to take care of this child."

Castor also loved her son, and she and her parents spent a lot of time caring for him, but the marriage between Rundle and Castor was troubled. Castor told Las Vegas authorities Rundle drank and gambled all the time, and he also kept a secret bank account. Rundle, meanwhile, portrays his ex-wife as someone who was struggling in life, and the stress caused by Richie's diabetes certainly did not help the marriage either.

The couple split in 1978, and the two agreed as part of

the divorce that Rundle would raise Richie, and Castor would continue on in life with her daughter Kelli.

"We decided we'll split up," Rundle said. "She told me, 'I'll take Kelli, and you take Richie.'"

It was a remarkable turn of events for Rundle. The man who'd abandoned two women and children, and who had conned and scammed his way through life, was now the only person looking out for a three-year-old diabetic. Rundle said he responded to the challenge, though, and he took on the responsibility of ensuring Richie got his shots.

"He was small, fragile and very self-conscious about his height," Rundle said of Richie's early life. "He would say, 'Daddy, I want to be big like you,' and I would tell him, 'Don't worry Richie—you'll grow.'"

"No more bars," Rundle said. "My life was dedicated to Richie. I did that, and yet he started getting more and more sick, and I got more and more hospital bills. It was hard for him. He would have severe insulin reactions where he didn't have enough sugar in his body."

Bill Rundle said he followed through on his efforts to be a decent person and a good father. To his mind, this meant taking care of Richie and not pulling off full-fledged cons on innocent people, and several witnesses would later attest that Bill Rundle did indeed take good care of his son. Richie was five in 1980 and just starting school, and the child continued to struggle with his diabetes. Around this time, Richie went into a coma and was briefly hospitalized before recovering.

"He'd be so active one day, burning up all of his sugar, and then I'd have to lower his insulin," Rundle said. "His ketones were high, and they just couldn't get a handle on it. I felt so bad for him. It was terrible."

Rundle was a single father caring for a diabetic child and driving a cab in Vegas. He relied on the help of babysitters and even an apartment complex manager to help him look out for Richie. He had hardly any money to support his sick child, and Rundle filed for medical bankruptcy after one well-known hospital in Las Vegas wouldn't take Richie because his father couldn't pay. Yet Rundle, in part through help from his parents, made sure Richie got his insulin shots.

But Rundle still found time to drink beer in his apartment, and he often gambled on sports even though he was broke and had a sick child. In 1980, a guy he gave a ride to in his cab told him he should bet a huge sum of cash on the Los Angeles Lakers to beat the Philadelphia 76ers in the NBA basketball finals.

"I was driving a cab, and this guy got in my cab and said, 'Do you follow sports?'" Rundle recalled. "I said, 'Yeah very closely.' He said, 'Well, tonight's game six of the Philadelphia 76ers-Lakers play-off series, and Kareem Abdul-Jabbar is not playing. Magic Johnson is playing center tonight, and this game is in Philly.'

"Philly was an eight-point favorite, and he said, 'There is no way Philly is going to win that game by eight points. Take my word. They are not going to win the game by that. I'm putting really big money on the Lakers.'"

Rundle was excited. It seemed too good of a tip to pass up.

"I dropped him off at all these sports books, and he laid all this money down, and I took him back to the airport," Rundle said. "I went home afterward, and I took every dime I could get my hands on. It was $1,650, and I went to Churchill Downs, and I bet it on the Lakers to win $1,500.

"The Lakers won the game straight up," Rundle said. "I was petrified the whole time. Absolutely petrified."

Being a parent is perhaps the greatest experience in life. But being responsible for a vulnerable, defenseless little child's life can also be a struggle. In 1980, Bill Rundle was a single father driving a cab and trying to support a diabetic child in Las Vegas. He'd endured a medical bankruptcy, and he was constantly worried that his work at a bottom-feeding, minimum-wage job shuttling tourists to and from the airport and the casinos would harm Richie because of a missed insulin injection while Richie was in the care of a babysitter.

Bill Rundle was hanging on, but he needed help. The elder Rundles, who were then living in an upscale mobile home park for seniors in Escondido, came to their son's rescue. Bill Rundle brought Richie to Escondido, and the Rundles were charmed by their grandchild. Bill Rundle decided to return to Southern California. He got an apartment in Escondido, and started relying on his parents to help with Richie.

The move to Southern California, however, was not without its awkward moments. Everyone in the Rundle family knew Bill Rundle was a lying cheat who'd embarrassed the family by going around and getting women pregnant and dumping them like trash.

"My uncle and all my aunts judged me for what I'd done," Rundle said. "Naturally, they found out about everything I'd done. They were polite to me, and they loved Richie, but they didn't want anything to do with me. I understood that. Forgiveness is hard. Some people can forgive. Some people can't."

Rundle took a job doing pool maintenance at Pool King and was promoted to supervisor. It was not a great job, but in Escondido, Rundle had his parents' help in looking out for Richie.

Richie got sick again at the end of 1980, and he was rushed to Palomar Medical Center in Escondido for a diabetic emergency. The child was gravely ill, and Bill Rundle and his parents prayed for their special little boy to recover. Seeing Richie in the emergency room, too sick to move, tore them all apart.

"Richie was in the hospital, and he was so sick I thought he was going to die," Rundle said.

Little did the Rundle family know, however, that the diabetic episode and his trip to the hospital would end up saving Richie. Emergency room physician Dr. David Minkoff took a special interest in Richie.

"David Minkoff stayed with Richie for two days in the hospital, and he didn't go home," Rundle said. "He didn't do anything. He just stayed right there in the hospital with Richie and got him well."

Dr. Minkoff was touched by the boy and agreed to take little Richie on as an individual patient. What happened next was remarkable: Richie got better.

"It was hard to believe, given how sick he'd been, but it turned out that this was the last time he ever had to go to the hospital," Rundle said. "Minkoff put him on a special diet, lowered his dosages, and he taught me how to better take care of him, and it was unbelievable. Richie turned around and got better."

By the time Richie was six, everyone around him noticed the difference. This Richie had a zest for life, and there was no denying it. He still got his insulin injections every day, but he wasn't sick anymore, and it was as if he was a different child. He had great energy, and after all of his illnesses and hospital stays and injections, it seemed as if Richie really appreciated just how special and precious life really is. He excelled in his first year of elementary school, and he loved baseball. Bill Rundle found himself amazed at Richie's progress from day to day, and his son was the one person in Rundle's life who loved him unconditionally. He realized Richie was a blessing from God.

"My life had changed," Rundle said. "Richie was getting better and better and better."

The elder Rundles also loved Richie dearly.

"My mom and dad were really close to Richie," Rundle

said. "They spent a lot of time with him. They had forgiven
me for what I had done, and Richie and I would go to their
house every Sunday for dinner, and we would play Scrabble. The kid was so smart I couldn't believe it. Richie had
my brain, but he was putting it to use. Everything he did
was good."

Rundle took Richie to pro sporting events almost weekly,
and Richie became a huge fan of the star-studded lineup of
the San Diego Padres in the early 1980s. Richie simply
loved going to see the Padres at Jack Murphy Stadium in
San Diego, and he marveled at baseball superstars Dave
Winfield and Steve Garvey. They were able to hit ninety-
mile-per-hour fastballs out of the park, and the tall, powerful yet graceful Winfield could snatch a line drive like no
other in center field. Richie himself dreamed of being a
player in the big leagues.

"The Padres were great with families, and they loved
the kids," Rundle said. "The players would come out in the
ballpark, and they'd sign autographs for Richie all the time.
He was just a sweet little kid. Blond hair, blue eyes, and
he loved Steve Garvey, Tony Gwynn, and Kevin McReyn-
olds."

Richie loved basketball, too, and his favorite team was
the Los Angeles Clippers. Rundle's job as a pool tech at
Pool King landed him some prized seats at the Clippers
games, and he brought his son along to take in the glim-
mering spectacle of live professional basketball.

"Richie played basketball at the YMCA in Escondido,
and Pool King had season tickets for the Clippers because
they'd built a pool for Clippers coach Paul Silas," Rundle
said. "Richie and I would get tickets all the time to the Clippers games, and we would get down to like the third, fourth
row, and see players like Bill Walton and Terry Cummings
and Tom Chambers. Those were some really great times."

By going to the sports games, the Rundle father and son
were repeating a tradition from some three decades earlier

when the elder Richard Rundle took his son to Dodger games in Southern California.

Richie was also doing great in school. He was eight years old and in the third grade when he entered an essay writing contest.

"He won first prize," Rundle said. "He was eight, he beat everyone else out in the entire school. I was so proud of him."

Rundle was enjoying fatherhood immensely. The joy of seeing Richie bloom was heartwarming, and very meaningful to him. Richie was his own flesh and blood, and it seemed the boy was put on Earth by God Himself to turn Rundle around and give him a shot at redemption in life. Rundle wanted to do right for the boy.

"Richie was my best friend by far, and, given how sick he'd been, I was trying to give him the best childhood I could," Rundle said. "He was a special kid. A really good kid, and God had given me a second chance in life by taking care of him."

6 . . . "MY DAD IS THE BEST"

Bill Rundle was on the right track. He was basically out on his own as a single father in Southern California, and with a little help from his parents, he was enjoying a nearly four-year run as a normal person who was not going around scamming people and leaving them emotionally broken.

Rundle started to desire more. He believed his job at Pool King was a dead-ender. He talked briefly over the phone to his third ex-wife, Amy Castor, about returning to Las Vegas with Richie, and was intrigued by the idea. Moving to Las Vegas, however, would mean he would have to leave behind the stability he'd found in Escondido, with the elder Richard and Willa Rundle helping him out with Richie, who was eight at the time. But he honestly believed he could make better money in Las Vegas than he was making at Pool King, and Richie might be able to spend more time with his mother.

Rundle decided to move back to Las Vegas with Richie, so he told his parents they were leaving, packed up their belongings from the apartment in Escondido, got on Interstate 15 in his old Mustang, and made the roughly five-hour trek east with his son.

They drove through the mountains and through dusty towns like Barstow and Baker and eventually into the barren Southern Nevada desert. Rundle drove past a couple of outpost casinos and a long stretch of billboard casino signs and into the southern stretch of the Devil's city. He believed he could raise Richie on his own, and remarkably, Rundle did just that. He had help from the Castors, but he mostly raised Richie in Vegas by himself.

His time as a single father in Vegas was not without its struggles. In fact, things started out tough for the father and son. They moved into what amounted to a skid-row apartment in a very tough section of downtown at Thirteenth and Fremont Streets. It is the type of run-down neighborhood where prostitutes walk the street, young men sling crack, people get robbed or murdered, and drunken losers ruined by alcohol and gambling walk up and down Fremont Street endlessly, without any hope of ever recovering.

Rundle moved into the neighborhood because he had very little money, and he could afford the rent here. He started driving cabs again, but he promised himself that as soon as he had enough money, he and Richie would move to a nicer area of town.

Surprisingly, however, despite the poor neighborhood, Rundle met there two of the nicest people whom he'd ever have a chance to know. Fred and Mary Ann Floyd were an older couple scratching out a living by managing the apartments, and they immediately started looking out for their new tenants—the single father who drove cabs to support his little boy Richie. Fred and Mary Ann Floyd sort of took Richie under their wing and looked out for him after school or when his dad was out shuttling fares.

"They [the Floyds] were just tremendous people, and they had one of the worst jobs in the world, managing that apartment building," Rundle said. "The scum that lived in there was unbelievable. The police were there every night. Drug dealers were everywhere. I said, 'I've got to get a better job, and I've got to get out of here for Richie's sake, and I've got to do it as fast as I possibly can.' "

Rundle said he remained close with Jake Castor, his ex-wife's father and Richie's grandfather. When he returned to Las Vegas, he looked Jake up, and Rundle said Jake told him that he knew someone at the Union Plaza casino in downtown Las Vegas who might be able to get Rundle a job. Castor urged Rundle to apply for a security job at the Union Plaza, and Rundle jumped on it, knowing that the position would be a huge score for someone with a history of conning people and a relatively spotty work record. The job offered a steady wage and, most important, health insurance for Richie.

"That day, Richie and I went to a movie, and when we came back, Fred Floyd told me, 'The security chief at Union Plaza wants to talk to you,'" Rundle recalled. "'He wants to talk to you right away,' and I'm figuring something went wrong with the background check. Fred watched Richie for me, I went back down to the Union Plaza, and the security chief said he had had two guys quit today, and if I wanted the job, it was mine. 'Oh, yeah, I want the job.' The benefits were great, and I had health benefits for my son."

Things were starting to turn around.

Working graveyard security meant that Rundle would have to make some sacrifices. He absolutely hated leaving Richie in anyone else's care, whether it was the Floyds, the Castors, or a babysitter. His son had to have his insulin shots, and he constantly feared someone would forget to give Richie a shot and he would get sick again.

"I would drop Richie off and work the graveyard shift, but I'd have to teach each babysitter how to give the shot, and that really bothered me because I was trusting someone else to do it," Rundle said.

Rundle stayed in regular contact with Dr. Minkoff in Southern California, and Minkoff suggested Rundle teach Richie how to inject himself with insulin. Richie was just eight and in the third grade, and his father was at first wary of the idea. But when Rundle sat down to teach Richie how to perform his insulin injections himself, Rundle was astonished at what happened.

"I taught him how to give himself the shots, and I let him practice with saline solution on my legs," Rundle said. "I showed him how, and it was amazing. He could measure the insulin faster and better than I could. Three units of this, twenty-four units of this, and then he took the syringe and gave himself a shot in the leg. He was able to give himself injections."

Rundle was overcome with pride and emotion as he watched Richie learn how to single-handedly perform an injection that would guarantee the child's well-being.

Richie truly was a special child.

By 1985, Bill Rundle was living a relatively normal life in Las Vegas. His new job as a security guard at the Union Plaza gave him a little bit of money to work with, and he and Richie moved to a better neighborhood on the far east side of Las Vegas on Jimmy Durante Boulevard, near Boulder Highway and the Sam's Town casino. The move got Richie out of what was arguably the worst neighborhood in Las Vegas.

Bill Rundle, meanwhile, was becoming a regular member of Las Vegas society. He made friends with a Las Vegas police investigator named Bob Roshak, and the two became close. Rundle played cards with Roshak regularly, and Roshak made a point of telling Rundle how impressed he was with Richie. Rundle also became close friends with a kind and established Las Vegan named Don Chalmers, and Chalmers and his wife helped care for Richie as well.

The Chalmers became very close to the boy, and they were amazed at how the child was able to give himself his insulin injections.

"Richie and I were doing really, really well," Rundle said.

That year, Rundle was working at the Union Plaza when a coworker introduced him to the woman who would become his fourth wife, Shirley Mullasgo. Shirley was a divorceé with a teenage daughter, Magda. Shirley was quite beautiful in her own special way. She had a rounded face and a classy aura about her. She dressed nice.

Shirley Mullasgo worked making change in the smoky, old-style casino to support her young daughter. She was a hard worker who knew what it was like to struggle. Shirley had been born in the Philippines in November 1938 to Nicholas and Demitria Mullasgo, the second of twelve children in a farming family. She had seven sisters and four brothers. The family was very poor in a country known for its abject poverty in rural areas. They basically had very little money at all.

"Nicholas was a good father, and he had to work hard to support his large family," Bill Rundle would later say. In addition to farming, "[Shirley's father] was a tailor and a musician . . . he was very good. He played the sax and clarinet and played in several bands in the Philippines.

"Even with a family of twelve children, the kids never lacked for food, clothing, or shelter," Rundle said of his wife's family. "Being the oldest daughter, Shirley would help her mom with cooking and cleaning, and she had a pretty good childhood in a very poor country. Their family was very close, and got along well. I have nothing but good memories and thoughts about Shirley's family."

Shirley had endured two miserable marriages in the Philippines, and given her upbringing, she was a woman keenly aware of how fortunate Americans are. She was thankful to have been able to come to the U.S. on a legitimate work visa, and she received her certificate of naturalization from the United States of America and the District Court of Nevada on July 19, 1985.

"She stayed in Glendale, California, with a doctor she'd known in the Philippines," Rundle said. "She looked for work in Los Angeles, but after two weeks, she moved to Las Vegas to stay [with another family she knew]." She liked Bill Rundle right away.

"She was a sweet person," Rundle said. "Not overly attractive-looking but super nice. We became friends. She'd been married twice before, and both of her husbands screwed around on her."

Bill Rundle introduced Shirley to Richie, and he quickly noticed chemistry between them. She laughed and joked with Richie, and asked him about his schooling at Joe Mackey Elementary School. Richie told her how he loved school, baseball, and basketball, and she was touched by his sweetness.

"Shirley loved Richie," Rundle said. "The first time they met, Richie liked her a lot. They got along so good it was unbelievable. It was like he was her son."

The relationship between Bill and Shirley's daughter, Magda, however, was initially rocky. Magda was seventeen at the time, and enrolled in the public Las Vegas High School, and Rundle said she didn't like him at first.

"She thought I was trying to take her mother away," Rundle said.

Bill Rundle said he took Shirley and Richie to Disneyland and the San Diego Zoo, where neither Shirley nor Richie had ever been before. Over time, Shirley became part of Bill and Richie Rundle's inner circle, and Bill Rundle said he fell in love with her and introduced her to his parents.

"My dad liked Shirley," Rundle said. "My mom hated

Shirley. I don't know if it was because she was foreign and Filipino. I don't know why. They did not get along at all, and as time went along, they argued."

Nonetheless, the couple married in 1986.

"Shirley and I got married at the Union Plaza wedding chapel," Rundle said. "It was a nice wedding. My best man was Don Chalmers, and all of our close friends were there."

Rundle said Shirley had only a couple of drawbacks as a wife. She had expensive tastes: She only bought the finest and most expensive products when it came to items like makeup, clothing, jewelry, and furniture. He said Shirley's prior marriages in the Philippines also had left her paranoid that he would cheat on her, and he said she was constantly checking up on him to make sure he wasn't having affairs with strange women.

"We got along fine, except she was so possessive," Rundle said. "She was so jealous, but she was the best thing that ever happened to Richie. I decided I was going to put up with it. It was so bad, though. She would spy on me.

"Here she was, five foot four, and I was six foot four, and she was 130 pounds, and I was 260 pounds, and I never laid a hand on her," Rundle said. "Nothing. I wasn't a violent person, but we had a little bit of a stormy relationship because she was possessive. Extremely possessive."

Others would later call this claim about Shirley Rundle a blatant and calculated lie.

Rundle also said his wife had an uncontrollable desire for nice belongings.

"I remember the first time I bought Shirley a piece of jewelry, and I thought it was really nice," Rundle said. "She didn't like it because she would only wear the real stuff—eighteen- to twenty-four-karat gold and diamonds. She wore very expensive pieces. She always had very expensive tastes and spent lots of money on her appearance. She wouldn't wear drugstore makeup—only expensive Lancôme, and she used lots of it. She would only carry [$400] handbags.

"Shirley's taste in clothes were just like her taste in jewelry and other things: only top-of-the-line," Rundle said. "She shopped at Neiman Marcus, Dillard's, and Macy's. Not at Sears or JCPenney, [and never] at Target or Kmart."

Still, Rundle described Shirley as a "good mother to Magda and a good mother to Richie."

In 1986, Richie Rundle was attending Jo Mackey Elementary School's Sixth Grade Center. He was excelling at everything he did. The principal of the school, Linda McMosley, took special interest in the child. The boy with long, straight blond hair and a small, wiry frame had significant health challenges, but it was impressive that he was able to inject himself with his own insulin shots.

Richie now loved the St. Louis Cardinals baseball team and former Padres shortstop Ozzie Smith, and he loved WrestleMania and Hulk Hogan and bowling. But he also loved school. McMosley took note of the fact, and she found him to be an extremely bright, kind, and thoughtful child who seemed to have a great future ahead of him.

The principal would later describe Richie Rundle as "almost perfect."

In 1986, Richie entered a contest where students wrote essays about why their dads were so special. Richie set out to win the contest for Clark County sixth graders, and in the apartment on Jimmy Durante Boulevard, the boy penned a letter about why he thought his dad Bill Rundle was the best father in the world.

The letter was titled "My Dad Is the Best." It reads:

I think my dad is the best. He's tall and I'm small, but size has nothing to do with love. It's how big your heart is that counts. My dad has a giant heart, so I guess he's pretty loveable!

My dad loves me. I should know! He works hard to take care of me. When I get sick, my dad takes better care of me than any other person could!

I have a disease, but my dad doesn't treat me like I have one. He treats me like a normal kid. That makes me feel good!

My dad takes me to the movies or to sports events when he has a chance to. I love my dad very much! When I do something bad, my dad sits down with me and teaches me right from wrong. I've learned from my dad to love—not to hate.

Signed:
Richard James Rundle
Mrs. Johnson AM
Jo Mackey

Bill Rundle was brought to tears by the letter, and after it was mailed in, the contest's judges called Rundle and asked if he and Shirley would attend a special ceremony at Jo Mackey. When Bill and Shirley showed up, Bill Rundle was named Las Vegas's Father of the Year.

That's right—Father of the Year. This was the same man who stomped all over Sarah Reitig's life, and it was the same man who married Sherri Grayson under a false name then left her when she was pregnant. Rundle himself couldn't believe it.

"Richie could write so nicely," said Rundle, who still gleams when he talks about the "My Dad Is the Best" letter nearly a quarter century later. "He told me he wrote about me because I told him what was right from wrong. He wrote in the letter about how I told him to love people and not to hate people and how he had diabetes and how I took such good care of him. I treated him like a normal child. It was an unbelievable letter.

"They gave me a plaque, and a county commissioner was there," Rundle said. "It was unbelievable."

7 ... BRINGER OF DEATH

Richie Rundle woke up on the morning of March 30, 1987, and got ready for school as he did every other morning. It was a beautiful sunny day in Las Vegas, and it was also the last day of Richie Rundle's beautiful life.

The eleven-year-old's father was just finishing up his graveyard security shift at the Union Plaza, and his step-mother, Shirley Rundle, was away visiting family in the Philippines. Richie, a straight-A student, got up that morning, got dressed, ate breakfast, and walked to the school bus stop just in front of the Coral Gardens Apartments on Jimmy Durante Boulevard. Richie and a small group of children waited patiently for the yellow Clark County School District bus to arrive and shuttle them to the Jo Mackey Sixth Grade Center as it did every morning.

Eleven-year-old Eli Scott stood near Richie. The two were good friends, and they both liked pro wrestling. Standing a short distance from the children was twenty-year-old maintenance worker Dewey Buckles. Buckles was blowing leaves with a blower at the front entryway of the

Coral Gardens. Buckles was a high school dropout and former member of the National Guard who was working maintenance to support his new wife who worked as a gift shop clerk on the Las Vegas Strip.

At 8:40 a.m., a 1976 Datsun 280Z sports car came barreling down Jimmy Durante Boulevard like a bat out of hell. The vehicle appeared to onlookers to be going too fast—way too fast. To some, it looked as if the vehicle was going as fast as sixty-eight miles per hour in a forty-five-mile-per-hour zone, and in a second, the car inexplicably swerved at the group of children waiting for the school bus.

There was no braking, and witnesses heard the car's engine revving like a monster.

The children were about to die.

The speeding car hit the curb where Richie was standing and went airborne like a massive metal bullet. The right front tire broke off from the impact with the curb. The word Michelin was printed in rubber on the sidewalk. The Datsun was now a killing machine, and Richie had only an instant to react.

"[He said] 'Watch out!' and pushed me into the street," Eli Scott would later recall. "I saw the car hit Richard, then [I] closed my eyes."

Richie Rundle pushed his friend out of the way of the car and saved little Eli Scott's life. Richie was not so fortunate. Dewey Buckles had jumped a retainer wall and tried to run to the children when he saw the car swerving in their direction. He barely missed getting there in time to save Richie, and Buckles was cut down as well. The impact from the catapulting vehicle severed his legs. A shoe was tossed into the air and came to rest hanging from a light pole. The Nissan ripped through its victims and smashed into another pole and cinder-block retainer wall.

The car's driver was a young, blond-haired woman. She

was upside down in the flipped vehicle, and she appeared to be dead.

The crash scene looked as if a bomb had gone off on Jimmy Durante. School books and homework were scattered in the street.

Eli Scott was safe. The child estimated that the rotating, flying Nissan missed him by about two inches, but Richie Rundle was dead at the scene. His little frame had been crushed and mutilated by the vehicle, and thrown nearly one hundred feet. The child who had warmed his father's cold heart, and who had fought so hard against diabetes and demonstrated such a strong will to live, was dead.

Little Richie was dead.

When police arrived, a child's haunting cry could be heard, and the boy was sobbing loudly.

"Richard!"

"Richard!"

Jonathan Baney had been working maintenance with Dewey Buckles. He'd seen the car head for the children, and he actually witnessed the crash.

"I saw two bodies fly up in the air," Baney said.

Baney ran a few yards and saw Richie's mangled, lifeless body. The shocking scene was too much to take. The boy was "all twisted up," he said. He then went to see if he could help Buckles, and found the dead maintenance man's severed legs, blood, and the remainder of his body down the street.

One of the first officers at the scene was Bill Rundle's longtime friend, Las Vegas police investigator Bob Roshak. Roshak started to investigate the car-versus-pedestrian crash before he saw Richie. The mangled, lifeless child in front of him was *his* Richie Rundle. He was the child he'd come to admire so very much. This child wasn't a stranger. This was his friend Bill's kid. The veteran cop, who had seen so many horrible things in life, was heartbroken as he stood in the middle of Jimmy Durante Boulevard.

"Richard was a good kid and a good student," Roshak told the *Las Vegas Sun* newspaper. "He was born a month after my daughter, and the children often played together for their first few years until Bill moved to California."

Roshak decided he should be the one to tell Richie's father.

On the morning of March 30, 1987, Bill Rundle was finishing up his security shift at the Union Plaza when a couple of coworkers approached him with alarmed looks on their faces. It was clear they wanted to tell him something.

"They called me to the security booth," Rundle said. "I was very close to Frank Metz, my sergeant, and he told me, 'You've got to go home right away. Don't drive your car. The security guards will drive you home.' I didn't know what was going on, and they wouldn't tell me."

Rundle knew in his heart something was very wrong. No one ever acted like this, and no one ever told him not to drive home. He prayed the most important person in life, Richie, was okay, as his coworkers drove him home.

"We got near Jimmy Durante, and I could see tons of flashing lights," Rundle said. "I knew something bad had happened. We pulled up there, and there is a police officer named Bob Roshak. I knew him. He drove cab[s] with me in 1974. His wife and my [ex-wife Amy Castor] were friends. He and I were friends.

"I said, 'Bob, what is going on? What happened?'" Rundle said. "He said, 'Richie was hit by a car.'"

Rundle looked at the crime scene and was shocked. He saw a car crumpled by a light pole and a smashed cinderblock retainer wall. A shoe was hanging from the light pole. His little boy was here somewhere, and he wanted to know where.

"Oh, my God!" Rundle exclaimed. "How bad is it?"

"He's dead," Roshak answered.

Rundle went numb.

"I was in mental shock at this point, so I went inside the apartment," Rundle said. "I asked, 'Who did it?' They said it was a cocktail waitress from Circus Circus. I asked, 'Was she drunk?' 'Yeah, she was drunk.'

"They told me she was going anywhere from fifty to seventy and hit him full bore," Rundle said. "Bob told me from what the witnesses had said that Richard pushed another boy, Eli Scott, out of the way because Eli didn't see the car coming. He pushed Eli out of the way, and the car hit him full bore. Knocked him over a wall, and I just couldn't believe it."

Rundle broke down in tears. The pain pulsed through his body, and life wasn't worth anything to him anymore. The pain he was feeling was the most searing, sharpest emotion on Earth. He was cut to shreds. His beautiful Richie, the child he was living for, was dead. The gift from God was gone after just eleven short years.

My Richie!

"I was completely crushed," Rundle said. "Everything I had worked for to straighten myself out had come to an end. Here Richie was doing so well healthwise and school-wise, and he was dead."

Shirley Rundle's family in the Philippines was called, and she rushed back to be with her devastated husband.

"I called my mom and dad and told them their grandson was dead," Rundle said. "It just tore me up. I also had to call the Philippines to try to find Shirley. Her mother was sick, and it was very hard for me to do. She said, 'I'll come home right away.'"

The driver of the car slowly climbed out of the vehicle at the crash scene. She was conscious, and a paramedic smelled alcohol on her breath. She had a broken nose, and was flown by helicopter to Sunrise Hospital.

The twenty-two-year-old Las Vegan was Corina King. She was young, thin, and pretty, with big, eighties-era blond hair. According to her friends and family, King was nice and charming in her everyday life. She took care of her friends' kids, and she was hardworking. She worked two jobs as a cocktail waitress, and everyone who knew her spoke very highly of her.

At the time of the crash, police alleged King was drunk. Her blood alcohol content tested at 0.14, and the legal limit in Nevada at the time was 0.10.

Las Vegas authorities charged her with felony driving under the influence of alcohol causing death. Investigator William Morrison said he estimated King was driving between fifty and sixty-eight miles per hour, but he believed the number was closer to sixty-eight miles per hour, based on the evidence he examined.

When he interviewed King at the hospital several hours after the accident, Morrison said King told him "that she was going down Jimmy Durante Boulevard, and a car had come at her, and she veered to the right to avoid it."

The detective said this account contradicted other witnesses, who said they didn't see another car coming at King's vehicle.

An examination of the Datsun by a Clark County, Nevada, mechanic found nothing wrong with the Datsun with one exception—the tires were extremely worn down. A police investigation and King's comments indicated she'd worked late, then stayed out all night at Tramp's Bar. She said she had a beer and four greyhound drinks—a concoction of vodka and grapefruit juice—and that she was not drunk when she left the bar at 8 a.m. King told authorities it was lack of sleep and lack of food that caused her to black out at the time of the crash.

"It's obvious that I wasn't able to drive," King said later. "But I didn't know I was that tired. I wouldn't have driven if I had known I wasn't able to drive."

She also said she had a hazy memory of the crash site.

"I remember a lot of people being around," King would later recall. "Everything's kind of . . . mixed up."

Authorities weren't buying it. Clark County prosecutor Scott Mitchell, a devout Mormon and son of a longtime football coach, believed there was a simple explanation for the crash: King had been driving drunk when she'd hit and killed two people, and she should go to jail for it.

Dewey Buckles was the first of the two victims to be buried. On April 2 he was memorialized in a beautiful service at the Mormon Church Fifth Ward on Eighth Street in downtown Las Vegas. Buckles's stepfather, Timothy Taylor, told *Las Vegas Review-Journal* newspaper reporter Warren Bates that Buckles had been a young man of high moral character. He had dropped out of high school in Oregon, and he was later a private first class in the Oregon National Guard. The young man had come to Las Vegas for a new start with his newlywed wife, and he had been planning on going back to school when his attempt to save Richie Rundle cut short his life.

When the grief-stricken family first heard of the crash, Taylor told the paper, "We were wondering, 'Why him?'" Dewey Buckles had been just "starting to put a life together."

But his family viewed the tragedy differently when they learned how Buckles had died trying to save Richie.

"It sort of changed our thinking," Taylor said. "We're all very proud of him."

Richie was buried next. His principal, Linda McMosley, told *Las Vegas Sun* reporter Ed Koch that the students at Jo Mackey were devastated by the loss. The principal also said she was not surprised to hear of Richie's heroics and how he saved the life of his classmate Eli Scott.

"If you told me that one of my students saved another

boy's life by risking his own, I'd say, 'That's Richard,'"
McMosley told the reporter. "It comes as no surprise to me
that Richard would do such a thing. He was kind, sensitive,
and caring. He suffered from diabetes, and I believe, because of that, Richard could see the suffering in others,
and he always tried to cheer them up.

"He was a straight-A student," McMosley said. "He was
almost perfect. Maybe because he had a short life, he was
destined to do so many good things in that limited time."

Bill Rundle was in a mind-numbing blur. He was com-
forted by one of his close friends, Dan Deever, on the day
of the accident and in the following weeks. The two men
picked Shirley Rundle up at the airport two days after, and
Rundle was thankful for her return.

"Dan Deever and I picked her up at the airport and we
all went back to the apartment," Rundle said. "I spent the
day telling her about how it happened, and she was devastated."

Shirley Rundle was an angel during this terrible time.
Bill Rundle was incapacitated by grief, and his wife com-
forted him in the face of insurmountable misery. Shirley
herself was heartbroken by the death of the little child
with such a glorious soul, and although Richie was not
her flesh and blood, Shirley had loved her stepson very
dearly, and grief over Richie's death brought her to her
knees.

"She truly loved Richie," Rundle said.

Rundle spoke with Ed Koch prior to the funeral. The
paper quoted Rundle in a story telling readers that the funeral would take place April 4.

"My son will be buried in a St. Louis Cardinals baseball jersey—it was his favorite team," Rundle said. "I'm
proud of my son and what he did, but I'm bitter over what
happened."

Rundle, according to the story, went to the funeral home
prior to the funeral and "placed in the young hero's coffin

a baseball pennant, an autographed photo of professional bowler Mike Aulby, and a photo of Bill and Richard together."

Richie's funeral was April 4 on a rainy day at Davis Paradise Valley Funeral Home. Burial followed at the Paradise Memorial Gardens cemetery. Richie's mother, Amy Castor, was then living in Ohio, but she and her daughter Kelli came to Las Vegas for the funeral. They were grief-stricken, like everyone else, and it seemed to Rundle as if the whole city of Las Vegas was at the funeral. The place was packed. Castor, and Richie's two sets of grandparents, wept openly. The profound grief and sense of loss enveloped the funeral with a heartbreaking sadness and the ghost of what might have been if Richie had lived. Mourners were overwhelmed as they paid tribute to Richie in a casket adorned with a St. Louis Cardinals flag and a banner that read, "Little Hero." Eli Scott was at the funeral, and the child appeared devastated in newspaper photos. Bill and Shirley Rundle were photographed by a newspaper photographer at the funeral reading a heartfelt card from Richie's fellow students titled "To the Rundle family." Later, a photographer snapped a photo of Rundle wiping a tear from his eye with Shirley comforting him at his side.

"We had the funeral," Rundle said. "My mom and dad came. The pallbearers were six friends of mine. Dan Deever, Don Chalmers, people I drove cab[s] with, my third wife's father, Jake Castor, and Fred Floyd. They all knew Richie, and they all knew what a sweet wonderful kid he was. This child never did anything bad in his life. He was the opposite of me.

"The funeral was nice," Rundle said. "We got tremendous respect for the community. Security guards from throughout Las Vegas took up a contribution and paid for the funeral. I couldn't believe people I didn't even know thought that much of Richard. Jackie Gaughan, [owner of] the

Union Plaza, kept me on the payroll, and I didn't work for a month. They cared."

Something remarkable happened in the aftermath of Richie's death. The entire city of Las Vegas and the state of Nevada grieved for Richie Rundle and Dewey Buckles. Las Vegas can be a cold, cruel city at times, and a lot of terrible things happen here without many people noticing or caring. People get murdered almost every other day in Las Vegas, and unless a celebrity or prominent person is involved, very few people pay attention to the cruelest human acts. But as news of the terrible crash that killed Richie Rundle spread, it was different. Richie's death was one of the most painful emotional episodes in Las Vegas's history, and the deaths of the child and the maintenance man changed the way Las Vegans viewed drunk driving.

People were outraged at Corina King. They were deeply affected by the emotional sadness of Richie's loss, and in death, Richie Rundle became the city's own son.

Richie's death was front-page news in the *Las Vegas Review-Journal* and the *Las Vegas Sun* newspapers, and it was the lead story on every evening newscast. Two heroes, killed too early in life: Richie Rundle had overcome diabetes only to be run over by a drunk driver, and Dewey Buckles had died trying to save Richie. They were young people who'd died because of their selfless, heroic acts, and they were the type of people whom the city of Las Vegas could be proud of.

The state of Nevada mourned, too. The Nevada Legislature took up the cause by passing a symbolic resolution labeling the child "a young boy with the heart of a giant." McMosley promised publicly in the *Las Vegas Sun* that she was "not going to allow this to be forgotten." Richie Rundle's fellow students collected hundreds of signatures for a petition reading, "Students at Jo Mackey are against drunk driving and students getting killed."

Students throughout Las Vegas studied Nevada's drunken

driving laws in their classes. Richie Rundle's textbooks were damaged in the crash, but school officials retrieved them for preservation in a trophy case at Jo Mackey's school library along with a plaque in honor of the child.

Carol Swan, who lived at the Rundles' Coral Gardens apartment complex, solicited donations and gift certificates for the families of the victims. The office of Congressman Jim Bilbray set up bank accounts for donations to the Rundles and the Buckles. On April 8, Clark County Commissioner Thaila Dondero awarded to their families two plaques honoring the victims. The Las Vegas Stars baseball team decided that once a year the ball club would hold a night in honor of Richie Rundle to increase awareness about the dangers of drinking and driving.

And the Clark County School District made sure Richie Rundle's name would live for decades to come by naming a brand-new grade school after the child. Richard J. Rundle Elementary School is now a place of learning in Las Vegas, and every year, the school holds an event called the "Rundle Roundup" to honor the life of Richie Rundle.

Corina King, meanwhile, wept and sobbed her way through court proceedings for the next seven months. She was clearly remorseful. She even vomited during one hearing. Bill Rundle attended her court proceedings and high-profile trial in December 1987, and Rundle turned out to be a regular media interview for reporters covering the case. During the trial, King took the witness stand and said she had not been drunk. She said it was a lack of food and sleep that caused the accident, but a jury convicted her of driving drunk, and she was sentenced by District Court Judge Del Guy to six years in prison.

"What's the cost of life?" the judge said as he sentenced King. "I don't know. I did consider this a non-intentional crime. Miss King does not fit the stereotyped image of what a drunken driver is."

Friends of King expressed relief at the sentence while

Sandy Heverly—president of a local group that advocates for stiff sentences for drunk drivers—denounced the judge's sentence. Rundle didn't think the sentence was enough.

"I think I've been cheated," Rundle told *Las Vegas Review-Journal* reporters Phil Pattee and Major Garrett. "I wanted ten years at least. I don't think that's too much to ask for two lives."

King decided not to appeal the sentence.

"I know I'm responsible for what happened," King said at her sentencing hearing. "I don't feel that the jury came back with a verdict because they were pressured. I don't think I've been treated unfairly."

8 . . . DEVIL'S CITY (THE GOOD LIFE)

Bill and Shirley Rundle trudged through their jobs for several years in the aftermath of Richie's death. They were grief-stricken, and Bill Rundle spent a lot of time wondering what his son might have accomplished if he hadn't been run over and killed by a drunken cocktail waitress while waiting for a school bus.

"I think he would have done something in sports," Bill Rundle said. "I think he would have been a sportswriter. He was too small to play. People told me he could have been a lawyer or doctor, but I never pushed Richie at all. I was just proud of who he was."

Rundle said he was a bitter person for years over his son's loss.

"I was angry," Bill Rundle said. "Even though I believed in God, I didn't realize what was happening. My faith wasn't strong enough. When Richie got killed, some religious person at the Union Plaza told me I was in a religious curse, and God was paying me back for this and that. I almost decked the guy. I was so pissed."

Bill Rundle kept mementos from his son with him in the years after Richie's death. He kept Richie's favorite baseball bat, a Louisville Slugger, and the plaque from the Clark County Commission. He kept a scrapbook with photos about Richie and news articles about his death in a shrine in his apartment. He cherished and treasured the items with his soul.

Bill Rundle said the grief from losing Richie never went away, but life got more bearable over time, and honoring Richie's life helped. He and Shirley went every year to the "Rundle Roundup" event at Richard Rundle Elementary School, to educate students about the hazards of drinking and driving. The Rundles took to the microphone during the event, and an outgoing Shirley told the children the heartbreaking story of Richie. Every summer, the Rundles went to Richie Rundle Night at the Las Vegas Stars baseball game.

These were special nights for Bill and Shirley Rundle. Photos of the couple show the two laughing and smiling in the baseball field's stands as Richie's memory was honored.

A former coworker and friend of Bill Rundle's, Thomas James Roach, went to the baseball games with the Rundles on two occasions.

"Every year, the Las Vegas Stars would sponsor Rundle Night in honor of Bill's son Richie," Roach said. "Every year, they would invite the entire [Richard Rundle] elementary school free of charge. And, they just kind of honored Richie Rundle. Bill would throw out the first ball, the first pitch, and it was just kind of a celebration night."

Roach worked with Bill Rundle in security at the King 8 casino. He knew that, years after Richie's death, the tragedy was still a central part of Bill's life that he was hesitant to talk about.

"[He talked about it] very seldom," Roach said. "Not often. Briefly after I first met him, he brought it up that that

was his son. And I had known about the case, the drunk
driving case, because I had read about it in the newspaper,
and I very vividly remember it. He brought it up, and talked
about it a little bit at the beginning [of our friendship], and
after that, he never spoke about it. I knew that he had a
bedroom dedicated in Richie's honor."

The memory of Richie Rundle stayed with Bill and
Shirley Rundle forever. The Rundles thought about Richie
daily, but they recognized if they dwelled obsessively on
the loss of the boy, they would not be able to continue to
honor the child's life. Bill and Shirley decided together
they were not going to give up on life in the storm of losing
Richie. They decided to recommit themselves to the family they had. Shirley Rundle, in particular, was a person
devoted to her family, and she spent much of her time with
her daughter Magda and her new son-in-law, Rodel Belen,
who worked as a cook at the Stardust casino.

Bill Rundle was eventually promoted to a management
position at the Union Plaza. In 1988, he and Shirley Rundle
bought a house in a nice section of East Las Vegas near
Flamingo and Sandhill Roads. It is a beautiful neighborhood featuring older, sixties-era Vegas houses and tower-
ing palm trees. In 1990, there was a managerial change at
the Union Plaza, and Bill Rundle was offered a choice: go
back to working security or be laid off. Rundle chose to be
laid off so he could collect unemployment. Shirley left the
Union Plaza as well, and the Rundles looked for new work
in Sin City.

The Rundles collected unemployment for a year, somehow kept their house, and gradually hired on at new casino
jobs. Bill Rundle got a security job at the King 8 casino on
Tropicana Avenue at Industrial Road. The casino, now under a different name, is a nondescript gambling hall sitting
in a sea of concrete long ago spread over the desert west of
the Las Vegas Strip and the MGM Grand. Down the road
is a huge complex of weekly rental suites, a porno outlet,

and a nice casino—the Orleans—which glows in the face of southwest Las Vegas residents streaming by it all day long.

At the King 8, Rundle made a lot of friends, and he was promoted to a supervisor position in security. He was responsible for looking for cheats or drunken derelicts who might stumble in and cause trouble, but he was often keeping his eye on the football and baseball games on the casino's television.

Rundle's friend, Thomas Roach, worked with him at the King 8. He said Rundle was an avid sports bettor, but didn't bet huge amounts of money.

"Oh, he was a big San Diego Chargers and San Diego Padres fan—anything that had to do with San Diego," Roach said. "We also bet on sports together, you know, on a small-time basis. Twenty, thirty bets . . . parlays, [which] a lot of us around the King 8 did for recreation.

"When he was at work and wanted to make a bet during his tour of duty, he would have one of the other people hanging around him at the King 8 or other friends go and make the bets for him," Roach said. "We all had our ups and downs. I suppose he was just like the rest of us. Some days were good. Some days were bad, you know. We just kept plugging away."

Shirley Rundle, meanwhile, got a job working the night shift at a change booth at the Stardust on the Strip. Roach got to know her while hanging out with Bill Rundle, and he was very impressed with her.

"Very bubbly and outgoing," Roach said. "A little more outgoing than Bill. She was always laughing and smiling and very friendly. More so than Bill because of her outward personality . . . just a great gal."

Bill Rundle said his life during this time in Las Vegas was largely normal, as was his wife's.

"Shirley's daily routine was like any other American: breakfast, lunch, dinner, and work," Rundle said. "From the

Union Plaza [and at other casino jobs] she was a good and conscientious employee, and a hard worker. She always put her family first. Our favorite things were eating out, going to movies, and traveling.

"Shirley was Catholic, and she went to church every Sunday, and sometimes morning mass during the week," Rundle said. "I attended Sunday mass with her, each week, for years. Shirley didn't have many friends, and she never went anywhere with the few she had. The best trait she had was her love for children. She was caring and giving to them all."

Bill Rundle, however, claims that his marriage was erratic in the years after Richie's death. It would be good for weeks on end, and he and Shirley got along great. But then, he said, the couple would fight for days, and the marriage was miserable. Rundle was slightly overweight, and drank a lot of beer at home in front of the television screen. He spent hours gambling on sports and watching football and baseball games in his creased, worn leather chair, but Rundle said Shirley constantly worried that he was cheating on her. Bill Rundle said his wife's intense paranoia and possessiveness caused a strain on the marriage.

"She would call me at home seven times every night while she was working," Rundle said. "Honest to God truth."

This would later be disputed.

Other witnesses said Bill Rundle was the dominant person in the marriage. One witness, part-time housekeeper Janet Bertrand—the woman who first noticed the garage door open—would later tell authorities Shirley Rundle was a soft-hearted, caring person, and she'd gotten the impression that Shirley waited on her husband hand and foot.

In the 1990s, Magda Belen gave Shirley and Bill Rundle an adorable little granddaughter named Gretchen. The baby was the apple of Shirley's eye, and Bill also loved the little girl dearly. After the loss of Richie, the Rundles viewed Gretchen as a second gift from God. They spent a lot of time with her, helping the Belens raise the child while Magda and Rodel were at work. The Rundles and the Belens were extremely close, and they often went on family trips together to places like Disneyland.

"I'd lost my chance with Richie because Richie died, and Gretchen was just the sweetest, most adorable child," Bill Rundle said. "I told myself, 'I'm going to take such good care of this little girl.'"

Shirley Rundle went from the Stardust to a job at the Luxor, and she remained in close contact with her siblings and parents in the Philippines. In 1993, the Rundles successfully petitioned the federal government for Shirley's ailing father, Nicholas Mullasgo, to come to the United States to live out his final years.

"I put up no objection to him coming over here," Bill Rundle said. In fact, he said, he took care of his father-in-law while Shirley worked the night shift at the casino.

"Nicholas Mullasgo—a really nice man," Bill Rundle said. "He liked boxing, and he and I got along super. It was fun being with him."

Sadly, Shirley's father didn't last long.

"He came over here, and it was unbelievable," Bill Rundle said. "We got him cured from what he had, and then he ended up dying from a heart attack a year and a half later because he was sick. He was terminal and died in Las Vegas."

The Rundles stayed in touch with Bill Rundle's parents as well. Rundle said he and Shirley drove frequently to Southern California to see the elder Rundles at the Lawrence Welk retirement park in Escondido, although Bill Rundle said Shirley and Willa Rundle argued frequently during their encounters.

In 1995, the elder Richard Rundle took ill.

"My dad was getting old," Bill Rundle said. "He was not in good health anymore. We went down to my parents' on Thanksgiving of 1995. We went out to eat, and my dad was sick, and I could tell. He always had a good appetite, and he couldn't even finish his food."

What happened next, according to Bill Rundle, was the type of good fortune a person could only dream of. Richard and Willa Rundle had been smart with their money over the years, and Richard Rundle had amassed a small fortune totaling hundreds of thousands of dollars in stock and cash. The wealth of the elder Rundles was later confirmed by Justin Rundle in testimony before a grand jury in Las Vegas.

"They seemed to be doing well," Justin Rundle said of the elder Richard and Willa Rundle. "They didn't flaunt money around extravagantly, but I know my grandfather was a hardworking man. He worked for many years, and I know that he . . . built up security for my grandmother."

The elder Richard Rundle, now facing death in 1995, said he wanted to provide for his wife and son after he was gone. Shortly before he died, the elder Richard Rundle gave his son, Bill Rundle, a huge some of money to buy a house in Las Vegas.

Bill Rundle said he and his dad agreed it would eventually be wise for Willa Rundle to come to live with Bill and Shirley at the soon-to-be-purchased house in Vegas.

Bill and Shirley Rundle gladly took the money and bought a spectacular, brand-new home in Las Vegas. The 1996 purchase was made prior to the real-estate boom in Vegas, and the Rundles were able to buy a massive three-thousand-square-foot structure with five bedrooms in a nice southwest Las Vegas neighborhood for just $180,000.

Bill Rundle prepared a shrine for his Richie, and he placed it in an upstairs office of the new home.

"About a week a later, my mom called and said, 'Your dad is at the hospital in downtown San Diego, and he has an intestine blockage, and he's on a breathing machine,'" Bill Rundle said. "Because of the damage he'd done to himself smoking, he couldn't come off of the breathing machine. My mom said, 'If you want to see him alive again, you better come down.'

"Shirley and I went to the hospital in San Diego, and we stayed with my mom," Rundle said. "Shirley and my mom seldom talked, but we went to the hospital. The doctor said he didn't think my dad could come off the breathing machine. I didn't want him to suffer, and he talked to my mother, and my mom said, 'Okay, take him off the breathing machine.'

"He died the next day," Bill Rundle said. "He was eighty-five. It was very difficult for me because he and I were very, very close."

Bill Rundle promised his father one thing before he died: He promised he would take care of his mother, Willa. She was old and frail, and she was going to need someone to look out for her, and Rundle's father needed to know she would be okay.

"I promised him he wouldn't have to worry about my mother," Bill Rundle said.

9 ... WILLA

In 1996, Willa Rundle was eighty-one years old and alone for the first time in her life. She was also in poor health, and after her husband's death, she started to consider moving from the Lawrence Welk mobile home park in Escondido to be with her son in Las Vegas. One of Willa's Escondido neighbors, Beth Borgal, was a good friend of Willa's. Borgal had mixed feelings about the idea of Willa moving. Willa couldn't really walk on her own due to problems with her legs, and she needed help with a lot of things, including her finances.

"Willa didn't know how to do anything with her money," said Borgal. "I helped her with her checking account. She didn't know how to do anything—her husband apparently had done all of that for her—but as I went on to help her with it, I thought that it was probably not a good thing since we were friends. I would know too much about her [financial] affairs, so I suggested that maybe she should ask her son to help her.

"It was mostly checking that I did, and at one point she

had $16,000 in the checking account," Borgal said. "I said to Willa, 'You don't need to do that. You better put that into savings or do something with it, but get in touch with your son.' [So] she did."

Beth Borgal was a big fan of the Lawrence Welk park. It is quaint, friendly, and a perfect setting for seniors. Golf carts buzz through the streets, and an active social network is in place for residents to enjoy in their golden years.

"We live in mobile homes, but we own our own lots so it's considered a condominium area, and she owned her own house with her husband," Borgal said. "It's a gated community of 458 homes.

"[Willa] was a personal friend, and she also attended the Bible study that I taught in Lawrence Welk village," Borgal said. "She lived there longer than I did . . . [and] Willa's [home] was a double-wide in good condition. A nice lot."

Borgal was concerned about her friend's well-being after Willa's husband, Richard, died in 1996. Willa had lost her soul mate, and now she was clearly aching with loneliness and grief.

"Willa was naturally very upset when her husband passed away, and she decided that she had [to] move to Las Vegas and live with her son Bill," Borgal said. "[I'd] met him only one time."

But while Borgal urged Willa to get her son to help her with her finances, Borgal did not think it was a good idea for Willa to leave the park and move in with her son.

"Her son wanted her to move to Las Vegas and be with him because he didn't feel as if he could keep running down and taking care of her affairs," Borgal said. "I tried to talk her out of it actually. I had seen other people that had moved out of the village, and gone to similar situations, and it didn't work out. So, I said to Willa, 'Why don't you just wait? You've got a little bit of money. Have somebody come in, clean your house and cook your meals.' She didn't drive at that time. She couldn't drive, but she had a [golf] cart.

"She could handle [the golf cart] really well," Borgal said. "[I told her,] 'You can get around in that cart, you can call your friends, we can have lunch together in the village, and you can get to the mailbox. But if you go to Vegas, where your son and wife work full-time, you're going to be stuck in a house and it's going to be an unhappy situation."

Beth Borgal came to believe Willa's son was persistent in his desire to get her to Vegas, and that Willa eventually gave in.

"She sold it," Willa's friend said. "She had a little bit of trouble getting it sold because of something to do with the title. As far as I know, that money went to Bill as well as other money that she told me about."

Despite Willa's health problems—she had trouble with her feet and legs—Borgal said Willa's mind was still sharp when she moved to Las Vegas in 1996.

"I thought her health was very good," Borgal said. "You know, we're all senior citizens and . . . some of us are more than senior citizens, but as far as her mind and her thinking were concerned, she was very bright."

Willa, who used both a walker and wheelchair to get around, planned to spend her last remaining years of life with her son and daughter-in-law in Southern Nevada's dry, warm climate. According to another neighbor of Willa's in Escondido, Ruth Williams, Willa up and "sold her home and moved to Las Vegas to be with her son."

Just before the move, Willa Rundle's grandson, Justin, visited Willa at her home in Escondido, and he also took note of some health troubles she was experiencing. Willa was taking large amounts of medication for swelling in her legs.

"The last time I saw my grandmother, she was actually very, very weak and feeble, and I did notice," Justin Rundle said. "I had empathy for her because she did a lot for me growing up. Her legs were very swollen and almost swollen to the point where it looked like they were full of water. Just very swollen. And we went out to dinner, and just walking down the steps of the mobile [home] park, she had to lean on me to get down because she couldn't use the walker on the steps . . . her legs were almost useless. She could walk, but not very good or far."

"My mother stayed downstairs," Bill Rundle said. "We moved her to Las Vegas in 1996, and I told Shirley and my mom they had to get along. I talked to each one of them separately, and I said, 'We are going to be living in this house together, so you have to get along.'

"For the first three months and afterwards, Shirley and my mom got along. Things were good, and I was happy," Bill Rundle said of his life at the new home on Poppywood Drive.

The Belens said they spent a little bit of time with Willa when they visited the Rundle home with Gretchen.

"Being she's an elderly woman, we tried not to bother her," Rodel Belen said. "My daughter would just run around and make noise, you know."

"Most of the time, [Willa] would be using a walker," Magda Belen said. "She moved in with them because Bill Rundle's father died and she [was] all by herself."

Willa was a wealthy woman at the time of the move. She and her husband saved heartily for nearly six decades, and the elder Richard Rundle had done well for himself over time in his management position at the Cadillac dealership. The elder Rundles had made smart investments and gave those investments the necessary time to mature, and after the elder Richard Rundle died, Willa Rundle had nearly $400,000 in her investment portfolio.

Beth Borgal tried to stay in touch with Willa following her move to Vegas.

"[I] continued to have contact her with about five months of letters back and forth," Borgal said. "Phone calls back and forth, and she was very lonesome because [she] had left all of her friends and her family, her husband [had died], and her son and wife worked a lot of hours."

Borgal said when she talked to Willa, Willa never mentioned any conflicts with Bill or Shirley. "As a matter of fact, she liked Shirley," Borgal said.

Yet roughly five months after moving to Las Vegas, Willa disappeared. Borgal said there eventually came a time when she could not get Willa on the phone.

"When I first contacted her after she left, she would always answer the phone, and she would call me, too," Borgal said. "But in about five months' time, nobody answered the phone. [You] couldn't get any answer at all, and eventually the letters started coming back just returned to sender."

Borgal said she called "many, many times," but she never got ahold of Willa again. "I would say I tried to call her once a week for a period of time," Borgal said. "Never got any answer. They had no answering service. Nothing."

Borgal said it just wasn't like Willa to stop communicating with her friends from the upscale mobile home park in Escondido.

"She wanted to be in touch with other people," Borgal said.

Magda and Rodel Belen said they also eventually noticed that Willa Rundle wasn't in the home anymore. When they asked about Willa, Bill Rundle explained to them, in the presence of Shirley, that Willa was vacationing in Europe, touring her native Austria.

"We heard it from them that she had moved to Austria, that, she, you know, she wanted to go back to her birthplace," Rodel Belen said.

Shirley and Bill Rundle were now living well at their home on Poppywood Drive. They both had low-level jobs at Vegas casinos—Bill at the King 8 and Shirley at the Luxor—and they had a massive house that was bought and paid for. Willa Rundle, the wealthy matriarch of the family, was reportedly touring Europe, and the Rundles—having their first taste of comfort as a couple—started to spend. They bought nice furniture, a big television, and Shirley spent a lot of money on phone bills due to calls to her family in the Philippines.

"Three hundred dollars a month for the phone bill," Bill Rundle said. "Calling and talking to her sisters all the time. Continuously."

Rundle spent his paltry security guard income on beer and gambling on sports. The couple had a lot of expenditures on credit cards. Shirley swiped her cards with ease at Vegas department stores, and the Rundles helped the Belens out with their financial matters, too. Bill Rundle said he helped the Belens make a down payment for a house, and he also helped them pay off credit card debt. Bill and Shirley Rundle also flew to the Philippines so Bill Rundle could finally meet Shirley's family.

"My first trip to the Philippines was in February of 1998," Rundle said. "I was able to meet all her brothers and sisters. I got along great with all [of] the family. Including sisters, brothers, nephews and nieces, and grandkids, there were over seventy relatives."

During the trip, Rundle said one of Shirley's sisters who had helped support her siblings and the Mullasgo family thanked Rundle for what she recognized as his willingness to take on the financial burden of helping support the Mullasgos who lived in the Philippines. It was a reference, Rundle said, to his wife's constant financial payments to her siblings in the country.

"[Shirley's sister] pulled me aside and said, 'Welcome to our family. You don't realize what you've gotten into,'"

Rundle quoted the sister as saying. " 'You have taken a great burden off my back. Now there are two families instead of just [one] to support this family.' "

With Willa Rundle absent, the couple took out a home equity loan on the house and used the money to purchase a PostNet franchise on West Charleston in northwest Las Vegas. Bill and Shirley viewed the private postal business as a chance to escape working in the casino industry once and for all. They quit their casino jobs, and they asked the Belens to help them run and manage the store. The franchise seemed like a lucrative opportunity at the time for the Rundles because the store location was in a busy, upscale part of Vegas where people were willing to pay extra money to stay out of the long lines at the overcrowded post offices in the fast-growing city.

In 1996, Shirley had decided she was going to do something very special for her husband. She persistently encouraged her husband to make up for his failed relationship with his first son, Justin. Shirley reached out to Justin, and Justin visited the Rundles in Las Vegas on three occasions starting in the fall of 1997.

"It was Shirley who orchestrated a very nice trip for me to come down there," Justin said. "Shirley took an interest in my father and I kind of coming back together. I think she wanted him to, you know, have a son, and I think it was very important [to] her to try to do everything she could to mend that relationship."

Justin said he'd always maintained a relationship with his grandparents, and he was aware that the Rundles were living in a home purchased with his grandparents' money. Justin said it was Willa—and not the elder Richard Rundle—who gave his father the money for the house on Poppywood Drive.

"My grandmother told me she was building that house for them," Justin said. "I was told by [Bill Rundle] and Shirley the house was built for them by my grandmother."

As a result of Shirley Rundle's encouragement, Justin Rundle traveled to Las Vegas from Southern California. It was an exciting moment for Justin, who'd basically been abandoned by his father when he was just a small boy. There had only been a few chances in Justin's childhood where he got to see his dad, and those were encounters that only unfolded when his grandmother demanded them.

"You have to understand, after the divorce [and up until] the time I saw him, he really kind of just faded out of my life completely," Justin said. "[My father] just wasn't interested for whatever reason. So anytime I would see him, except maybe one time, it was with my grandparents. They would pick me up, they would drive me down [to Vegas], and they would take me to a motel on the way in and say how excited my dad was to see me.

"But . . . my grandmother was kind of like the liaison in between, kind of like pushing me onto his lap," Justin recalled.

Even given the pain and self-doubt the abandonment caused for Justin as a child, he looked forward to his trip to Las Vegas to get to know his father better. That excitement, however, morphed into the cold reality of his father's emotional callousness upon Justin's arrival in Vegas. There were times during the trip when Justin felt his father wasn't very excited to have him around. There was also an uncomfortable tour of Vegas during which Justin was shown all the memorials to Richie—the son Bill *hadn't* abandoned.

"I was taken to a grave site, and I was taken on like a little tour," Justin said. "I was taken to . . . Richard J. Rundle Elementary School, which was a very awkward thing for me. I went over to a cemetery. It wasn't too far from the school, and even though I know they had an urn with ashes of my grandfather there in the bedroom of the house, there was a grave site for Richie, and there was a headstone for my grandfather.

"Bill told me that my grandmother's wishes were to be buried next to my grandfather, and that they wanted to keep a family plot. They had three spaces . . . I guess like grave sites or whatever you call them, next to each other. I believe there was a headstone for Richard [my grandfather] there, with maybe part of the ashes there and part at the house, and then [a headstone] for Richie, then an empty one that hasn't been used. That was supposed to be for my grandmother.

"I got a tour of the house," he said. "I had never been there. There was a shrine to Richie in the office, and in that shrine, there was . . . a picture of him, a baseball that was signed by a Cardinals player, a jacket, a hat, and a baseball bat."

Justin was uncomfortable over all of the information he was given about Richie. He also found himself uncomfortable in the presence of his father in general.

"My dad sat me down and told me, 'Go through the movies, and find a couple movies you want to watch, and bring them down, and we'll watch them,'" Justin recalled. "I guess that's just what he wanted to do [was] watch movies. So he went downstairs, and I was looking at [the] movies, and I chose a couple.

"When I went downstairs to rejoin them, he had a big-screen TV constantly broadcasting sports," Justin said. "It's kind of weird, but I can't stand sports. I'm just not into them. Not my thing. And that's all that was on. Baseball games. Football games . . . That's all he would watch. I kind of was like, you know, here's the movie, can we watch the movie? What was on was of no interest to me."

Justin said he was hurt by his father's lack of emotional attachment to him.

"If I had a child coming up that I hadn't seen in a while, personally I would turn the TV off," Justin said. "I have a daughter, and I'm very active in her life. I would have spent time with me. So, as a father myself, it struck me as kind of weird how he wasn't as close as he could be. It was the first visit that we had in so long.

"I don't necessarily want to call it a coldness, but there was like a distance between us as to where it seemed like, you know, he had his wall up," Justin said. "I tried my hardest to talk to him about stuff in the past, and [I asked] questions that I wanted to know, like, 'What happened between you and Mom?' His side of the story. He had his explanations which to this day, I regard as garbage."

At the time of the 1997 visit, Justin was under the impression that his grandmother was living with Bill and Shirley. But during dinner, Bill Rundle asked him a question that took Justin by complete surprise.

"We were eating dinner, and he looked over at me while he was sitting at the head of the table, and he asked me if I'd heard anything from my grandmother," Justin recalled. "He asked me in just a very matter-of-fact way. 'Hey, have you heard from your grandmother? Has she contacted you?' And, you know, I thought it was a very strange question for me because I thought she was living there."

Justin told Bill and Shirley no, he hadn't heard from his grandmother, and then Bill Rundle revealed to him that Willa was touring Austria with a male nurse.

"He told me that she had gotten kind of ornery in her old age, and she was a sassy woman anyways," Justin said. "Basically, she had taken off with a male nurse that was looking over her care."

Bill insinuated that Willa was having a relationship with her male nurse during their tour of Austria.

"I thought [it] was ridiculous," Justin said. "He had specified that . . . she's from Austria, and I know that she was very, very proud of her Austrian heritage, so, he said she was going back to Austria to retrace her roots, which was strange to me."

Justin questioned how Willa could tour Austria. After all, the last time he'd seen his grandmother, her legs had

been so swelled up she could barely walk. Still, he had no
indication, or even a suspicion, that anything criminal had
unfolded, and he said he had no reason to even think about
calling the authorities.

In 1999, Justin visited his father and stepmother again.
This time, he was with his fiancée.

"My father had mentioned that finances were tough,
and things were not going that well, and that they were
working," Justin said. "Both were working as many hours
as possible."

Despite the financial problems, however, Shirley repeatedly gave Justin cash when her husband wasn't around.

"My father said finances were bad, and Shirley would
always, when I was there, come up to me and . . . slip me a
hundred bucks, two hundred bucks," Justin said. "She
would put it into my pocket and would be like, 'Don't tell
your father.' "

Simultaneous to his father's talk about financial troubles
were Shirley's proclamations that the Rundles were considering the purchase of a PostNet franchise. The figure floated
for the franchise was $50,000, and Justin questioned how
Bill and Shirley could afford the hefty price tag if his father
and stepmother were having money problems. After all,
Bill and Shirley were no longer working in the casinos.
They'd quit their jobs shortly after Willa had arrived.

"I was curious," Justin said. "I had asked him a couple
times [previously], 'Dad, you know, can you send me down
a couple hundred bucks. I want to get something for my
daughter' . . . and [it was] 'Oh, I can't do that right now.
Things are just so rough.' Blah blah blah . . . Yet Shirley
was talking about a $50,000 investment. When I asked
how they would get that kind of money, I was informed
that [they] might have to sell [a] ranch [Shirley] owned in
the Philippines."

Justin noted during the trip as well that Bill and Shirley were constantly going out to eat. He estimated that the couple prepared only one meal a day in their home.

Also during the 1999 trip, Justin again found himself alone with his father, and Justin asked how his grandmother was doing.

"My fiancée gave me time with my father, and he was kind of making an effort to open up a little more," Justin said. "You could see it a tiny bit. Again I inquired about my grandmother, and he informed me that he spoke with her a month before I came. Basically . . . He said that she was fine, but she was kind of short with him on the phone. [He said she] was almost displaying like a defiant attitude. That's what he told me."

Two years later, Justin talked to his dad on the phone, and Bill Rundle told him the PostNet business that they'd spent $50,000 on was tanking.

"He told me the business was doing extremely poor, that they were in the red, and things were bad," Justin recalled. "Basically . . . the business wasn't even breaking even. It was a total loss."

The topic of his grandmother's whereabouts became outright awkward during Justin's final visit to see Bill and Shirley in Vegas in 2001. Rundle, during the visit, was checking a sports pager "every thirty minutes" and screening his calls at home, Justin said.

"He informed me that if I were to call [in the future], to call collect," Justin said. "He told me to have the operator say it was me on the machine, because there were a couple of people they were trying to avoid. This was an issue. It was definitely something [where] they did not want to answer the phone."

Rundle changed his email address around this time.

"It was Honybun for a while and then, for some reason, he changed it to Hurricane," Justin said.

Justin said that during the 2001 visit, they went to

breakfast at the Orleans casino, and Bill was at the buffet
line when Justin decided to ask Shirley about his grandmother.

"I said to Shirley, 'Honestly, you guys haven't heard
anything from Willa?'" Justin recalled. "'I mean, it's just
so strange to me, this whole thing. Is there anything you
know?'"

The expression on Shirley's face caught Justin's attention. She seemed pained by the question.

"And there was . . . a bit of difference in Shirley that I
noticed," Justin said. "She looked at me with a concern of
some kind in her eyes. Maybe she knew I wanted to know,
and I was dying to know. But again, I had no reason to
think any foul play or anything. And she started to tell me
something, and that's when my father returned."

"Justin, your grandmother was real tired," Shirley said
before being cut off by her husband.

"She wanted to tell me something," Justin said. "There
was a moment where I really felt a connection between
Shirley and myself . . . that she wanted to tell me something. I had an idea that it had to do with my grandmother,
and maybe [she was going to tell me] the truth."

10 ... LASSEN COUNTY

Susanville, California, is a scenic, charming, small city in the northeast corner of the state. To the southeast, down Highway 395, is the famous western gambling town of Reno, Nevada, and farther down the road is the spectacular resort town, Lake Tahoe. The area is both pretty and historic: There is a classic old theater in downtown Susanville, and part of the Susanville's charm can be found in the city's history, its origins in the mining and logging industries. In fact, about twenty miles away the town of Westwood boasts a statue of mythic logger Paul Bunyan and Babe the Blue Ox carved out of logs.

Susanville is located in Lassen County, a huge, rural, remote, and remarkably beautiful county that offers magnificent views of the snowy Cascade Mountains and the Sierra Nevadas. There are expansive western blue skies, high-desert meadows, the Lassen County National Forest, the Honey Lake National Wildlife Refuge, and the massive Eagle Lake about fifteen miles to the north. Along Highway Number 44, out traveling in a northwest direction through Northern California, motorists come to a little lake known as Poison Lake. On August 20, 2001, Cottonwood, California, contract logger Dana Spooner and his wife, Connie, were traveling through this area, moving equipment, when they stopped at a small pull-over area on the side of the roadway.

"West on 44, and we seen like a red rug or something lying along the side of the road within probably, oh, forty feet of the edge," Dana Spooner said.

The logger got out of his vehicle and inspected further.

"I got out and walked over to it to try and decide what it was," Spooner said. "I went alone. I walked up to what would be the east side of it . . . and it was a red-like velour blanket. Something was obviously rolled in it, and it had three cords tied around it where it was bound. I went to the other end of it. I lifted a loose flap of the blanket up, and there was a person's legs and feet."

Spooner was briefly startled, and he noticed the body seemed particularly pink to him. He rushed back to his vehicle and used a satellite phone to call an interagency dispatch number, which led to a call to the Lassen County Sheriff's Office. Patrol Deputy Benny Wayne Wallace, a deputy for thirteen years, was dispatched to the site of the body on Highway 44 near Poison Lake. It was a remote area that Wallace knew well.

Wallace was first to the scene, and he observed there a body wrapped in a red blanket.

"I observed what appeared to be two human feet pointing down toward the ground," Wallace said. "I backed away, secured the scene, and waited for my investigators to arrive."

Sergeants Bill Ceaglio, John Mineau, and David Martin of the Lassen County Sheriff's Office arrived and determined that the body in the velour blanket was about fifty feet from the roadway. Three nylon cords secured the blanket around the deceased. The cords were approximately a quarter-inch in diameter.

"One [rope] secured the blanket around the victim in the area of the calves of the legs," Wallace said. "A second was in what appeared to be the waist area of the victim, and a third was way up high—I would say in the neck/chest area.

"We proceeded to do a crime scene investigation, collecting, cataloging, and photographing evidence," Wallace said. "A videotape was made."

The men processed the crime scene under a beautiful Northern California sky in a desolate stretch of the Golden State.

"A remote area of western Lassen County," Lassen County Sergeant John Mineau said. "The highway runs predominantly east and west and is one of the main thoroughfares between Susanville and Redding. It's largely a logging area."

The area is uninhabited, with lot of trees, lots of open meadows, and grasslands. It didn't seem like an appropriate place for death, given the natural beauty of the surrounding scenery. The detectives automatically suspected they were dealing with a homicide given the way the body was tied up and seemingly dumped alongside the roadway in a hurried manner. Whoever had dumped the body must have been in a rush, because it appeared to be a haphazard place to dispose of the remains. Just a few more minutes of effort dedicated to concealing the body might have delayed its discovery for a significant period of time. Instead, the person who dumped the corpse had basically left the body in the red blanket within plain sight of the roadway. The officers slowly made their way to the body, and the red blanket was unraveled. The victim was a small woman with black hair, and she was wearing a pink and blue nightgown. She was wrapped not only in a blanket but also a very bloody blue and white sheet. The investigators examined the head of the victim and found disturbing evidence. It appeared the woman had had some sort of dramatic trauma to her head, and something was in her mouth.

"I observed that the victim had a green towel that appeared to be stuffed quite deeply into her mouth," Wallace said.

Whoever stuck the towel in this woman's mouth had obviously wanted her to die. This was evident because of how far down the towel was shoved into the woman's throat. It was a coldhearted, mean-spirited act of murder. The investigators contemplated the possibility that the woman had been hit in the head with some sort of blunt object, causing the lacerations to the head. If she had still been alive after that, the towel might have been put in her mouth to stop her from moaning and groaning.

"The victim had quite a large quantity of blood on the back of her head," Mineau said. "As the body was moved, I observed what appeared to be large lacerations to the back upper portion of her head."

There was something else the investigators noticed: The woman had no identification on her, and she wasn't wearing any jewelry. The detectives thought she might be a vagrant, and without knowing who she was, it would be difficult to determine exactly what had happened to her. A representative from Walton's Mortuary in Susanville drove to the remote scene, picked up the body, and the nameless victim was transported back to the mortuary in Susanville. An autopsy was performed the following day by Washoe County, Nevada, Medical Examiner Ellen Clark. Fingerprints and dental X-rays of the woman's teeth were secured. The cause of death was determined to be blunt force trauma to the head, and her skull had been brutally fractured. The victim's age was estimated at forty-five to sixty years old.

The Lassen County detectives, in the following days,

set out to find out who the woman was, but in the coming weeks, the detectives became very frustrated in their efforts to identify her. The victim's fingerprints were entered into computer databases, but those searches turned up nothing. A flier was distributed to law enforcement with a description of the victim, but the sheriff's office got no response.

"Actually, one of the things we have available to us is called the TRAK system, and what that stands for is Technology to Recover Abducted Kids," Mineau said. "We use it quite extensively in California, and it's widely used in Nevada. You scan a photo, and send a text along with that photo [to other police agencies]. In this case, what we did is we put a flier out initially with no photo saying that we had an unidentified deceased female and then [provided] some basic physical descriptors. It had her estimated age. We sent that out throughout California. We also sent it to some agencies in Northern Nevada.

"The next step we took was we used the California law enforcement teletype system," Mineau said. "We put in physical descriptors, and we ran searches that way to see if we could get any potential matches to somebody who might have fit this description."

The detectives released details of the unidentified body to the media, including the *Lassen County Times* newspaper and a local television station, but they came up with nothing again. With no identification, the victim's body was cremated.

11 ... SPEAK FOR THE DEAD

Justice, and only justice, you shall pursue.

—Deuteronomy 16:20

Sheila Huggins carries a badge and gun as a homicide detective for the Las Vegas Metropolitan Police Department, and her job is to catch killers in the Devil's city.

The forty-seven-year-old detective is small in size—barely five feet tall—but she is a dynamo of a human being. She is charismatic, funny, and a country girl through and through. Huggins was raised on a ranch with her three younger brothers, on the open expanse of the Northern Nevada range in Elko—a dusty cowboy, ranching, and mining town that looks as if it fell straight out of a Copenhagen snuff ad. Elko is about a five-hour drive northeast of Las Vegas. Huggins's parents, Jim and Paula Fieselman, are ranchers, and Jim Fieselman raised his daughter to be a buckaroo.

"You don't call them cowboys in Elko," Huggins said. "They are buckaroos. You wear a certain type of pants, a certain type of boots, and the saddles are specific to this area. In Elko you are talking about Old West buckaroos."

Huggins was born in Cottonwood, Arizona, though she

spent much of her childhood in Colorado. Her dad was employed as a truck driver on a ranch, and when Jim Fieselman's employers bought another ranch in Nevada, Fieselman moved his family to Elko to manage the property.

"My dad is a serious cowboy," Huggins said. "He's a tall, good-looking, handsome man [with] piercing blue eyes, a handlebar mustache, and he wears cowboy hats and boots all of the time. He has a great work ethic, and he thinks work is a necessity."

"I was a teen growing up on this humongous ranch," Huggins said. "It was fifty miles long and thirty miles wide, in Elko, and they asked my dad to manage it. It had several different outpost ranches, little segments, and we managed one called Devil's Gates. I moved there when I was probably a freshman in high school."

Jim Fieselman made it clear to his daughter that she was expected to do everything a man did on the ranch, and Huggins literally lived the Western rancher's life as a teen on the open range.

"I had two cows to milk, and that was just for us to drink," Huggins said. "I was the one who went out on the range with my dad. We'd have breakfast, milk the cows, and then we'd be off to ride for days. You have to remember we still lived thirty miles outside of town, so we were isolated, and I spent a lot of time with my parents. We basically went to town in Elko very little. Once a week, except to school."

Huggins learned on the ranch the true realities of the world and how to survive in it. She was to show no weakness, work hard, and remember that life can slip away in an instant.

"I was taught never to be afraid of hard work, and growing up on a ranch taught me to be prepared for whatever happens," Huggins said. "You see things go bad with one of your animals, and you deal with it."

Huggins is also extremely close to her mother, who

was a housewife and also waitressed to help support the family.

"To this day, my mom is my best friend," Huggins said.

At the age of eighteen, Huggins met the first love of her life. Jimmie Lee Vincente* lived in Elko, and Huggins was head over heels in love with the dark-haired Italian. Vincente was interested in law enforcement and was subsequently hired as a police officer in Las Vegas. Huggins loved Vincente dearly, and she followed him to Las Vegas. The couple married and had a wonderful son, Tyler, but life was not easy for the rancher's daughter in the big city. She'd gone from life on the open range to living in a small apartment in urban Vegas. She barely got out of the apartment, and over time, she became frustrated because her new husband was hardly ever home.

"I was in love, and that is what kept me in Las Vegas, but I hated it at first," Huggins said. "The city was very impersonal to me. Nobody smiles at you. Nobody talks to you. Where I come from, you drive by in your old truck, and people wave. It wasn't like that here. You move here, no one knows anything about you, and you are just a face."

A few years into the marriage, it was clear to Huggins that the union was not going well. The couple soon divorced, and Huggins found herself alone in Las Vegas.

To cope with the fear and insecurity of being a single mother in the big city, she said she relied on a life lesson from the ranch: always deal with all your problems head-on. To support her son, she got a job as a clerk at the Clark County Detention Center, and she worked at the booking desk in the downtown den of concrete and steel bars that serves as home to criminals ranging from pickpockets to cold-blooded killers. She didn't know it at the time, but the

* Denotes pseudonym

job at the jail would change her life forever. Huggins made a lot of friends who were cops, and over time, the diminutive country girl from Elko contemplated becoming a cop herself in Sin City.

"It hits me all of a sudden one day that everyone in law enforcement is [part of] a family," Huggins said. "Even though I wasn't a cop, when I was working at the jail, all the cops would come and talk to you. 'Hi, Sheila, how you doing?' They'd be bringing in some fighting drunk to be booked, and it was fun. It was exciting and cool."

Huggins entered the Las Vegas police academy in 1988 and graduated that year. The rancher's daughter was a long way from Elko. She was assigned to Patrol, and instead of rounding up cattle on the range, she was tasked with corralling human animals. She wasted no time making her way up the chain of command in the Vegas police force, and she worked as a detective in narcotics and vice.

"I went to Vice, and I posed as a whore," Huggins said. "I'd walk the streets in prostitution stings, but I'm from the country, and I had to get used to the language these johns would use. These guys would ask me if I've got paper in my crib, and I'm like, 'I ain't got no paper in my crib,' and I'm thinking to myself, 'What are you talking about? What do you mean "Paper in your crib?"' They'd call me a momma baby, and I'm like, 'Momma baby? Isn't that someone who sucks their thumb and cries for their momma?'"

She worked undercover in Narcotics, and over time, she came to hate it.

"You know why I really started not liking investigating dope?" Huggins said. "I couldn't go to any cop functions because I was undercover, and I would be answering my phone, and it would only be crooks on the other end. You would meet with these drug dealers and be talking to them, and you would talk to them about their families, and they had lives, too, but they just had a weird job—selling dope—and my job at that time was to buy dope from them. You'd get to know them, and pretty soon they'd be dumping their issues on you, like I had a fight with my old lady, stuff like that. So I'd meet some of them sitting there undercover, and I felt like saying, 'Run. Don't you know I'm a cop?'"

Huggins's fellow officers took notice of the small woman's bravery and also her larger-than-life personality. She said she never really worried about the dangers of her job, but during one traffic stop early on in her career, it struck her that there were times when her small size left her at a disadvantage physically. The moment arrived when she was alone in the middle of the night, and she encountered a massive criminal suspect named "Wolf" during a traffic stop. The man was wanted on charges of chopping off his girlfriend's kid's fingers.

"He was a big mean fightin' dude," Huggins said. "I get him out of the car . . . and he's just looking at me, and you could tell he was trying to figure out what he's going to do. Running would probably be the worst for me because I'm so short I can't catch anybody.

"I told him, 'I need you to step in front of my car and put your hands behind your back,'" Huggins said. "I knew the other officers were coming, but it was then that it hit me that the size difference between me and this guy was unbelievable."

Wolf was arrested and carted off, and Huggins realized that in most instances the size difference between her and a suspect was no big deal.

"You still got to talk to them nice and soft and make sure they don't kick," Huggins said. "I don't want them to bite me, either. I've always believed you can figure your way out of pretty much any situation without going to shit, and that's true. There are a lot of cops who get into fights or altercations when they don't have to. Being a good cop has nothing to do with being a tough guy or with big macho skills. It's people skills."

There are a lot of Las Vegas homicide detectives who find that a job in the elite unit is a real drag over time. The demands on an individual are immense, and the time away from one's family is extremely difficult. The cycle of murder never ends in Vegas, and the job can wear on you. The dead body calls come in at all hours, and a homicide detective regularly walks through life like a sleep-deprived zombie. The job takes a toll on your family, your body, and your psyche. It's murder, mayhem, and cruelty around the clock. The Devil is busy in Las Vegas, and it's a homicide detective's job to keep him in check as much as is humanly possible.

Don Tremel, fifty-one, has lasted as a Vegas homicide detective for fifteen years. Everyone around him says he's about as good a detective as you'll find. He is an intense individual who stands about five feet ten inches tall. He's got straight brown hair and a face seemingly chiseled out of granite. Tremel was born in Dearborn, Michigan, and grew up there. He was one of four children raised in a strict Catholic family. His dad, Don, worked for decades in the gasoline and oil business, and his mother, Mary, was a housewife who occasionally worked at Sears to help make ends meet. Tremel loved playing baseball and hockey as a kid, and he said his parents instilled in him early that he was expected to follow the rules of the family and society.

"The rules were the rules, and I was the oldest, so I was always the first one to break the rules and experience what it was like to be disciplined by my dad," Tremel said. "You know, grounded for the rest of your life."

Tremel and his wife, Cindy, have two sons, and Tremel is as tough on his kids as his dad was on him. He likes to stay fit, but the physical drain of being a detective means he has to find some way to relax. When he does get some downtime, he sucks down a few beers, flips on the television, and watches his favorite Detroit Red Wings skate up and down the ice in Hockeytown USA.

"The real toll on you as a homicide detective is the time away from family and friends," Tremel said. "Getting up in the middle of the night, getting dressed, getting to the scene and functioning in a working mode when you are tired is the hardest.

"You might not get any sleep for three days, depending on the type of case and how fast things are developing," Tremel said. "You can't just say, 'I'm tired, I'm going to go home and rest, I'll take care of it later,' or 'I'll be back in a couple of hours.' You can't do that, and in the summertime, when it gets really, really hot here, it will wear you out. I'm finding it harder and harder the older I get."

Tremel is proud to be a police officer. With law and order, there is civility, and human beings have a chance to blossom. But at the same time, all of his years investigating homicides in Las Vegas have left Tremel a hard-liner for people who don't like to cooperate with the police.

"You get a person shot dead in the street, and nobody saw nothing," Tremel said. "They are motherfucking you because you are there, and they don't want you there, and I've seen so much of that that I'm like, 'Well, okay, it's your neighborhood.' "

Detective Don Tremel has investigated literally hundreds of homicides and caught countless cold-blooded killers. He stopped keeping track long ago, but of all the cases he has solved, there is one that gives him the most satisfaction. The victim's name was Brooklyn Ricks, a small, beautiful girl who was working at a video store in Las Vegas on August 12, 1995. After finishing her late shift on a hot Vegas night, she jumped in her car and headed home.

Hours later, a construction worker discovered Ricks's brutalized body hidden under a pile of debris.

"He hears moaning," Tremel said. "There is a pile of debris or whatnot, he moves the debris away, and there's Brooklyn bound and gagged, bleeding, underneath this pile of debris, and within minutes, she died."

Tremel was outraged. She was an innocent, defenseless victim.

"A violent death," Tremel sad. "Beat about the head and face, and this probably rendered her unconscious. She was tied up, her hands were bound with a six-pack plastic ring thing, and she had like a Wonder Bread bag gagged in her mouth. Raped. This guy had his way with her, and then he brutally beat and disposed of her like a piece of garbage."

Tremel and his fellow detectives vowed to catch the killer. In questioning Ricks's coworkers, the name Gregory Boland came up almost immediately. Boland was a customer at the store who'd made regular advances to the victim, according to witnesses. Video from the store on the night in question showed Boland talking to Ricks before she left the store.

"We surmised that he flagged her down, she stopped, he probably coldcocked her, and he got her in his truck," Tremel said.

A pubic hair was found on the victim, and it was linked to Boland. It turned out that the killer had just been released from a Colorado prison for abducting and raping another woman. He's now on Nevada's death row.

"We have to speak for the dead," Tremel said. "No one else will. No one else is going to go out and work for them."

There are times when Las Vegas lives up to its reputation as Satan's city. It can be a place where drug dealers kill one another with impunity, husbands kill their wives in suicidal drunken rages, and prostitutes are cast aside along the highway outside of the city in the scrub brush of the barren Clark County desert.

To keep the sanity, the city relies on the 2,500 officers of the Las Vegas Metropolitan Police Department, and the job of catching the city's killers falls to a half dozen police detectives at the police department's homicide section. In 2002, Homicide was headquartered on West Charleston Boulevard.

Las Vegas Police Sergeant Rocky Alby supervises a team of six detectives out of twenty-four in the office. Alby is a longtime cop who worked his way up through the ranks, including assignment on Gangs and Juvenile, Sex Assault, Patrol, and the Detective Bureau. He was an integral figure in the creation of the Las Vegas police CAT unit, or Criminal Apprehension Team. The unit, in conjunction with the FBI and other police agencies in the Las Vegas Valley, spends every day hunting down fugitives who come to Vegas for one last thrill.

Alby, like most everyone in Homicide, is a no-nonsense cop on the job.

"My own personal theory of case management is I try to do as much as I can to help the homicide detectives I supervise during the first seventy-two hours after a murder," Alby said. "Whatever I can do to help, I try to do, and then I get out of the way. After the first seventy-two hours, I start scaling back. I need to start prepping myself for warrants because we do a lot of search warrants. I usually do the search warrants. I'll get the search warrant done and out of the way and filed at the courthouse. I also may take digital photos or statements from nonessential witnesses."

Alby, however, is not just a sounding board for the detectives he supervises. He is actively involved in his detectives' murder cases, and there is clearly a hierarchy to the work under Alby. He runs a tight ship because he knows his work is very, very important, and one misstep can cost a case and feasibly set a killer free.

"There is discussion," Alby said. "Whenever we get one that is unsolved, a whodunit case where the suspect is not identified really quick, we will sit down and say, 'Okay, what direction are we going? What has been done so far, what hasn't been done, and who are the most likely suspects? Where is the physical evidence? What can we do with the physical evidence at the scene?' Sometimes you have to look at a case and decide if it is going to be a case solved by witnesses or if the case is going to be decided by forensic evidence.

"Some people have a difficult time with this job," Alby said. "They get too emotionally wrapped up in the violence that took place or the individuals who get killed. For reasons I can't explain, it doesn't bother me at all. I have the ability to turn it off and just say okay. I find that I spend very little time trying to understand why anything happened and just accept that it did happen and not worry about it."

Alby said in August of 2002 he was very fortunate to have two devoted detectives like Huggins and Tremel working for him. The two detectives have chemistry as an investigative unit.

"Don Tremel, like myself, seems to be able to distance himself from a case, so he doesn't dwell on it, and he can turn it off and not get emotionally involved," Alby said. "He's really good because he can pace himself. Maybe somebody will beat him to something, but over the long haul, he is consistent, thorough, and very, very little gets by him. If you were to take an unsolved case from him, you could look it over, and it would be real thorough. At the end, you would say, 'I don't know what else I could do here because he's already done everything else.' He's in there for the long haul."

Alby said Huggins is different, but she is just as effective.

"Sheila works at a much faster pace," Alby said. "Because of the time she spent as a narcotics detective, she has the ability to talk with people and to bond with them in a much closer fashion. Sheila goes in close. Some suspects seem to bond with Sheila because she is a people person. Don is 'Tell me what I need to know, and I don't care about your dog,' while Sheila will say, 'What kind of dog do you have?' Sheila is more willing to try long shots."

One long shot that paid off for Huggins unfolded in the 2004 case of a longtime Las Vegan who was found brutally bludgeoned with a toilet tank cover in a home where he was house-sitting. The detectives learned the victim had been in the company of a transvestite prostitute on the night he was murdered, but the investigation was at a standstill when it came to identifying the killer.

"Sheila went to all the gay bars during the evening hours," Alby said. "These were places where other cops would have been very uncomfortable, and Sheila struck up conversations with bartenders, and she frequented the bars daily. Sheila was able to get people to call her back with little tiny pieces of information here and there. Little tiny pieces of description of the suspect, and within three to four weeks, we had a street name. Then, we had a real name, and then we had the car he drives, and he's in Southern California. Then we caught up with him, and he confessed. Sheila was a driving force behind that."

12 ... BLOOD

On August 22, 2002, Magda Belen was horrified to find what looked like a huge bloodstain underneath a throw rug in the home of her mother and stepfather, Shirley and Bill Rundle. Las Vegas Police Missing Persons Detective Thomas Marin obtained a telephonic search warrant and he called more detectives and crime scene analysts to the Rundles' home on Poppywood Drive. Las Vegas Police Crime Scene Analyst Yolanda McClary photographed the bloodstain and processed the home for further evidence. A DNA sample was later taken from Magda Belen by Las Vegas Police Lieutenant Tom Monahan.

"We took some miscellaneous items [from the home] . . . some mail that showed the Rundles did live there, some receipts, a phone book, and some swabs were completed by CSI," Marin said. "Samples of the stains on the carpet [were taken] to help us determine whether or not it was human blood.

"Magda . . . provided me with an Internet address that

she believed belonged to Bill Rundle," Marin said. "[Detective] Gary Sayre made contact with bank representatives to retrieve [bank surveillance] photos and [bank] statements."

On the morning of September 12, 2002, Las Vegas police Homicide Detective Don Tremel and Sergeant Rocky Alby were sitting in the police department's homicide office on West Charleston Boulevard waiting for Detective Sheila Huggins to arrive. Alby, Tremel, and Huggins were on call, meaning that the next homicide case reported to police would be theirs to investigate.

Huggins was late. While Tremel and Alby waited for her, Alby picked up a copy of the *Las Vegas Review-Journal* newspaper and read a front-page story written by reporter Mike Kalil. The story was about the disappearance of Bill and Shirley Rundle in August, and Kalil quoted police sources saying blood was found in the Rundles' home. Kalil also documented in the story how, some fifteen years earlier, the couple had endured the tragic death of Richie Rundle. And now the Rundles were missing. Alby showed the article to Tremel, and Tremel was intrigued because he vividly remembered the grief the city of Las Vegas felt from Richie's death.

"I remembered the name Rundle from when his kid got killed," Tremel said. "It was a huge deal. Richie was a young, innocent kid killed by some drunk while he was waiting for a school bus. For Christ's sake. What's safer than that?"

Huggins walked into the office as Tremel finished the article. He threw the newspaper at Huggins.

"Here's our next case," Tremel said.

Huggins was flustered from trying to get to work on time. She read the article, and she questioned out loud why the missing persons detectives hadn't called homicide detectives three weeks earlier.

"I read the article, and I was mad," Huggins said. "For one, they found blood, and it's in the paper. I was confused as to why they hadn't called us. I got pissy about it."

Huggins rang up Missing Persons and talked to Marin. She learned the missing persons detectives weren't sure what they had, and Marin told Huggins the police were about to execute a second search warrant on the Rundle home. The homicide detectives asked to be included in the search, and Marin agreed.

Huggins was fired up. She wanted to help solve the mystery.

"Don looked at Rocky [Alby] and said out loud, 'Oh boy, we just dangled the carrot in front of the mule,'" Huggins recalled.

The detectives arrived at the home on Poppywood Drive, and missing persons detectives were already there with crime scene analysts. The homicide detectives were briefed on all of the facts. The Rundles hadn't been seen since August 17 and there were thousands withdrawn from the couple's bank accounts. The Rundles' Buick Regal with tag HONYBUN was missing, and in the garage was the note on the door saying,

Alarm is set! Be home 09-06. Emergency trip to the Philippines.

Shirley Rundle's daughter, Magda Belen, met with the homicide detectives and repeated for the detectives her grave worries about the whereabouts of her mother and stepfather.

"Magda was suspicious of what happened to them from the get-go," Tremel said.

Huggins said she seemed to bond with Magda Belen. Belen immediately struck her as a very classy woman, and Huggins, being close to her own mother, could only imagine

the terror Belen was feeling at not knowing where her
mom was. Huggins felt great sympathy for Belen when she
interviewed the woman.

"Magda is a very sweet lady," Huggins said. "I got to
know her, and she was extremely worried about her mom.
She felt about her mom the way I feel about my mom. I talk
to my mom almost every day, and so did she. She depended
on her mom, and her mom was her good friend. They did
things together, and if I were Magda, I would have known
something was wrong, too. I went off what she felt, because who would know better than her?"

The detectives decided to run a team of crime scene
analysts through the home again. Senior Crime Scene Analyst Daniel Holstein and two other CSIs, Kristen Gramma
and Charity Green, carried out the forensics investigation.
Holstein, a soft-spoken, large man with dark hair and kind
demeanor, is a thirteen-year veteran investigator, and his
colleagues respect him greatly. He is highly regarded
throughout the Las Vegas police force for his ability to find
fingerprints or interpret blood patterns. Holstein, Gramma,
and Green did a walk-through of the home with the detectives, and they observed the bloodstain Belen had discovered underneath the throw rugs in the living room.

"I looked around the house, and I took some notes,"
Holstein said. "Once I was done with that, then I started to
do photography. I photographed the entire residence, and I
made some more notes. After that, I started to do further
documentation and processing and collection of evidence."

The bloodstain was a major focus of attention for the
police and the CSIs. Holstein wrote down the layout of the
living room where the stain was located.

"There were two tables with a sofa in between," Holstein
said. "There was a square coffee table in the center of the
room which was on top of a throw rug. Over in the corner
there was a recliner, a [white] leather-type chair. Partially

on the throw rug, and on the carpet, was where the blood-stain was located. There was a flower-colored chair that was next to the coffee table, [and it] was later told to me that [this chair] was not [normally in this room]."

Samples of the blood were taken, and then Holstein sprayed the stain with a special protein-based stain, leuco crystal violet, to turn it bright purple. The purple stain enhanced the visibility of the original bloodstain so that the investigators could examine it better.

"When you see blood, sometimes it will start to fade," Holstein said. "It looks like a reddish-brown stain, but when you use an enhancement, the enhancement will turn it purple. A lot of times, something doesn't seem real obvious, or you can't see [it] with the naked eye, [but] when you enhance it with the leuco crystal violet, it becomes more prevalent in terms of pattern recognition."

The bloodstain was large. The size of the stain convinced the detectives they were investigating a felony assault, a murder, or murders.

"I didn't think it was from a bloody nose," Huggins said.

"There was a significant amount of blood," Tremel said, concerned. "It told me they didn't cut themselves. I figured they were probably hurt pretty bad. Very suspicious."

The detectives scoured the home for any clues, and Huggins tried to learn as much as she could about the couple through what she observed.

"When you walked into that house it was totally Shirley inside," Huggins said. "The decorations and art told you she had good taste. The stuff in there probably cost more than they could afford, but she had good taste. It was classy in the home, and it was very clean.

"The pictures in the home were all in nice gold frames," Huggins said. "One of the only things in the whole house that told me Bill Rundle even lived there was a white leather chair in the living room that looked like someone was sitting in it every day. It was in front of a big television. There were sports magazines next to the chair on a table, and there were notebook pages that were like betting pages. You knew that was his chair."

One thing that struck Tremel, Huggins, and Alby was how incredibly normal the Rundles looked in photos. These people weren't gangbangers or crack dealers on Fremont Street. The home was filled with family snapshots of happy times at resort parks and at birthday celebrations. The detectives were amazed at the volume of family photos in the Rundle home, and it told them how highly Shirley valued family.

"We went through the pictures of the family album and stuff," Alby said. "He's a big guy, very big, who seemed like an ordinary type of individual. His house was nice and clean, and there were no substance abuse problems."

"A big, dopey guy with glasses," Tremel said. "Those were my thoughts about Bill Rundle exactly. The neighbors couldn't believe they were missing. They were totally normal."

The detectives found a walker and wheelchair in a closet of the Rundle home. They found an empty gun case in the closet, too. The officers considered the possibility the missing gun was used to shoot someone in the living room. The detectives searched the upstairs of the home next. They entered an upstairs office and found a desk covered with paperwork. To the right of the entryway was a cabinet full of memorabilia honoring the life of Richie Rundle.

"The Richie room," Huggins said. "That's what we called it. It was basically a shrine to Richie. There was a desk in the middle of the room cluttered with paperwork and bills, and there was an easel with a big art sketchbook. Inside the shrine there were glued pictures, newspaper clippings about Richard Rundle Elementary School, and there was the 'My Dad Is the Best' letter in a frame."

Huggins read the letter, and she was touched by Richie's words.

"My daddy is the best," Richie had written.

"When I do something bad, my dad sits down with me and teaches me right from wrong," Richie wrote. *"I've learned from my dad to love—not to hate."*

Huggins found some of the Rundles' checkbooks in the Richie room. One checking account was in the name of Bill and Willa Rundle.

"I remember us saying, 'Who is Willa?' " Huggins said. "We thought this might be Bill's mom."

The detectives inspected the couple's massive master bedroom and bathroom on the second floor. They noticed Shirley's belongings were all present in the home, with the exception of her purse. All of the dresser drawers used by Shirley were full of clothing and neatly arranged. In Shirley's medicine chest, there were several medication bottles in her name. According to the labels, they were medicines Shirley needed to take every day. Shirley actually kept a yellow notepad near the bathroom sink documenting the medicines she was supposed to take, and when she was supposed to take them. The last entry on the note pad was for August 16. All of her cosmetics and cleaning products were on the vanity.

Meanwhile, most of Bill Rundle's belongings seemed to be missing from the master bedroom and bathroom.

"There was only one pair of men's underwear left in the home," Huggins said. "His side of the bathroom cabinet was empty, and Shirley's was not. There was none of Bill's stuff there, and all of Shirley's stuff was still there."

One item in particular caught Tremel's attention in a walkway in the upstairs of the home. The detective noticed a tan-colored velour chair covered with a pink bedsheet. Tremel pulled the sheet back, and he was surprised to see a dark maroon splatter on the chair. It was another large bloodstain that was not discovered during the first search of the home by police and CSIs, or by Magda Belen.

"Come look at this!" Tremel yelled.

The detectives rushed to the walkway, and they inspected the chair. It was definitely blood.

"Don was upstairs just kind of looking around, and he noticed there is a sheet over a chair," Alby said. "He hollers at me, I go up and I look . . . and there was blood on it. The chair definitely looked out of place."

The tan chair with blood on it was Shirley's chair. Magda Belen told the detectives the tan chair was usually located in the living room, but someone must've moved it upstairs and replaced it in the living room with the floral print chair near where the blood was found underneath the throw rugs. Holstein photographed the tan chair, and he processed it for evidence. He gathered samples of the maroon stain on the chair for testing, and he sprayed it with the leuco crystal violet. The stain tested positive for blood.

"Once we took the sheet off, I photographed the chair all the way around on all four sides," Holstein said. "Once I'd done that, then I looked at the bloodstain itself. And then, using a ruler, I put the ruler next to the chair, and I photographed the chair."

The investigators carried the stained chair downstairs and placed it in the spot of the living room where Magda first found the blood. The bloodstain on the chair and the bloodstain on the floor fit together like two pieces of a puzzle.

Holstein, Tremel, Alby, Green, and Gramma continued to closely scrutinize the blood-splattered chair, and they observed a large urine stain in the seat as well. This, in combination with the blood, indicated someone had been either gravely wounded or murdered in the chair.

"A lot of the time, if you die a violent death, you void your bladder, and that was Shirley's chair," Huggins said. "That's when our sergeant and the missing persons sergeant had a little discussion and it was decided we would take the case."

The detectives discussed the contents of the note found in the garage. It seemed very curious to the detectives. If the Rundles were going to take an emergency trip to the Philippines, it seemed highly doubtful they would have let their family know via a note left on a garage door. It was much more likely that they would have called the Belens, perhaps from their cell phone on their way to the airport if they were in a hurry.

"I thought the note was bullshit," Alby said. "Nobody writes a note saying they are going to the Philippines. I don't leave town without telling my mom I'm leaving. It seemed totally out of character for them."

Detectives Huggins and Tremel thought the note was bogus, too.

"I knew whoever left that note was trying to buy time," Huggins said.

The detectives and crime scene analysts completed their processing of the home, and they gathered on Poppywood Drive to contemplate what scenarios could explain the evidence. They knew very, very little about the Rundles at this point. They had two missing people on their hands—the couple had now been missing for a little more than three weeks—and they appeared to be very normal individuals. The Rundles were certainly not dope dealers, or prostitutes, or involved in risky behavior, yet there was blood on Shirley's chair, and it appeared someone had tried to conceal the chair by moving it upstairs, covering it with a bedsheet and then replacing it with another chair in the living room. The circumstances seemed highly suspicious.

"We had two missing people, and in our mind, one of them is dead and the other one's gone, or it could easily have been that both of them were dead," Huggins said.

"We discussed it at length," Alby said. "We questioned whether an unknown third party could be responsible for the Rundles being missing, and there was no evidence of it. We didn't think a third party would go to the trouble of moving the chair and covering it. The weapon, whatever it was, had been taken or moved.

"The vehicle was missing, which was not unusual, but it is kind of rare that the suspects take a vehicle," Alby said. "At the time, there was some home invasion robberies going on in Las Vegas, but what we had in front of us really didn't fit a home invasion robbery. There were no signs of forced entry. There was no ransacking to the extent that it looked like someone was looking for valuables."

The detectives were leaning toward the possibility that Bill Rundle had killed his wife and fled.

"I thought it was very suspicious," Tremel said.

"When we left there we thought she was probably dead, he probably did it, and he is now on the run," Alby said.

On September 18, 2002, veteran *Las Vegas Review-Journal* reporter Mike Kalil—one of the best reporters in the city—sought to advance the Rundle story even further in the pages of Nevada's largest newspaper. Kalil reviewed the facts that were known at the time, and he homed in on the fact that Bill Rundle's son, Richie, had died saving the life of another boy, Eli Scott, some fifteen years earlier. Kalil decided to seek out Scott for an interview about the Rundles, and he tracked Eli down by phone in Florida, where he was working as an exterminator.

To Kalil's surprise, Eli Scott told the reporter that he'd talked to Bill Rundle by phone just a few weeks prior to when the couple vanished. Scott said he'd called Bill Rundle simply to catch up, and that Rundle had sounded fine.

"He was more than happy or excited to hear from me—he was ecstatic," Scott told the paper.

News about the blood found in the home was now public, and Scott, then twenty-seven, said he doubted something was terribly wrong because of the good mood Rundle had seemed to be in when he talked to him.

"That's why this whole thing is kind of hard to take," Scott told the paper. "I just keep thinking about how happy he sounded on the phone, and now they're gone . . . It's so strange that they're gone, considering they were a part of the biggest thing that's ever happened to me."

Scott also reflected in the article on the accident that took Richie's life, and the heroics that saved his own.

"I think about it every day," said Scott, who also noted that he wrestled in high school. "I think Richie would've liked that I wrestled. We were both so into [pro wrestling]."

Eli Scott added that he wished he could say thank-you to Riche Rundle. "Thanks. That's the only thing I could possibly say to him if I had the chance. He gave up his life for mine."

13 . . . FAÇADE (MANHUNT)

In the forty-eight hours after the search of the Rundle home, the team of Las Vegas investigators quickly realized they were in the middle of a huge case. The local paper and television stations were calling, and bigger news organizations would be calling soon. The story had all the hooks for the media. Bill Rundle had once been named "Father of the Year" in Las Vegas because of son Richie's essay. Richie, the boy who died tragically young, cut down by a drunk driver. Fifteen years later, Bill and Shirley Rundle seemed a totally normal couple who lived in a nice Las Vegas neighborhood. Now they were missing, and there was blood in their home.

It was a hell of a story.

The best reporting on the case was done by the *Review-Journal*'s Mike Kalil and Michael Squires, who were the first journalists to pick up on the mystery. Local television stations gobbled up the story next, and then *Dateline NBC* expressed interest. A news crew from the national television show was in Las Vegas to prepare a series of docu-

mentaries on Las Vegas homicide detectives, and when the
Rundle case surfaced, the Las Vegas police administration
gave *Dateline*'s camera crew complete access to the detectives working the Rundle murder investigation.

"Usually I find that . . . the media kind of gets in your
way," Sergeant Rocky Alby said. "They [*Dateline*] brought
with them their own little sets of problems. Sometimes you
had to have them wait outside, and as things developed
throughout the case, we had to travel. We told the *Dateline*
guys, 'Keep up if you can, because we are not going to slow
down,' and they did a good job, but it was a little bit of a
pain to have them photographing us in the office. It's always
a little unnerving to have [a] guy in there with a camera in
your face."

Then *Good Morning America* called. They wanted to
do a story on the Rundle disappearance, too.

"I didn't think it was going to get as big as it did, and I
didn't realize it was going to turn into the manhunt it did,"
Detective Sheila Huggins said. "I didn't think it would be a
big deal, but it was. There was a lot of interest in what happened to Bill and Shirley."

Dateline NBC producer Daniel Slepian is a visionary in the
field of television documentaries. He was one of the first—if
not the first—person to come up with the idea of following
homicide detectives around with small, portable, handheld
cameras for the purposes of filming murder investigations in
real time. Today, the practice is widely used on shows such
as *The First 48*, which uses cameras to trail homicide detectives during the first forty-eight hours of a murder investigation. Slepian, however, started using the technique back in
2002, when he was working on a series for *Dateline* called
"Vegas Homicide." The smaller cameras, he said, allowed
him to film the detectives' actions in a less intrusive way
than would normally be the case, with a full camera crew.

"It was just me and a video camera," Slepian said. "I went to Vegas, and I would wait for [homicide detectives] to call me. When I got a call, I got to follow them everywhere, often starting at the crime scene. It was a real-life *Law & Order.* I think it is true that we were the first to do it, and for network television, it was rare, if not unique, to do not only documentation of a homicide investigation in real time, but to also film the crime scene and then present the story with absolutely no narration or correspondent. Instead, the actual events and the witnesses involved told the entire story in real time with no narration."

Slepian, thirty-eight, has traveled across the country and back dozens of times to cover murder stories for *Dateline.* Born and raised in Westchester, New York, the tall, slender, and soft-spoken producer has a true appreciation for just how awful human beings can be, given his experiences working for the news show.

"I've been to forty-some states for stories," Slepian said. "Last week I was in Indiana, New Hampshire, and Kentucky in five days. It's very, very difficult, but it has given me a front-row seat to some of the weirdest, most outrageous stories about people doing the craziest things. I see a slice of life I wouldn't have otherwise seen."

Slepian was granted access by Las Vegas police to film homicide investigations, and in September 2002, he was in the Las Vegas police homicide office—also known as the bullpen—when he first heard about Bill and Shirley Rundle. Slepian knew right away that the case was going to be extremely interesting.

"I was in the homicide office when Bill and Shirley went missing," Slepian said. "Richie had been a hero all these years earlier, and the fact that this guy was Father of the Year was intriguing to me. I said, 'This is going to be an interesting one.'"

Little did he know how interesting the case would become. Slepian spent the next month with fellow *Dateline* producer Anthony Galloway filming every investigative move by Detectives Huggins, Tremel, and Alby. His efforts ended up producing one of the most compelling television documentaries that was ever made about a murder investigation.

"The Rundle story was told all through Don [Tremel] and Sheila [Huggins], and by the characters who lived it, through their own words," Slepian said. "We were trying to be a complete spectator."

The detectives continued their investigation into the whereabouts of the Rundles by carrying out the basics of any missing persons case. They interviewed friends and immediate family members of the Rundles. One of Bill Rundle's former coworkers at the King 8 casino gave them some insight into Bill Rundle and what he was like.

"Bill was a very friendly guy on the job," Thomas Roach told authorities. "He had his private side that he didn't talk too much about, like what he did on the weekends. Bill never discussed that too much, but while he was on the job at work, very likeable, very polite. He was a good security guard. He was, you know, a very honest man."

Roach was a close enough friend that he was invited to the Rundle home, and like other witnesses, he took notice of the nice house Bill and Shirley lived in.

"He had bought a new home and he liked it—he enjoyed it," Roach said. "He never discussed finances, but we assumed that after his father died, that he probably had gotten some life insurance money. I knew that he had a bedroom dedicated in Richie's honor . . . Shirley is the one who had mentioned . . . [that] Richie's stuff was in a bedroom in their new home."

Roach said after Rundle moved his mother, Willa, to Las Vegas, Rundle quit his job in security. Before he quit, though, Rundle talked of plans for a small business.

"He told me that he was contemplating going into the T-shirt business," Roach said. "He and Shirley were going to go over to the Philippines [to] buy a bunch of T-shirts and open up a T-shirt shop in Las Vegas. It apparently never materialized."

Roach figured that after Rundle left the King 8, the two would stay in touch. They were friends after all.

"Normally when people leave the King 8, they quit or something, they always stop in and say hi," Roach said. "It was like a small family. But when Bill quit, he never stepped foot back into the King 8 again. He never came back down and said hi. I would say probably about a year went by before I finally commented about what the heck ever happened to Rundle? You know, what happened to him? It was like he fell off the face of the Earth. No one ever saw him again after he quit."

The police entered the Rundle information into all the relevant police computers and databases, including entering details of the white Buick with the HONYBUN tag into a national police database. The CAT unit constantly monitored cell phone numbers and credit card transactions for any indication that the Rundles were alive. The homicide detectives spent a great deal of time reviewing the couple's financial history. The missing persons detectives had gathered a lot of information from the couple's bank records, and when pieced together, the records showed a very ugly financial picture. The Rundles were on the edge of the financial cliff. They were stone-cold broke, and they owed a lot of money. Most important, the couple's three bank accounts at Bank of America were all empty. The accounts had been drained of thousands. The bank's investigator, Pat Doran, helped police secure all records of the Rundles' transactions, and they showed a series of cash withdrawals starting in May. Those cash withdrawals, combined, totaled more than $18,000, and the withdrawals continued right up to the disappearance.

The first withdrawal had occurred on May 10. The other withdrawals had been on June 17, July 26, July 30, August 1, and the last was on August 17—the last day Bill and Shirley Rundle had been seen in Las Vegas. Doran pulled security video from the branch outlets where the withdrawals were made, and the videos each showed Bill Rundle alone at the counter collecting the cash. Shirley Rundle was nowhere in sight during any of the transactions.

In total, Bill Rundle withdrew $18,300 in cash in the twenty-three days prior to the couple's disappearance.

One transaction was particularly troubling to authorities. They'd learned from Magda Belen that the Rundles were incredibly fond of their granddaughter, Gretchen, and they had set up a small trust fund for the girl. Yet two weeks before the Rundles disappeared, Bill Rundle raided his ten-year-old granddaughter's account. He took $1,700 cash from it and left merely $31 in Gretchen's trust fund.

The Rundles' credit card bills were simply staggering in size. There were twenty different credit card accounts totaling more than $90,000 in credit card debt. Credit card billing statements showed that the couple used the credit cards to take trips, and that Shirley paid for all kinds of clothes and furniture at high-end Las Vegas department stores with her plastic. It looked to the detectives like money was flying out the door of the Rundle home, but none was coming in. The couple was accumulating debt, and neither Bill nor Shirley was working.

The cops were initially baffled as to how two retired casino workers with little income could afford to live the way they'd been living. Shirley Rundle got less than $1,000 a month in Social Security, and Bill Rundle was bringing in no cash at all. They assumed the money supporting the family must be from the PostNet business, but when they analyzed the business, they found that the Rundles had taken out a home equity loan on their house, and they'd paid approximately $55,000 for the PostNet store franchise on West Charleston. Interviews with the Belens indicated the store was not doing well. In fact, it was tanking. It was a complete loss, and in March of 2002, the Rundles had been on the edge of financial disaster.

"Magda and her husband were basically running the PostNet, and it was a nice store in a nice area of town on Charleston Boulevard in a shopping complex known as Boca Park," Huggins said. "But [the Rundles] paid an ungodly amount of rent for it and it was a complete flop."

Authorities found paperwork in the Rundle home for a loan taken out on the Rundles' Buick prior to their disappearance. The loan was through Wells Fargo bank for a little less than $13,000.

"We were seeing they had huge financial issues," Tremel said. "Huge issues. They had a huge house, too, and it was well furnished. There was no cheap stuff in that house. I probably shouldn't judge like this, but I work my ass off, and I couldn't afford the stuff they had. Meanwhile, the work history we had for him was a security guard at the King 8 casino."

Tremel said other financial records showed Shirley Rundle was sending a lot of money to her family in the Philippines. The detectives noticed that the financial transactions were extensive.

"A lot of wire receipts," Tremel said. "She was wiring a lot of money over there, and I mean lots . . . Stacks of wire receipts that were inches thick, so you know she was sending a lot of money, and that didn't help issues."

The detectives briefly entertained the possibility that the couple had simply given up because of their huge debts. Perhaps the Rundles went missing on purpose, and maybe they were enjoying a fresh start somewhere else.

"The amount of money they were spending had us all asking, 'How are they doing it?' " Huggins said. "There was nearly $100,000 in credit card debt. The house had been refinanced, and the money from that was all gone, and there were recent purchases where they'd bought tons of furniture. New furniture, and they were sinking.

"The thought crossed my mind that maybe they'd just had enough," Huggins recalled. "Could they have staged this and left town? It was one possible scenario besides murder."

But Magda Belen insisted to the detectives that the Rundles would have never abandoned their loved ones in such a fashion.

They would never leave their cherished granddaughter behind without at least saying good-bye.

When it comes to catching killers, Las Vegas police have a huge resource available to them in the form of the Criminal Apprehension Team. The team is known to the local cops as CAT, and it consists of agents from the Federal Bureau of Investigation and veteran detectives from local police departments throughout the Las Vegas Valley. The local detectives and the feds work together to search for major felons in Southern Nevada, and they have some of the most sophisticated financial tracking software and law enforcement resources available to them at the FBI's headquarters on East Charleston Boulevard. Much of their technology is kept a secret, for a reason.

Early on in the Rundle investigation, the Las Vegas detectives contacted CAT for help in trying to track the Rundles. They figured establishing a financial trail tracing Bill and Shirley would be difficult because it seemed likely they might have thousands in cash with them. But to the detectives' shock, CAT reported back to them within days that monitoring of the Rundles' credit cards showed someone was using Bill's credit card to buy gas and to pay for stays at a string of Holiday Inns along the West Coast. One gas purchase had been near Susanville, California. Another transaction was for a Holiday Inn in Reno, and a third for a hotel in Portland, Oregon. When police checked the receipts and store surveillance videos, they learned that Bill Rundle had made each of the gas purchases. This showed that Rundle was definitely alive and well, but there was no sign of Shirley. He was alone at the hotels. Rundle was now a prime suspect in his wife's disappearance. He certainly wasn't in the Philippines, as the note had indicated.

"Now we know," Tremel said. "He's alive. We thought he was heading to Canada. We [were] getting this information a couple of days after the actual purchases, and it looked like he was possibly heading that way. Everything was pointing to a suspicious death . . . and yet he was not trying to hide himself. He was using his credit card and his own name. It was strange."

Nevertheless, Bill Rundle was clearly on the run.

14 ... LIES

The evidence was mounting against Bill Rundle. There
was blood in the Rundle home, all his stuff was gone, his
wife was nowhere to be found, and yet financial transactions and security videos indicated he was alive and well
in northern Nevada, California, and Oregon. The detectives and forensic analysts focused their attention on the
note that had been left on the garage door, and an analysis
of the handwriting showed it had been written by Bill
Rundle.

Despite presumably having a large amount of cash on
him, he was using credit cards in his own name. The detectives figured it was only a matter of time before they caught
up with him or some trooper stopped the Buick Regal with
its HONYBUN license plate, but in the following two
weeks, Bill Rundle left no evidence of where he was.

"It was a period of about fifteen to sixteen days, and we
were thinking for sure he'd gone to Canada," Alby said.
"There was plenty of time for him to do that."

The detectives were also waiting for DNA tests from

the lab on the blood samples from the home. While they waited for the tests and for some sign of Rundle, Tremel and Huggins set out to learn as much as they could about the Rundles through interviews with witnesses. They reviewed interviews conducted by missing persons detectives, including the interviews with the Truedsdales and Janet Bertrand. They suspected that the Filipino extortion story given to David Truedsdale was bogus. It sounded ridiculous, and they knew the note on the door about the emergency trip to the Philippines was not true. When they interviewed Janet Bertrand, the housekeeper, she told them something interesting.

"There was just a lot of tension in [their] house," Bertrand said of the relationship between Bill and Shirley Rundle.

Bertrand told the police she admired Shirley, but she'd felt Shirley waited on her husband hand and foot. Bertrand said she felt uncomfortable around Bill.

"I think she [Shirley] was afraid of him," the housekeeper told authorities.

"We started digging," Huggins said. "The maid gave us some insight into his personality, and how he was, and how he treated Shirley. It helped us in trying to determine if he could be responsible for this. According to the maid and Magda, Bill didn't do much, and he ordered Shirley around a lot. People were saying less than flattering things about him."

Police also got more information from Steven Williams, a friend of the Rundles who used to watch sports with Bill. Williams, whose wife was also from the Philippines, said that the couple occasionally went to the Rundles' home for dinner, and they, too, noticed the way Bill Rundle seemed to order Shirley around.

"He seemed like he was a dominant type just because of the way . . . he always loud talked her," Williams told police. "He'd down talk her. Me and my wife would just look at each other . . . but you know, it's none of our business."

The way Rundle talked to his wife was so noticeable, Williams said, that he and wife talked about it when they'd leave the Rundle residence.

"Do you hear the way Bill talks to Shirley?" Williams would say to his wife. "He seems like he doesn't respect her. I think he just wants her as a servant or something . . . the way he talks to her."

The detectives tracked down Richie's mother, Amy Castor, and she talked very openly about the bad way Rundle had treated her during their five-year marriage.

"She didn't like him at all," Huggins said. "She said he refused to work. She did all the work, and he would rather stay home, and she [grew] tired of it. He bet all their money, controlled the money, and he controlled her."

The detectives traveled to Southern California and met with Bill Rundle's second wife, Sherri Grayson. They were shocked at the story Grayson had to tell.

"She's very shy and she's very sweet," Huggins said. "He'd married her under a false name, and then he immediately moved her to Vegas from California, away from her family. He gets her pregnant, and he abandons her. Can you believe that? It floored me.

"How do you pull off something like that?" Huggins said. "That takes a real shyster. A real con man."

The detectives also tracked down Rundle's first wife, Sarah Reitig, in Southern California, and they got a similar story from her. Rundle had lied to Reitig and controlled their money.

"He's a controller, and he wants to be waited on," Huggins said. "It's his way or the highway, and then when he gets tired of the life he's living, he hits the road and just walks away."

The detectives were convinced that the Bill Rundle everyone knew from a distance—the middle-class guy, the

Father of the Year, the guy who'd lost his kid to tragedy, the middle-aged man who'd married a Filipino immigrant and who lived in a nice house in southwest Las Vegas, was actually a bad guy. He was a coldhearted deceiver. He was a complete fake who'd broken the hearts of all the women in his life through deception. And, now there was blood in his home, and his fourth wife was missing.

"We were thinking, 'What is wrong with this guy?'" Alby said. "He had this whole Dr. Jekyll/Mr. Hyde–type personality where he is living these lies. I don't know how he kept them all straight. He has no feeling or compassion for the people he comes into contact with, and he destroys their lives. He's done that his whole life.

"It's almost like he's got this one side that he wants the public to see," Alby said. "A loving father who lost his child. Father of the Year. That's one side, but he's got another side where he's a compulsive gambler who hasn't done much with his life. He married all these women and abandoned them, and it looks like he's now murdered his wife and is on the run."

During their interviews with Reitig and her son, Justin, there was one other fact that stood out to detectives. Justin Rundle recounted for authorities how Willa Rundle had moved to live with the Rundles in 1996, and he hadn't seen her since. His eighty-seven-year-old mother, Willa Rundle, Bill Rundle had told people, was touring Austria with a male nurse.

"With every witness, it got weirder and weirder," Huggins said. "Then we started hearing about Willa, and we started to wonder: 'Where's Willa?'"

15 . . . WHERE'S WILLA?

Detective Sheila Huggins had a growing certainty that Willa Rundle was not roaming the hills of Austria with a hot young male nurse. Willa was an old lady when she'd moved to Vegas five years earlier, and there was no death certificate for her on record anywhere. Willa Rundle had been a rich woman when she moved to Vegas, with more than $300,000 in her bank account, but a few months after moving in with the Rundles, she was gone. Given the blood found in the Rundle home and the growing suspicion that Shirley was dead, Detectives Huggins and Tremel decided they needed to find out what had happened to Willa.

They inspected her Social Security records, which showed that Willa was still receiving $1,200 a month in a bank account that was jointly shared by Bill and Shirley Rundle. As soon as Willa's Social Security checks were deposited, the Rundles spent the money almost immediately.

More alarming were the details of what had happened to Willa's huge cache of money. Financial records inspected by authorities showed that someone claiming to be

Willa had called her stockbroker in 1998 and had all of her stocks sold and transferred into an account registered to Bill and Willa Rundle. Presumably, the person who'd called the stockbroker had been female, because it seemed doubtful that Bill Rundle could have pulled that off on his own.

Could Shirley have done that?

The money was repeatedly transferred from Bill and Willa's account to Bill and Shirley's account. Over the next two years, the Rundles burned through the money. By August of 2002, all of the nearly $320,000 was gone. The detectives were amazed at how fast the Rundles had spent Willa's cash.

The authorities contemplated other witness testimony about the whereabouts of Willa. In his interviews with authorities, Thomas Roach—Rundle's coworker at the King 8—said Rundle had quit his job at the casino after his mother moved to Las Vegas. Although a long period of time passed before he saw Rundle again, Roach told authorities that he eventually stumbled across him in church, long after Willa had moved to Las Vegas.

"I just asked him how his mother was doing," Roach said. "And he says, 'Oh, fine, she's vacationing over in Europe.' I said, 'Well, that's great that a lady of her age can still physically be able to be in good enough shape to go and enjoy herself in life.' And he said, 'Oh yeah, she's doing just fine.'"

This was not the first time that Bill Rundle had claimed his mother was in the mountains of Europe with a man. When Rundle courted Sherri Grayson nearly two decades earlier, he'd told her entire family they couldn't meet the elder Richard and Willa Rundle because they were in Austria, which of course was untrue.

Now, Huggins and Tremel wondered, was Rundle telling the same lie to hide Willa again?

Huggins was particularly focused on Justin Rundle's

memories of the dinner in Las Vegas with Bill and Shirley Rundle, where Bill had asked Justin if he'd heard from his grandmother as she traveled in Europe.

"I thought [the idea of Willa traveling abroad] was ridiculous," Justin said. "He had specified that . . . she's from Austria, and I know that she was very, very proud of her Austrian heritage, so, he said she was going back to Austria to retrace her roots, which was strange to me."

When Justin had questioned how his grandmother, who could barely walk, could tour Austria, Shirley had privately said: *"Justin, your grandmother was real tired."* Justin was sure that Shirley had wanted to tell him something, but was interrupted by his father's return.

Detective Huggins was dumbfounded by this information. It seemed to indicate Shirley knew what happened to Willa. The more Huggins learned, the more she was convinced that Willa was dead.

"I remember sitting at my desk and checking through all the records and realizing we can't find her," Huggins said. "She's supposedly moved in with them, but no one's seen her. Her passport hadn't been used, so where is she? I was sitting at my desk, and I knew she was gone. She's dead, too. I just knew it. She's dead, too."

16 ... SEAHAWKS

Slowly, the Vegas heat of 2002 started to dissipate, and by late September, there were at least some small signs that it was going to cool down in the Devil's city for a few months.

A preliminary blood test from the blood in the home was returned on September 20, and it was learned that the blood on the chair and floor was likely from Magda Belen's mother. Forty-four days after the Rundles went missing, the detectives got some very important information: Blood on the floor and chair in the Rundle home was confirmed through forensic testing as belonging to Shirley Rundle.

"There was the very real possibility Shirley's dead," Detective Sheila Huggins said.

Huggins made a difficult phone call to Magda Belen. Huggins had kept in regular touch with Belen, and she'd given her updates on the case. Now she was honest with Magda in letting her know everything was starting to point to the likelihood Shirley was dead.

"I'm refusing to believe that she is dead," Belen told

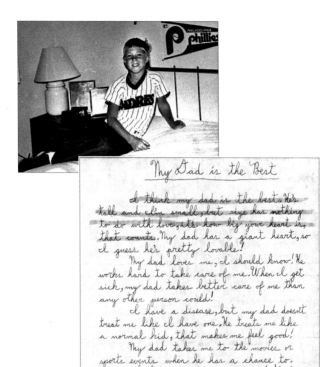

My Dad is the Best

I think my dad is the best. He's tall and I'm small, but size has nothing to do with love, it's how big your heart is, that counts. My dad has a giant heart, so I guess he's pretty lovable!

My dad loves me, I should know! He works hard to take care of me. When I get sick, my dad takes better care of me than any other person could!

I have a disease, but my dad doesn't treat me like I have one. He treats me like a normal kid, that makes me feel good!

My dad takes me to the movies or sports events when he has a chance to.

I love my dad very much! When I do something bad, my dad sits down with me and teaches me right from wrong. I've learned from my dad to love not to hate.

Richard James Rundle
4475 Jimmy D'wanty Blvd #395
458-7780
Mrs. Johnson AM
Jo Mackey

TOP LEFT: Richie Rundle, circa 1987. *(Las Vegas Review-Journal)*

RIGHT: The essay that earned Bill Rundle the award for Las Vegas's Father of the Year. (Clark County Sheriff's Office)

The scene of the crash that killed little Richie Rundle while he waited for the school bus. A maintenance man, Dewey Buckles, was also killed.
(*Las Vegas Review-Journal*)

Bill Rundle hugs a mourner at his son Richie's funeral.
(*Las Vegas Review-Journal*)

Bill and Shirley Rundle are pictured in court during the trial of the motorist accused of killing Richie Rundle. (*Las Vegas Review-Journal*)

Bill Rundle (and portrait of Richie in the background) from a 2002 news article remembering the fifteen-year anniversary of Richie's death. This photo was taken just months before Rundle and his wife Shirley disappeared. (*Las Vegas Review-Journal*)

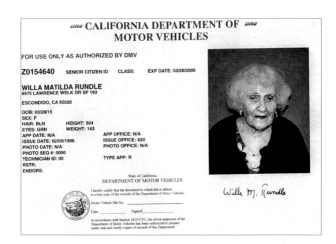

Willa Rundle, Bill Rundle's elderly mother, is pictured in her driver's license photo. The senior citizen moved into her son's home in 1996 but went missing a few months later. (Clark County Sheriff's Office)

Bill and Shirley Rundle's large suburban home in Las Vegas. The couple went missing from the home in August 2002. (Clark County Sheriff's Office)

The note found on the interior door of Bill and Shirley's garage after they went missing. (Clark County Sheriff's Office)

A Las Vegas police crime scene photo documenting the blood on Shirley's favorite chair.
(Clark County Sheriff's Office)

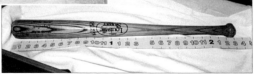

Richie Rundle's baseball bat, which was found to have been used by his father to kill Shirley. (Clark County Sheriff's Office)

ABOVE:
Shirley Rundle's body was
discovered dumped alongside
the road in Lassen County,
California.
(Clark County Sheriff's Office)

RIGHT:
Shirley Rundle's jewelry, including two expensive gold watches, was
pawned by Bill Rundle in Seattle for $3,900 following Shirley's death.
The jewelry was eventually recovered by Las Vegas police.
(Clark County Sheriff's Office)

Bill and Shirley Rundle's Buick Regal, with license plate HONYBUN,
discovered in a Seattle storage garage. Shirley's blood was found in the
trunk by Las Vegas police. (Clark County Sheriff's Office)

Bill Rundle is pictured in a Las Vegas courtroom during his murder trial.
(*Las Vegas Review-Journal*)

Convicted killer Bill Rundle during his death penalty murder trial.
(*Las Vegas Review-Journal*)

TOP LEFT: Las Vegas police homicide Detective Don Tremel. (Photo by Sheila Huggins)

TOP RIGHT: Las Vegas police homicide Sergeant Rocky Alba. (Photo courtesy of Sheila Huggins)

LEFT: Las Vegas police homicide Detective Sheila Huggins. (Photo courtesy of Sheila Huggins)

BOTTOM LEFT: Nancy Lemcke of the Clark County Public Defender's Office, one of Bill Rundle's defense attorneys. (Photo by Nancy Lemcke)

BOTTOM RIGHT: Curtis Brown, chief deputy public defender for the Clark County Public Defender's Office, who also helped defend Bill Rundle. (Photo by Nancy Lemcke)

Dateline NBC. "She would only be officially dead to me if I see her dead body.

"Although all of the investigation is pointing towards [Bill Rundle as a killer,] still my mind is not set that it's him," Belen told producer Daniel Slepian.

Huggins took photos of the blood spatters and stains on the chair and floor of the Poppywood Drive home, and she drove to the Clark County, Nevada, Coroner's Office on Shadow Lane in downtown Las Vegas. Huggins met with Dr. Larry Simms—a tall, distinguished man with a beard, who used to practice general medicine in Tulsa, Oklahoma. Simms was now the head medical examiner for all of Southern Nevada, and he told Huggins that the blood-stains documented in the photos were likely the result of a homicide or near-fatal bloodletting.

"I didn't expect to learn much when I went to see Dr. Simms, but he gave us the opinion that Shirley had suffered a severe, if not fatal, injury," Huggins said. "We just didn't know by what means. We were assuming a gun, because the gun was missing."

The detectives knew Shirley had been gravely wounded, at a minimum, and there was no evidence that Bill had been hurt. Huggins said that as each piece of evidence was gathered, the detectives became more and more convinced that Bill Rundle had killed his wife, and was now on the lam. Shirley and Willa's whereabouts remained mysteries.

"We started to believe we had enough to get a warrant for Shirley's death," Huggins said.

In September 2002, Las Vegas police homicide detectives started drafting an arrest warrant application for Bill Rundle. The detectives, in the affidavit, outlined the case up to that point, from the details of the Rundles' disappearance to the blood found in the home. They documented Rundle's past relationships with women, specifically his ex-wives Sarah Reitig, Sherri Grayson, and Amy Castor, and they detailed Dr. Simms's findings regarding the

amount of the blood loss. Huggins said that when the affidavit was presented to a judge, she wanted the judge to see
the same pattern of facts that had convinced the detectives
Bill Rundle was a killer.

The following are excerpts from the affidavit in support
of arrest drafted by Huggins:

> *State of Nevada, County of Clark:*
> *Sheila Huggins, being duly sworn, deposes and says:*
> *That she is a police officer with the Las Vegas Met-*
> *ropolitan Police Department, being so employed for a*
> *period of 14 years, [and was assigned] to investigate*
> *the crime of murder committed on or about August 18,*
> *2002, which investigation has determined William*
> *James Rundle as the perpetrator. Declarant developed*
> *the following facts:*
> *On August 20, 2002, at approximately 8 p.m.,*
> *Magda Belen called Las Vegas police dispatch and*
> *asked that a patrol vehicle meet her at Poppywood*
> *Drive. Mrs. Belen told dispatchers that she was at her*
> *mother and step-father's residence and that they were*
> *missing under suspicious circumstances. Patrol [offi-*
> *cers] responded and contacted Magda Belen. Inside*
> *the garage they observed a note hanging on the door to*
> *the house stating "Alarm is set! Be home 9-06. Emer-*
> *gency Trip to Philippines!"*
> *Ms. Belen insisted that officers check the inside of*
> *the home because she knew her mother would never*
> *leave for even a day without telling Belen. The patrol*
> *officers requested a locksmith and entered. Inside, the*
> *officers found no persons and nothing seemed out of*
> *place. Dispatchers called all area hospitals and found*
> *no record of the Rundles receiving medical attention.*
> *Belen told officers that the Rundle car was also gone*
> *from the garage—officers left a contact card at the*
> *home and secured the residence.*

On 8/21/2002, Magda Belen filed a missing persons report for William and Shirley Rundle. [Belen] went to the Missing Persons Detail and discussed the report with detectives. With a bank statement provided by Belen, these detectives contacted Pat Doran at Bank of America. Doran told detectives that the Rundles had several accounts, business and personal. Doran noted that the money market account had several recent and large withdrawals . . . All of the transactions showed that William Rundle had withdrawn a total of $18,300 in cash in the period of 23 days.

Mrs. Belen told the detectives at Missing Persons that she had last seen her mother and step-father on the seventeenth of August. She told detectives that her mother was very close with her daughter, Gretchen, and that she would never go days without calling. Mrs. Belen told Detective Marin that she wanted to go back inside the home.

The discovery of the blood was documented in the report.

Photographs and swabs of the apparent blood stain were collected. Several personal items, such as a daily planner and a note written by Shirley Rundle were collected. The note was dated 8/18/2002 and talked of a dream she had the night before [about family members in the Philippines].

The September 12 search was documented in the report, which also provided extensive details on what else the detectives found in the Poppywood home.

All rooms of the home were photographed and searched. In the master bedroom several items of interest were worthy of note. It was apparent to detectives

that Shirley Rundle was an immaculate housekeeper
and organizer. Every item in the drawers were neatly
folded and arranged. There were drawers that were
obviously dedicated to Shirley's personal clothing, and
drawers for Bill's clothing. Very few items of Bill Rundle's personal underwear items were left in the dresser
designated for him. Only one pair of men's underwear
could be seen. Numerous drawers were completely
empty. All of the dresser drawers dedicated for Shirley
were full of clothing and neatly arranged.

In the master bathroom, there were separate areas
and vanities dedicated for Shirley and for Bill. In the
medicine chest of Shirley's area, there were several
medication bottles in her name, which she needs to take
every day. She had written the times and dates she was
taking her medication on a yellow note near the sink.
The last entry appeared to be at 4:35 p.m. on August
16. All of her cosmetics and cleansing products appeared to be on the vanity. On Bill's vanity, there were
a few things, and the medicine cabinet designated for
him was almost empty with no personal medications.

The closet that connected to the master bath was
large and neatly arranged. In the far back, several
suitcases were on the carpeted floor and there were
small impressions in the rug that appeared to be from
a suitcase that was no longer there. A search of the
closet revealed a small black carrying bag that contained the factory box for a Smith and Wesson
.38-caliber revolver, cleaning equipment, and numerous rounds of ammunition. In a plastic bag containing
numerous .380 and .38-caliber cartridges was one
.38-caliber cartridge case. The gun was missing. A
check of gun registration shows that William Rundle
is the registered owner of a Smith and Wesson .38 revolver.

In the center room of the second floor is an office-

*type room that has a desk and some computer equip-
ment such as a printer and fax machine. The room is
decorated in memorabilia of William Rundle's deceased young son. There are several items of personal
paperwork in the room, such as a death certificate for
Richard Rundle, William's father, and a Social Security letter for Willa Rundle. There are no items of personal identification in this room or anywhere else for
William Rundle. No tax returns, no checks, or canceled checks, no bills or personal phone books. There
are several personal items of Shirley Rundle, including
a deed of ownership for land in the Philippines.*

*In the garage on the first level, in [an] open box, a pair
of men's sandals were recovered and impounded. Pre-
sumptive tests on the bottoms of the shoes showed positive for blood. Magda Belen describes those sandals
as Bill Rundle's favorite shoes.*

The report detailed the hunt for Bill Rundle using records from his credit cards.

*A grand jury subpoena for the credit cards of the Run-
dles was applied for to ascertain if there was current
activity. Missing Persons also conducted a request
through Interpol for any passport activity on either
passport of the Rundles. The vehicle and the couple
had been entered into NCIC as missing endangered
adults. Detective Marin also advised homicide detectives that he had received a call from a citizen that had
been driving to the San Diego area on or about August
20 and had observed a vehicle that had the plate "HO-
NYBUN." He saw the vehicle on Interstate 15 in California, going in the direction of San Diego. He did not
remember the driver. Information regarding the Rundles' disappearance was released to the local media
and aired citywide.*

Detectives Tremel and Huggins went to the Wild West Casino and contacted Douglas Woodbury, who had worked in security for years at that location. He was casual friends with William Rundle, when Rundle had worked there. Woodbury told detectives that he had not seen Bill Rundle for [years], since Rundle quit his job as a security officer. Woodbury told detectives that Rundle came into the casino on August 17 and talked for a while, then left. He found it very odd, as Rundle had not talked to him for years.

On 9/16/2002, [Amy Castor's father] contacted the police . . . [and said] William Rundle was a drunk and a liar. He stated that he did not trust him and thought he used Richie's high-profile death to generate sympathy and media attention for himself. He also stated that Rundle was a very heavy sports gambler and spent more money than he made.

Detective Huggins phoned Detective Howard Bradley from San Diego County Sheriff's Office. Huggins asked Detective Bradley to respond to Lawrence Welk Drive in Escondido, California. This was the last [known] residence of Rundle's parents. Bradley spoke with a tenant, Ruth Williams, who knew Willa Rundle very well. Williams told Bradley that she had been close friends with the Rundles and that after Richard Rundle Sr. had died, Willa Rundle sold her home and moved to Las Vegas to be with her son. She had not seen or talked to her since. Detective Huggins asked Magda Belen if she knew William's mother. Belen stated that she had met her years ago, and that she only stayed with William and Shirley Rundle for a few months. When family members would ask about her whereabouts, Rundle would explain that she had moved to Austria to travel [through] Europe in her old age. Willa's friend, Williams, told Detective Bradley that in

1996, Willa was very ill and used a walker to get around. A California driver's license check shows that Willa Rundle is 87. There is little explanation why William Rundle is controlling and spending her Social Security checks that are deposited into their joint account. An Interpol notice was sent to ascertain if Willa Rundle's passport was used to enter Austria or any other European country.

Detective Huggins [was contacted by Sarah Reitig]. She told Detective Huggins she had been married to William Rundle 30 years ago and had a son. Sarah said she found out during her marriage that Rundle lied to her about his employment. . . . Sarah also said that her son, Justin, was extremely concerned for his grandmother, Willa. Justin would ask Bill Rundle how to contact his grandmother, and Bill would tell him that it was impossible as she was touring Europe.

Detective Huggins contacted Sherri Grayson, and she told the detective that Bill Rundle married her under a fraudulent name of William Randau. During their short, year-long marriage, Rundle told her that he was employed with Metropolitan Life Insurance. He also told her that his parents were living in Europe. When Sherri became pregnant, Bill left her one day and never came back. Sherri's parents helped her find [out that Bill's parents actually] lived in California. Sherri said Bill had taken all of their money from their checking accounts, wrote bad checks, and had never worked for Metropolitan Life Insurance.

[Amy Castor, Bill's third wife], and mother to his son, Richie, told Detective Huggins that she had been married to Bill from 1972 to 1978. She stated Bill was extremely controlling and was mentally abusive. She stated that he did not work for the last several years of their marriage and would stay drunk most of the day.

When she left him, she said she found out that he had a bank account under his name that she did not know about, and that he was a heavy sports gambler.

Dr. Simms' opinion was that the amount of blood loss and area of pooling blood suggested a large wound that would require immediate emergency medical treatment. Hospitals were checked for Shirley Rundle's admittance with negative results.

The detectives also wrote in the affidavit about how they were trying to trace Rundle's whereabouts.

Because William Rundle could be in possession of his laptop computer and accessing his email, a subpoena will be served on his Internet provider. The cell phone information of William Rundle has been requested through subpoena. The note left on the garage door has been submitted for handwriting analysis to determine if it is similar to known handwriting of William Rundle. Additionally, homicide detectives have contacted FBI special agents who requested legal attaches in Manila, Philippines, [for] any information on entrance or exit by the Rundles using their passports.

The arrest warrant was obtained from Las Vegas Justice of the Peace Tony Abbatangelo even though authorities had no idea where Shirley's body was. A huge factor in the cops' ability to secure the murder warrant was Dr. Simms's opinion that the bloodstains in the Rundle home were so large that they were likely the result of a homicide.

"It was somewhat weak in nature because we didn't have a whole lot," Sergeant Rocky Alby said about the warrant application. "We had to come to a lot of conclusions. We had to establish it was her blood. Dr. Simms at the coroner office gave us a huge break because he was able to articulate that the amount of blood at the scene was consistent with someone probably dying. That helped us a lot to get enough probable cause to get the arrest warrant."

The warrant was a crucial step for police. It meant the full powers of federal authorities could now be brought to the manhunt for Rundle, since he'd crossed state lines. Michael Adams, a special agent with the Federal Bureau of Investigation in Seattle, was asked by the Las Vegas CAT unit to follow up on the financial transaction in Seattle, at an apartment complex called the Mediterranean in the Lower Queen Anne area of the city.

"My primary responsibility was to conduct a fugitive investigation in an attempt to locate Mr. Rundle," Adams said. "I was first contacted by a detective with the FBI's violent crimes squad in Las Vegas, and the information I received led me to an address in the Lower Queen Anne area of Seattle . . . It's a commercial district with various businesses, banks, and an apartment complex.

"I asked the clerk, and I found out Mr. Rundle, according to the records, stayed there for about a month's time," Adams said. "He was not still there. He had checked out. I then reported that information back to the detectives I'd been in contact with [in Las Vegas]."

Las Vegas CAT called Adams back a few hours later and informed him of another financial transaction by Rundle at a storage facility called Urban Self Storage. The storage facility was located at Twelfth and Madison Streets. Rundle was at Urban Self Storage either to make a purchase or rent storage.

"I went to that storage facility, and I contacted the clerk," Adams said. "The clerk opened up their records and, sure enough, confirmed he [Rundle] stored a vehicle there."

The clerk was a man named Burney Campbell, and he recalled for authorities how, on the morning of September

5, he'd received a call from a person identifying himself as Bill Rundle.

"[Rundle] asked us about our storage facilities for vehicles," said Campbell. "It was primarily for storage—not for parking. This individual showed up. I took him down to the annex, and I showed him where the vehicles were . . . [We had] a deal—buy one month, get one free. In this particular case, storage for a month was $150."

The storage clerk secured the deal for the car storage with the tall, older gentleman.

"Mr. Rundle said that would be great," Campbell said. "However, he wanted to extend that, and he actually paid me for three months, and I gave him the one month free. Basically, it was for four months. He showed me [his ID] and I thought that I had taken a picture of it, because we normally put that into the files. . . . [But] unfortunately, when I went back to look at the file, I couldn't find it."

Campbell said he and Rundle chatted about Vegas during the encounter, specifically about the Star Trek Experience tourist attraction at the Las Vegas Hilton.

"I'm somewhat of a *Star Trek* fan, so I was trying to build a rapport with Mr. Rundle, as I do with everybody who comes in," Campbell said. "And, I said something to the effect of . . . 'They're doing the *CSI* thing there.' And Mr. Rundle told me that the cast comes out to [the Las Vegas desert] to shoot the [show] . . . [but] they do most of it in Hollywood. I told him I was kind of disappointed in that."

Then Rundle blurted out some information that really caused Campbell to remember the tall man in the dark parking garage who wanted to store the white Buick Regal with license plate HONYBUN.

"He said his wife recently passed away, and he couldn't bear the memories that were associated with Las Vegas, so he was relocating to Seattle," Campbell said. "He just said he [was going] back down there to [Las Vegas] to get the rest of his things."

Special Agent Adams asked Campbell to show him the car. The storage clerk walked him down one flight into the basement of the dark, concrete storage garage.

"I saw the Buick Regal with license plate Nevada HONYBUN," Adams said. "It was just one level beneath the street level there. [The structure] was fully encased in concrete. Very dark. I called [the detectives] in Las Vegas, and I told them I found the car parked in that storage facility."

The trio of Las Vegas detectives, Rocky Alby, Sheila Huggins, and Don Tremel, were at the Foothills Express Bar and Restaurant in Las Vegas when Alby got a call on his cell phone.

"They found the vehicle," Alby told the other detectives in a conversation recorded by the *Dateline* cameras.

Huggins: "Is it in the downtown area? Do you know?"

"Seattle," Alby said.

The detectives were ecstatic at the news. They had a warrant, and now they had the car. It was a huge break. They hopped on a flight to Seattle with Crime Scene Analyst Yolanda McClary and *Dateline* producers Daniel Slepian and Anthony Galloway in tow. The next morning, they were exhausted and excited at the same time as they drove through the streets of Seattle in the direction of the parking garage.

"We're thinking, 'We are going to catch him,'" Alby said.

The detectives sensed their prey was nearby. They drove through Seattle with the Space Needle in sight. Every time they saw a male figure walking down the street, they wondered if it was him. It was possible. They knew he'd been in the area.

"This is the stuff you live for as a cop," Alby said. "You have hot information to go on and you are on the move. We are looking on the streets for him, because we know we are so close. You almost felt like you could sense him."

The detectives decided they would first go to the parking garage to see the car. The *Dateline* cameras were rolling as they walked into the garage. They noted it was very dark and somewhat spooky in the bottom floor of Urban Self Storage.

"Creepy," Huggins said.

The detectives walked down a slight incline, and the white Buick Regal with the HONYBUN tag came into view.

Finally.

"There it is," Huggins said.

"The long awaited," Tremel said. "No, he wasn't trying to hide this, was he?"

As Slepian filmed the detectives in the bottom floor of the garage, he couldn't help but think that the images he was capturing were groundbreaking. He was thrilled by the experience of being a spectator to a real-time murder investigation, and his heart was racing.

"We were filming in real time, and you have to remember that we didn't know where Bill Rundle was, what he was going to do, and if we were going to find him with the car," Slepian said. "We didn't know if he was a danger to others. We didn't know what happened to his mother. It was a mystery, and the detectives kept saying, 'We've got to get this guy.'

"The power of being there in the moment was so extreme," Slepian said. "This is what these detectives do every day, and I was reminded that it's not only searching for the bad guy—it's dealing with a grieving daughter and the emotion that comes along with that, too.

"As an observer, from my perspective, as we were walking into the garage, there was a suspense because you just didn't know what was going to happen," Slepian said. "A

Silence of the Lambs–type moment. It was dark and wet, and for all we knew, he [Bill] could've jumped out of the corner—out of the shadows. My heart was beating very fast."

Huggins walked to the rear of the vehicle as Slepian's camera recorded her actions. She bent over the trunk and sniffed. There was no noticeable scent of decaying flesh in the air. The detectives decided they needed a search warrant for permission to get in the car, and the warrant was going to take some time.

"Oh, I want to get in there so bad," Huggins said.

The team of Las Vegas investigators learned from CAT that Rundle had a bank account in Seattle in his own name. It was agreed that Detective Huggins and Crime Scene Analyst McClary would go to the bank to see what they could find out about Rundle's account while Alby and Tremel waited for the warrant and a locksmith in the parking garage. Huggins and McClary drove away from the vehicle, disappointed about having to leave the scene before seeing what they would find in the car. Huggins knew, though, that their time in Seattle was precious, and they had to use it wisely. She and McClary arrived at the bank and inspected the bank records and a safe deposit box rented by Rundle. Inside the safe deposit box, the investigators found three different passports. One was in the name of William Rundle, and two different ones were in the name of Shirley Rundle. There were also two leather credit card holders in the safe deposit box, filled with the Rundles' credit cards. There were dozens and dozens of credit cards in the wallets.

Next, the investigators retrieved video surveillance images showing Bill Rundle at the bank counter.

"We got surveillance video," Huggins said. "He was alive and well." The video showed Rundle wearing a Seattle Seahawks hat, and looking tired.

Huggins interviewed a heavyset bank clerk with dark hair who remembered visiting with Rundle at the counter of the bank.

"He told the lady at the bank he lost his wife and he was getting a new start in life," Huggins said. "He said he was going to get Seattle Seahawks tickets because he was really into football, and he was saying how excited he was to be in a town with a professional team."

Meanwhile, Alby and Tremel waited patiently for the warrant at the storage facility. When the detectives finally got the warrant, they called a locksmith, and the car's front door was jimmied without causing damage to the vehicle. Tremel looked like a bloodhound on the scent as the door cracked open. He climbed into the front seat, and he noticed the car was very clean. He found a receipt for a Holiday Inn in Seattle in the front of the car.

The detectives popped the trunk and rushed to the rear of the vehicle carrying their flashlights to see if Shirley's body was inside.

It wasn't, but the evidence they found was still damning.

"Right here!" Tremel said. "Look at this! We've got blood in here! It looks like blood, anyways."

There, right in plain sight, was a large bloodstain soaked into the fuzzy gray cloth of the right side of the trunk interior. The detectives knew the bloodstain was another huge find.

"Where did he dump her?" Alby asked Tremel.

"I don't know, but that confirms she was in the trunk of this fuckin' car, and she was definitely dead," Tremel said.

Tremel pulled out his cell phone. He dialed Huggins's number as fast as he could, and Huggins took the call inside the bank.

"Sheila . . . hold on to your skivvies," Tremel said.

"Okay," Huggins said.

"Trunk's open, and there's blood in it," Tremel said.

"Okay!" Huggins said.

Huggins and McClary returned to the storage facility and processed the vehicle for forensic evidence. Crime Scene Analyst Yolanda McClary described the processing of the scene and the finding of the blood.

"I photographed the Buick with HONYBUN tag—the interior and exterior, and I collected some evidence," McClary said. "The interior of the vehicle was actually extremely clean. On the center of the seat was a folded black towel and a can of aerosol fragrant spray. There was a Kleenex box on the front passenger floorboard, and there was a small, little, clear plastic box that contained .38 bullet cartridges. Live ammunition, and I collected the cartridges.

"The trunk of the vehicle . . . had in it . . . another aerosol can, a fragrance-type can, and a little cleaning kit that looked like it came with the car," McClary said. "And then, on the right side of the trunk, on the carpet, way in the right corner of it, was a fairly large apparent bloodstain. I took a sample."

The blood was tested, and it was indeed Shirley's. Finding Shirley's blood in the trunk of the Buick was a huge deal, and the detectives knew it. Things were really coming together. The thrill was palpable as the detectives milled about the car in front of the *Dateline* cameras. The bloodstain was undisputable evidence of a crime. Everyone knew it, and they all knew they would probably remember this moment for the rest of their lives. Each detective and McClary had spent decades in the Las Vegas police department, and this was the kind of moment they lived and breathed for. It was what they got up for every morning. People like Alby, Tremel, Huggins, and McClary were put on this Earth by God himself for this very purpose: to search for evidence and find it.

They had Shirley's blood on the chair, which had been hidden from view in the home on Poppywood Drive. They had Shirley's blood on the floor in the living room, and now there was another large pool of it in the trunk of the Rundles' vehicle. It was evidence that her body had been transported in the trunk, and on top of all the forensic evidence, they had evidence of Bill Rundle's flight from Vegas and the bogus note in his handwriting. He was using his credit cards while he was on the run, and this showed he was definitely alive and well.

The detectives were thrilled at the strength of the case they were assembling. But at the same time, Huggins knew she had to call Magda Belen and tell her there was little doubt that her mother was dead. Huggins dreaded making the call, which was recorded by *Dateline* cameras.

"Hello Magda, it's Sheila Huggins. I just want to let you know where we are at, and what's going on with the case."

"Okay," Magda said.

"My partner, myself, my sergeant, and the *Dateline* crew is also with us—we flew to Seattle last night [because] we had a lead that Bill was up here," Huggins said. "We found the car."

"You did?" Magda said.

"Yes," Huggins said. "We are processing the car right now."

Magda sobbed over the phone.

"Are you okay?" Huggins said.

"Yeah," Magda said.

She then asked about her mother.

"There's no sign of your mom here," Huggins said.

Magda sighed.

"There's some blood in the car," Huggins said.

"In the backseat?" Magda said. "In the trunk?"

"In the trunk, pumpkin."

Sighs and sobs were heard.

Bill Rundle had caused an immeasurable amount of pain, and left his entire family tortured over the unknown for months. The Belens were suffering in Las Vegas, in grief-stricken misery, while Rundle was apparently moving on with his life and talking about relocating to Seattle. The detectives knew they had to find Rundle, and his wife's body. If they found Shirley's body, no matter what the circumstances, they doubted Rundle could lie or explain his way out of it.

The Seattle Police Department helped the Las Vegas detectives check an inventory of pawn receipts in Seattle the following day, and they got a hit. A pawn receipt led police to a Seattle jewelry dealer on Leroy Avenue, about five miles from the Space Needle. The detectives met with a man named Gerald Ralph Olson, who described himself to the police as a precious metal buyer.

"I do some refining," Olson said. "I buy gemstones as well. At one time, I was voted the best place to sell jewelry. I use it in my ad."

Olson recounted for the detectives how he'd met with Bill Rundle on September 2 in Seattle. The man from Las Vegas brought a cache of nice jewelry to the meeting.

"He was a tall, older gentleman," Olson said. "A fairly good-sized guy . . . He told me that his wife had died, and he was from Las Vegas, and he just couldn't stand to be in town anymore since she died, and he was also an avid sports fan, and he liked the sports atmosphere in Seattle," Olson said. "He was talking about moving to Seattle, or maybe he had already. That was the impression I had.

"He showed me a bunch of jewelry, and I basically evaluated it," Olson said. "I ultimately made him an offer."

Rundle showed the precious metal buyer a pendant, hoop earrings, some gold items, at least a couple of diamond rings, and a couple of very high-end gold watches. There was a ladies' Rolex watch and a ladies' Audemars Piguet watch in Rundle's collection. All of the jewelry was in good condition, and Olson gave Rundle a check for $3,900.

The jewelry was definitely Shirley's.

"[Olson] had her watch, and it had Shirley's name on the back of it," Huggins said.

The detectives interviewed a number of restaurant clerks, hotel employees, and bartenders who'd encountered Bill Rundle during his stay in town. The detectives were amazed at what they told them: that Rundle—their suspected murderer—was using his own name, presenting himself as a grieving widower, and talking about settling down in Seattle.

"He stayed in a hotel, and he even sent flowers to one of the little checkout girls after telling her this sad story," Huggins said. "He brought her flowers one day, and it creeped her out."

Rundle told the same story to a bartender at TJ's, a Seattle bar.

"He told the bartender his wife died, and how sad he was," Huggins said. "He said he had too many memories in Vegas, and he couldn't stand to live there anymore. He only said Shirley died, and he was going to start a new life. He wanted everyone to feel sorry for him."

The detectives kept hearing witnesses tell them that Rundle was interested in the Seattle Seahawks football team. He talked about the team a lot. They asked the FBI to contact the Seattle Seahawks to see if there was any evidence of Rundle going to the games, and to their shock, there was.

Rundle was a season ticket holder.

The Seattle Seahawks kept a customer account file for Bill Rundle that showed he paid $434 for the tickets.

"I was angry," Huggins said. "Magda Belen was back in Las Vegas wondering what happened to her mother, and he's buying season tickets to Seahawks football? His wife is out there somewhere, rotting away, and he doesn't care. He's moving on.

"It makes you sick," Huggins said. "The more I learned about him, the more I was convinced he was a total psychopath. How narcissistic can you be? This guy thinks the world revolves around him."

The detectives returned to Las Vegas with a lot of evidence but still no Bill Rundle. The FBI was ready to stake out the next home game for the Seahawks, against the Denver Broncos the following week, but although they didn't know it yet, Rundle wasn't going to be there.

He was on his way to Disney World.

The Las Vegas detectives were disappointed to leave Seattle without catching their prey. They'd gathered an incredible cache of evidence against Rundle during their four days in Seattle, but they still needed to catch him. They knew they were close to him, and they thought Rundle was still in Seattle when they boarded a plane to fly back to Vegas. The detectives held out hope that the FBI would catch him at a stakeout of the Seahawks game, but any hope that Rundle would be arrested at the football game evaporated within days of the detectives arriving back in the Devil's city.

On October 11, fifty-four days after the Rundles' disappearance, the CAT unit documented a credit card transaction showing Rundle had stayed the night at a Holiday Inn in Fredericksburg, Virginia. The detectives were crushed. Their prey was clearly on the run again. They had been so close in Seattle, and now he was on the other side of the country.

Huggins and Tremel were frustrated that they seemed always to be one step behind Rundle. Huggins decided that waiting for Rundle to leave more evidence of his whereabouts through financial transactions wasn't enough.

She was going to try a long shot.

"We knew he had an AOL account, and through the help of the CAT unit, we got his screen name—Rraven111," Huggins said.

It was an obvious reference to another football team—
the Baltimore Ravens. Huggins entered *Rraven111* into her
buddy list on her AOL account, which meant that she
would be alerted anytime *Rraven111* was logged on to his
computer at the same time she was.

Sure enough, what she hoped for happened: She was
logged on to her personal computer at the homicide detail's
office on West Charleston Boulevard when her computer
alerted her that *Rraven111* was online, too.

Huggins sent *Rraven111* an email in the hope he might
respond to her. Her first email to Rraven111 read:

"Woo Hoo are you a Ravens Fan?"

There was no response.

Huggins waited several minutes before typing up a second message. Alby walked into the office as she was typing
up the next email.

"Guess who I'm talking to, or [at least] trying to?" Huggins said to her sergeant.

"No. Are you really?" Alby shot back. "So he's on[line],
huh?"

"Yep," Huggins said.

Alby called the CAT unit to alert them to the fact that
Rraven111 was online. Huggins, in her next email, decided
to make it clear to *Rraven111* that the writer was a woman
who liked football.

"I was going to play the sex card," Huggins said.

The second email read:

*"Guess ur not wanting to talk to a girl that loves the
game . . . boo hoo."*

Huggins was again frustrated at the lack of a response.
She knew it was a long shot, but she felt like Rundle was
right there in front of her, and there was nothing she could
do about it.

"I wanted to reach through my computer screen and
grab him," Huggins said. "It was driving me nuts."

But as Huggins's frustration mounted, her fortune shifted

like the desert wind. CAT called Alby back and informed him they had been able to trace Rundle's whereabouts through his online computer usage and his IP address.

"He's at a Days Inn in Orlando!" Alby yelled out.

All of the detectives' actions, including Huggins's Internet search, were recorded by Anthony Galloway for *Dateline* as they happened. Daniel Slepian was in New York City when Galloway called him to give him the news.

"He goes, 'You are not going to believe this, but I was rolling when she found him online,'" Slepian recalled. "It was an amazing moment."

17 ... INTERVIEW

Detective Sheila Huggins couldn't believe the good fortune she'd had. Her decision to put Bill Rundle's computer screen name, *Rraven111*, on her AOL buddy list had brought an end to a two-month-long national manhunt for the fugitive. Huggins's long-shot gamble was aimed at locating Rundle through his online computer use, and the gamble was a winner. Now it was time to collect.

Florida FBI agents had succeeded in tracking down and apprehending Bill Rundle at the Orlando hotel, and he was being held in the Seminole County Florida Detention Center. Huggins and Detective Don Tremel boarded a red-eye flight from Vegas to Orlando to go interview Rundle, and *Dateline*'s Slepian met the detectives outside the jail. The detectives arrived in Florida at 8 a.m. on October 12, 2002. They were tired, and the humidity they encountered was intense.

"It was very hot and humid, and I was running on adrenaline," Huggins recalled. "It's like ninety degrees with two hundred percent humidity, and I was having a bad hair day. My hair was flat, my makeup's running, and I had to go buy a hair clip so I could keep the hair out of my face. I'm thinking, 'Great. I'm going to be on *Dateline*, and I look like I've been rode hard and put away wet.'"

The detectives arrived at the jail shortly before noon. They were escorted into an interview room while Slepian waited outside in the parking lot. Rundle was brought in. He was in an orange jumpsuit and handcuffed at the wrists and ankles. Nearly two months after the blood had been found in Shirley Rundle's home, the detectives finally sat face-to-face with their prey. Their initial impression was that he certainly didn't look like a killer; he looked like a tired, overweight grandfather wearing dorky glasses, a completely normal man, and Tremel thought to himself that Rundle's regular guy appearance was probably his greatest asset. It was the reason Rundle had been able to get away with so much for so long.

"If I could tell what a crook or killer looks like, we'd be out of business, but we can't," Tremel said. "Bill Rundle is the perfect example of that. Looking at him, who would think it? He definitely does not look like a killer. He looks like a grandpa."

The detectives had three goals for the interview: to get Rundle to confess to killing Shirley, to find out where her body was, and to discover the fate of Rundle's mother, Willa.

"I wanted to know where Shirley was, and I wanted to know for Magda," Huggins said.

Huggins led the interview. The detectives expected Rundle to invoke his right to a lawyer and say nothing. This, however, was not in Rundle's nature. The man believed he could talk his way out of anything, and the detectives were blown away at what he had to say to them.

The following are excerpts from his 108-page statement:

"In my personal belongings, I have a four-way nasal spray," Rundle began the interview. "I haven't had a chance to take my heart medication or anything. I'm having a lot of trouble breathing right now, and it's affecting me. . . . [but] I will answer any question you ask me."

"Okay," Huggins said.

"As truthfully and completely as I can," Rundle said.

"I appreciate that," Huggins said. "Tell me what happened leading up to you leaving Las Vegas."

Rundle made it clear that he first wanted to talk about criticisms he'd read in the paper from his third wife, Amy. His wife had apparently told a newspaper reporter that he was a drunk, and Rundle didn't like that.

"My ex-wife said I was a drunk," Rundle told the detectives. "Which, I drink, but, you know, she said . . . I didn't work the last year or so [of our marriage], and let me tell you, I was raising Richard by myself. I got custody of Richard because she deserted him when she found out he had diabetes when he's two years old. I raised him from when he was two until 1987 when he was killed by the car by Corina King.

"[At that time] I was looking for somebody," Rundle said. "I had had such bad luck with wives. I just had bad taste in [women.] So, I met Shirley at the Union Plaza. We fell in love, and we got married. Her daughter [Magda] was very jealous of me right away because they had just come over from the Philippines. And, I could understand that. I was as good with Magda as I possibly could be.

"Shirley and I worked at the Union Plaza," Rundle said. "This is the sole truth . . . She was such a good person, but she was the most jealous and possessive person.

"She'd been married twice [in the Philippines]," Rundle said. "I just really cared so much about her . . . but she had a terrible, terrible temper. A terrible temper. She would hit me with bottles. No matter what I said, it was not good enough. She thought I was having an affair with every woman I ever saw or worked with. She was just a super jealous person."

Despite this picture of Shirley not matching up with anything they'd heard from anyone else, the detectives were ecstatic that Rundle was talking at all, and they did little to interrupt him. Rundle told them a lengthy narrative of how he and his wife bought their home on Poppywood Drive with his parents' money, and he talked extensively about Shirley's relationship with his mother, Willa. He said the relationship between his mother and wife was a stormy one.

"Okay ... in 1995, my dad—who was just a wonderful man—became ill," Rundle told the detectives. "I promised him that I would take care of my mom. He wanted her to come to Las Vegas, and I said, 'I think that's a good idea.'

"[But] Shirley and my mom never got along," Rundle said. "They never got along. So, my dad died ... January 16, 1996, and, my father was a very, very generous person. He liked Shirley a lot, so he bought us a home."

"He left you money or something?" Huggins said.

"Yeah," Rundle said. "So we paid cash for that house ... on Poppywood."

Rundle told the detectives that his mother came to live with them in 1996, and that Shirley and Willa bickered constantly after Willa's arrival.

"My mom came to Las Vegas so she could stay with us," Rundle said. "Shirley wasn't crazy about that, but [we had] a beautiful new home out in that area, and Shirley said 'Okay' to my mom living with us." Bill continued to paint himself as the peacemaker between the two women. "I [told Shirley], 'Look, we'll try to make this work.'

"My mom stayed in the downstairs bedroom," Rundle said. "My mother was very, very sick. By that, I mean she walked with a walker, and she was in severe pain, and she took heavy doses of morphine to alleviate the pain."

"Um," Huggins said.

"Okay," Rundle said. "My mother and Shirley got into quarreling and the worst fights. This was, oh, I would say,

March of 1997. And my mother and Shirley got into a terrible, terrible fight. I mean, screaming and pushing and
shoving. It was tearing me apart that this was happening. I
don't know if it was because Shirley was jealous of my
mother, but there was no reason to be. We'd sit down, we'd
play a simple board game at the table, Clue or Scrabble,
and Shirley and my mom were yelling back and forth that
each other was cheating at Scrabble and that I was helping
and . . . I just went, 'Oh my God, what's going on?'

"Well, this next part you're gonna find hard to believe,
but this is the gospel truth," Rundle claimed, setting up his
bombshell for the detectives.

"Okay," Huggins said.

"Shirley started upping my mother's morphine medication," Rundle said. "I had no idea this was happening. Her
morphine tablets were in capsule form. [Shirley] told me
this."

"Like the little powder inside the capsule?" Huggins
asked.

"The powder—yeah," Rundle said. "And, she [Shirley]
admitted this to me after this happened. She was taking
the capsules and putting . . ."

"More?" Huggins said.

"A lot more morphine in each capsule, and then she put
them back into my mother," Rundle said. "This was right
after that big fight I told you about that they had."

Huggins and Tremel were shocked at what Rundle was
saying. They had walked into the interview room expect-
ing Rundle to invoke his right to an attorney, and now
Rundle was telling them this amazing account: that his
missing wife, Shirley, had killed his missing mother.

Again, the detectives decided to just let Rundle talk. It
sounded implausible; everyone they'd interviewed had described Shirley as a docile, caring woman. She was not the
type of person to murder a defenseless elderly woman with
morphine. But Rundle, in his interview, blamed everything

on Shirley. He said a few months after his mother moved to Las Vegas, he found his mother dead in her bed in the home on Poppywood Drive from a morphine overdose.

"You actually found her passed away?" Huggins asked.

"Yes," Rundle said.

"Okay," Huggins said.

"Yes," Rundle said. "And, I confronted Shirley about it, and she was just as callous and cold as could possibly be. I said, [whispering], 'We've got to call the police,' and Shirley begged me not to . . . She told me that she could take care of everything."

Rundle claimed Shirley promised him she would dispose of his mother's body. Rundle said he went to work at the casino that day instead of calling the police, and when Rundle returned home later that afternoon, Willa's body was gone. He asked Shirley what she had done with the body, and Shirley said she'd hired two Filipino acquaintances to get rid of the corpse.

Rundle said he had no idea what Shirley and the two men did with his mother's body.

"This is my fault," Rundle said. "I let her take care of what she wanted to do. I don't know the two people involved [but] they were both Filipinos—male Filipinos. They disposed of the body."

The detectives were incredulous at the account. Shirley, a petite woman of five feet four inches, was described by every witness they'd interviewed as a sweet, loving woman. Now Rundle was telling them Shirley had fought constantly with her eighty-seven-year-old mother-in-law, and that she'd not only poisoned the old woman with morphine, but had dumped her body God knew where.

"The whole time, I'm thinking bullshit, bullshit, bullshit," Huggins said.

The detectives pressed Rundle further on the whereabouts of his mother's body, but he gave them nothing.

"Do you know where?" Huggins said.

"I have no idea," Rundle said. "That's the truth. I do not know where."

"I'd hate to see your mom out in some [unmarked] grave somewhere," Huggins said.

"We made a story up that she went to Austria traveling," Rundle said. "Okay. Uh, we completely were at fault for using her Social Security money. We used it to pay bills."

"What were you thinking when Shirley said she'd take care of the body?" Tremel asked.

"That she would get rid of the body," Rundle said.

"And that didn't bother you, the fact that maybe she was thrown in a Dumpster or something?" Tremel asked.

"Oh, I don't think they did," Rundle said. "You can't throw the body in a Dumpster."

"Why did you leave her like that?" Tremel said. "Your mom?"

"It's terrible," Rundle said. "Terrible judgment. I chose the wrong side." Once again, he painted Shirley as the one in the wrong.

"But you have no idea where she would have put her?" Huggins said.

"I have no idea," Rundle said.

"Did you ever think of calling the cops?" Huggins asked.

"Uh, I didn't," Rundle said. "I'll tell you something, she told me that if I had done that, she would tell the police and everybody else that I had given her the idea, uh, about my mother."

"Okay," Huggins said.

"And it was kind of a blackmail, you know," Rundle said.

The detectives didn't believe Rundle, but they didn't want to say anything that would cause him to stop talking. They waited patiently for him to start talking about the death of his wife, and he didn't disappoint. In a stoic, un-emotional tone, he spoke of the events leading to the killing of his wife, and he said the events started with the money problems the couple had.

He portrayed his wife as someone who couldn't wait to spend their money.

"She had eleven brothers and sisters," Rundle said. "I was close to all of them. Every single one of them, [and she] would mail six, seven, eight, nine hundred dollars to them in the Philippines. And that's a lot of money when you're not working."

He described how his wife spent thousands of dollars on phone calls to her siblings in the Philippines.

"I told her, 'You've got to limit your calls,'" Rundle said. "She wouldn't limit her calls. The bills were two hundred and seventy-five to three hundred dollars every single month. You can get all of those bills and check on them. They're all to the Philippines, and some of them an hour and a half, two hours."

Rundle also blamed Magda and Rodel for being huge financial drains. He said he and Shirley had given the Belens approximately $50,000 over the last decade, and this included $15,000 for a home down payment. In 1997, Rundle said he gave the Belens $27,000 to pay off credit card bills and $14,000 for clearing up a vehicle lease.

"How'd you get that money?" Huggins said.

"That was from the money that my father had left," Rundle said. "It was continuous with them . . . [our] giving them money."

Rundle admitted to the police that he and Shirley had spent nearly all of his mother's money after Willa's death. As his parents' life savings got smaller and smaller, he came up with an idea to make more money: he was going to buy a PostNet store.

"So the store opens," Rundle said. "Rodel quits his job. Magda quit her job. Well, the store didn't do real well. It couldn't support four people. It just couldn't support four people.

"So, we took out a second mortgage on our house," Rundle said. "Plus Shirley had every credit card you could possibly have. Dillard's, Penney's, Macy's, Sears. Every one. And they gave her large lines of credit. She would go over there and she would buy . . . clothes that she would send to the Philippines in boxes. Then . . . she wanted to make herself look younger and, you know, she looked fine.

"It was just a terrible situation," Rundle said. "I told Shirley, 'We've got to stop spending. We've got to stop this.' I said, 'There's no money. It's all gonna be gone' . . . I said, 'We'll have nothing.' "

"Did she know what kind of money she was spending?" Huggins said.

"Of course she did," Rundle said. "She knew exactly what she was spending."

"What about bankruptcy?" Huggins said.

"I talked to her about bankruptcy," Rundle said. "I talked to her, but she was worried about it ruining her credit."

Rundle then portrayed Shirley as a domestic abuser with a drinking problem and a controlling woman who assaulted him. She "would yell and scream" at him constantly. She threw objects at him, and he said Shirley once threatened to kill him in his sleep.

"Were there people [who] ever saw [Shirley] throwing things at you?" Huggins said.

"No," Rundle said. "It was done inside the privacy of our house." Despite this so-called constant abuse, however, Rundle gallantly said he never retaliated. "I would not hit her back. She was five-foot-four. I was six foot four. I was almost twice as heavy as she was.

"She would pound me," he said. "I'm not kidding. When she would drink champagne, she would pass out on the couch, and that's when the stuff would stop. And then she'd be mad for three days after that."

Rundle said the couple's financial problems and domestic fights came to a head on the night of August 17, 2002.

He wanted the couple to escape their financial nightmare by running away to the Philippines, and, at first, Shirley was willing to go. But, Rundle said, Shirley got drunk on the night of the murder, and the two started arguing.

"We were going to leave a note for Magda to go and sell everything," Rundle said. "I was ninety percent sure that [Shirley] had agreed to go . . . [and then] on Saturday night, she started drinking. She was drinking real heavy, and she started in on me on everything about what I had done, and how I was taking her away from her granddaughter. How I was doing this and how I was doing that. She took the champagne bottle, and she continually hit me. She hit me and hit me, and she broke my arm."

"With the champagne bottle?" Huggins said.

"With the champagne bottle," Rundle said. "I couldn't get her to stop hitting me. Absolutely nuts. When I got to Seattle, I had to go to the hospital. I couldn't even move my arm from where she broke it."

"Did she hit you anywhere else on your body?" Huggins said.

"She hit me everywhere," Rundle said. "As many places as she possibly could. And, then, she threatened that she would kill me during my sleep. So I couldn't get her to stop."

Rundle documented for the detectives the moment he killed his wife.

"I went into the closet. I took out a baseball bat, and I hit her once," he said.

"With the baseball bat?" Huggins said.

"Yes," Rundle said. "With the baseball bat . . . She fell into the chair when I hit her. Blood was coming out of her . . ."

"Of her head?" Huggins said.

"Her head," Rundle said. "So I said, 'Oh, my God! Look at this! Jesus Christ.'"

Rundle first said it was just "a" baseball bat in the closet.

But when pressed further, he admitted the bat wasn't just any bat. It was a special bat.

It was *Richie's* bat.

The detectives found this account curious as soon as they heard it. Why would Rundle, a man approaching sixty, keep Richie's baseball bat stored in a downstairs closet when Richie's shrine was upstairs? Rundle, when pressed, came up with a bizarre explanation: He claimed that he kept Richie's bat in the closet because he liked to go to a nearby park and use it to hit fly balls to local kids.

"I hit fly balls to the kids and stuff like that," Rundle told the cops. "The bat was in the closet because we were using it all the time. That was Richie's bat. So, the bat, I washed it off, and I took it, and I replaced it in the china closet."

The detectives were mortified at the idea of Rundle killing his wife with his dead son's bat, and they didn't believe Rundle's account that the bat just happened to be nearby by chance. They believed he'd stashed it downstairs as part of a premeditated plan to murder his wife, and that the killing wasn't some spontaneous act of passion or anger. The detail about the bat was important information. Now they finally had the murder weapon. The detectives immediately sent Senior Crime Scene Analyst Daniel Holstein back to the home on Poppywood Drive to get the bat. Rundle, meanwhile, showed no emotion when he talked about killing his wife with Richie's bat. The story seemed rehearsed to the detectives. It was clear that Rundle was pining for a manslaughter scenario, a heat-of-passion crime, and not calculated murder.

"I got her body into the trunk of the car," Rundle said. "I knew I could never clean it up, so I switched chairs. I put the chair downstairs upstairs and the one upstairs downstairs. I put a couple throw rugs over the stains that were there so they wouldn't be visible to the naked eye without looking.

FATHER OF THE YEAR

"Obviously, the [police were] gonna find it," Rundle said. "I knew that. So . . . when I got her into the trunk, I cleaned up as much as I could of what had been there.

"Then, I went upstairs," Rundle said. "I took my medication. I took some clothes. One suitcase. A laptop. My .38, which has never been fired, ever. Small odds and ends . . . Pictures of Gretchen, and pictures of Richie."

Rundle said he wrote the note about the emergency trip to the Philippines and put it on the interior door of the garage. He tried to get some sleep that night, and he fled in the Buick Regal the next morning to Reno, then Portland, and then Seattle.

"In [my] briefcase, there are Seattle Seahawks tickets," Rundle said. "I bought Seattle Seahawk tickets."

"Season tickets?" Huggins said.

"Yeah," Rundle said.

"Oh, okay," Huggins said.

"Cheap," Rundle said. "Lower [deck]. Four hundred dollars."

Rundle then told the detectives exactly what they were waiting for. He said he'd dumped his wife's body along a rural road just over the California state line traveling from Reno. He could not name the exact location, but he described where he dumped Shirley's body to the detectives, and he mentioned reading about the discovery of the unidentified Asian female in the *Seattle Times* newspaper.

"I didn't hide it," Rundle said of his wife's corpse. "I just wanted it found right away. I figured they would be able to identify it."

Huggins knew the police were now just one step away from having a very good case against Rundle, and her heart was racing. She got up, walked out of the interview room, and called Alby in Las Vegas.

"I think it was on a Saturday," Alby said. "I got the call, I left my home, and I went back to the office. I was looking on a map to try and see what county it could be. I'd pick a county and make a phone call to the police there. If they didn't have any cases of unidentified, deceased females matching Shirley's description, I'd go to another county in that region of California and call them. After a few calls, I'm telling an officer from Lassen County what she looked like, and he said, 'My God, I think that sounds like the unidentified female who was found.' Same height, weight, and physical description. He emailed me a photo of the body. I looked at the photo, and I said, 'It's Shirley.'"

18 . . . BLUDGEONED

> When I hit her she was by the chair standing. She saw me coming. She fell back into the chair, and she was bleeding. I don't think she was alive, and I sat right there and I looked at what I had done.
>
> I said, "I've got to cover this up, and I've got to run."
>
> —Bill Rundle

In May of 1998, Bill Rundle said, he and his wife, Shirley, hatched a plan to get at his mother's life savings of $300,000. According to Bill Rundle, the plan involved Shirley calling Willa's stockbroker in Escondido and posing as Willa. Shirley put in a sale order on the stock, and the transaction went through. Willa Rundle had no say in what happened to the money, because she'd been dead for nearly a year.

"My mom's money ended up in our joint bank account because Shirley called and said she was Willa Rundle to my mother's bank in Escondido," Rundle said. "She called Bank of America investments, and Shirley put in a sell order. They didn't do anything to verify the sell order. They said the check would be there in three to four days."

When the cash arrived, the Rundles started spending it like sailors in a whorehouse. They burned through that huge chunk of cash, $300,000, in just two years. They spent the majority of the money on furniture, travel, Rundle's sports gambling habit, and on Shirley's relatives in the Philippines. Rundle said a significant portion of the money went to the Belens to help them out when they were in a financial bind.

The following is Rundle's description of how he and Shirley burned through his mother's $300,000.

"We bought a franchise—a PostNet for $55,000," Rundle said. "It was a good investment, but it didn't work.

"Shirley sent hundreds and hundreds of dollars to the Philippines," Rundle said. "Hundreds to this brother. Hundreds to that brother. Hundreds to this sister, and I got to the point where I didn't care anymore.

"Shirley racked up $300 a month in phone bills calling and talking to her sisters all the time," Rundle said. "Continuously. We gave [a lot to] Magda and Rodel—we gave it to them even though it wasn't ours to give.

"We gave them [the Belens] approximately $15,000 for a house down payment," Rundle said. "We paid for their landscaping. We paid $28,000 on their credit card bills. It doesn't take long . . . It just happens.

"We ate great," Rundle said. "Money for food, for the business, and for the furniture. The bed set we had was incredible. You should see the bedroom furniture we had. [Shirley] couldn't have a regular king-size bed. She had to go to May Company and get the most beautiful, expensive furniture she could get.

After going through most of Willa's money, Bill Rundle said he came up with a plan to stop the spending. He said he laid out for his wife a schedule for living on $30,000 a year in expenditures, but he said the plan proved fruitless.

"I set up a system on how we can make our way out of this," Rundle said. "We could lock in on $30,000 a year. We can live on $30,000 a year. Well, she couldn't live on $30,000 a month. I'm exaggerating a little bit, but it was close."

A lot of the couple's remaining money went to monthly credit card payments. By August 2002, the money was nearly all gone, but the Rundles kept living the high life. There was roughly $25,000 in the couple's bank accounts, and they had nearly four times that amount in credit card debt. The situation was starting to seem hopeless, and the Rundles talked about selling the home and moving to the Philippines.

"Things were building up," Rundle said. He presented himself as helpless in the face of his wife's spendthrift ways. "It got to the point where . . . we had about $25,000 left in cash. We now owed on the house. Shirley had run up the credit cards. She just bought and bought and bought and bought. Her brother-in-law ran a Toyota company in the Philippines, and there [would have been] no problem with me getting a job there. They would have loved to have had an American salesman working there, and we had enough money to buy a nice house there. I could have had a job. She could have had a job and we could have a house in the Philippines. Everything would have been fine. Shirley was ready to leave Magda and everything because she realized we had nothing left."

But Rundle said that as he and his wife were about to make their escape from the mountain of debt, Shirley Rundle backed out. She couldn't leave her daughter and granddaughter behind for the Philippines.

"Shirley wouldn't sell the house," Rundle said. "She wouldn't do it. She didn't want to go to a lower style of living, period. None. I was willing to go, but then she had second thoughts. She didn't want to leave Gretchen. We had the passports. I said, 'I don't want to leave Gretchen either, but I've given you every option in the world, and you won't do what I say to do as far as the money is concerned. We are in debt where we can't possibly pay this off. It's impossible.' "

The stress from the debt blew out like lava bubbling in the depths of a volcano on the night of August 17. Rundle said Shirley was drinking at the home on Poppywood Drive, and they quarreled about money. Shirley, Rundle said, was swigging champagne, and she was angry about their predicament. Then, he claims, Shirley, at just five feet four inches tall and 130 pounds, attacked him with a champagne bottle even though he was twice her size.

"It came to a head that night," Rundle said. "We both were drinking. She hit me with a champagne bottle. Then she hit me again with the champagne bottle."

Rundle was pissed. He stormed off, then went to a closet and retrieved a Louisville Slugger bat. Not just any bat, either—it was *Richie's* bat. A memory of Richie's beautiful life, yet Rundle used it to unleash a flurry of violent hatred on his wife. He pulled Richie's bat back and with every ounce of strength in his body, he bludgeoned Shirley again, and again and again in the living room of their home.

"I'd been hit and hit, and I was tired of it," Rundle said. "I picked up the bat and I cracked her in the head with it. She was stunned, and I hit her again. Then I hit her again. And I probably hit her two or three more times. I totally lost it. I snapped. I had had it.

"When I hit her, she was by the chair, standing," Rundle said. "She saw me coming. She fell back into the chair, and she was bleeding. I don't think she was alive, and I sat right there, and I looked at what I had done. I said, 'I've got to cover this up, and I've got to run.'

"My mother was dead," Rundle said. "My father was dead. I had nothing left. Shirley was gone, too, now, so I put a blanket over her in the chair. I packed up the little stuff that I had that I wanted to take. I took her jewelry, and I took the things I thought I could sell. I put her in the trunk of the car. The next morning, at 6:30 a.m., I left the house. I put a note on the door. It said we had an emergency. We are going to the Philippines. We'd be back by September 6, which was in time for Gretchen's birthday. So, I put her in the trunk, I covered her up, I tried to get some sleep, and then I drove north.

"I felt terrible about it," Rundle said. "You don't know

how bad it was. My wife was dead, and I knew I wasn't going to get away with it."

Rundle sped north in the Buick Regal, the HONYBUN tag gleaming in the blazing desert sun for all to see. He knew he was screwed. There was no way to explain the blood in the home. He drove to Reno and booked a night at a Holiday Inn. He immediately went into the bar and started drinking. He ordered a beer and watched a *Monday Night Football* game on television while his wife's corpse rotted in the trunk of his car in the parking lot.

"I was so worried about them finding a body in the trunk in my car in the parking lot, so I had a can of Lysol, and every hour and [a] half, I'd go out there and spray it in there," Rundle said. "It was terrible. I had so much guilt, and so much remorse. That was a Monday night, so I stayed and I watched the football game in the bar there."

It was a real bitch for Bill Rundle. He couldn't sleep, and he was paranoid. He decided the next morning would be the day he and Shirley parted from each other forever.

"I went to sleep and I got up at six the next morning, and I decided I was going to go to Seattle," Rundle said.

"I was driving on some obscure highway [the next day]," Rundle said. "It was from Reno to California, some deserted place, and I stopped and pulled over near Susanville. I took her body out of the trunk. She was in a blanket, and I put it alongside the road. I didn't throw it down the hill or anything like that. I knew someone was going to find it. I just wanted to be away from her."

Rundle felt a huge sense of relief come over him as he sped away from his wife's cold, dead body. He drove to Portland and spent the night there, then drove on to Seattle the next day, and he spent the next ten days in a Holiday Inn in the city. He decided to spend some time in one of America's most gorgeous cities.

"I liked Seattle," Rundle said. "I was like, 'Well, if they are going to get me, they might as well get me here.'"

Rundle rented an apartment at the Mediterranean apartment complex on Queen Anne Avenue North in Seattle. Every day, he walked from his apartment to a Kinko's with Internet access, and he spent hours and hours surfing the Internet on his laptop. He gambled regularly on football and baseball games through online betting sites. He said he usually bet $10 or $20 on each game. He also surfed some online Asian porn sites. He read every story in the *Las Vegas Review-Journal* about the manhunt for him. He knew the police were looking for him from reading the online news stories, and he also knew the cops didn't know yet he was in Seattle.

"I got a bank account under my name," Rundle said. "I could have gotten on a plane the first night after I killed my wife and gone to St. Kitts, and I'd still be in St. Kitts because there is no extradition. But I didn't want to. I was tired. I was worn out. I never used an alias. I was using my own credit card. I knew I was going to get caught.

"Every day, I typed in reviewjournal.com and . . . I followed everything about me in there," Rundle said. "I found an article in the *Seattle Times* two days later—two days after I got to Seattle—and it was about a body discovered on the side of the road [near Susanville]. The Las Vegas police didn't know anything about it.

"The [California authorities] thought it was a vagrant who had been camping out in the area, but I knew right away," Rundle said. "It was Shirley, and I felt terrible."

But if Rundle actually felt any remorse over leaving his wife's bludgeoned body on the side of the road like a piece of trash, he still felt no need to keep any memories of his life with her.

"Shirley's jewelry? I pawned it in Seattle. I sold it," Rundle said. "Everyone [who I met in Seattle] asked me when

I was in Seattle what I was doing there, why I was there, and I told them my wife just passed away. I told everyone that, and I never changed it. I wasn't going to tell them I'd just murdered my wife."

Rundle says he knew he was going to get caught. Given this, he figured he might as well enjoy himself.

"I had this $18,000 left in my pocket, and I knew I wasn't going to get to see [much more in life], so I bought season tickets to the Seahawks. I knew I was going to go to prison or get killed."

But Rundle's account regarding his time on the run is full of contradictions. Despite his claims that he was just waiting for the cops to catch up with him, he discarded his Buick in a storage facility parking garage, and he switched to cash. He stopped using his credit cards for eight days, and he regularly read books about changing one's identity to facilitate a disappearance.

"I knew they were near, ready to get me . . . and so I decided I would stop using my credit card in Seattle. I knew I had to get rid of the car," Rundle said. "I put the car in three months' storage in Seattle. I got the car out of the way, and then I rented another one.

"I met with a guy who rented cars with only cash deposits," Rundle said. "I gave him six hundred dollars, and he gave me a Ford Escort. I told the guy I was planning to go to Portland. I meant Portland, Maine, but I didn't want to get in any trouble with the guy, so I didn't tell him which Portland I was talking about."

Rundle left Seattle a week before Las Vegas detectives arrived. His first stop was in Missoula, Montana, where he spent the night.

"People say I was running around having the greatest time of my life after I'd killed my wife . . . and I say, 'What fun can you have in Missoula?'" Rundle said.

But of course, he didn't stay in Missoula. The next

morning, Rundle drove his newly rented Escort to Rapid City and the Black Hills of South Dakota. There, he took a tour of Mount Rushmore. While Magda Belen and her daughter were grief-stricken in Las Vegas over Shirley's unknown fate, Rundle was spending an October afternoon marveling at the faces of George Washington, Thomas Jefferson, Theodore Roosevelt, and Abraham Lincoln carved into the side of a mountain.

He'd been there once before with Shirley.

"I did take a tour of Mount Rushmore," Rundle said. "I already killed my wife, so what more trouble could I get into? I certainly wasn't going to hurt anyone else."

Rundle drove to Washington, D.C., next.

"They had a huge convention in town, and I couldn't get a room, so I went south to Virginia and North Carolina," Rundle said. "I didn't go to Hilton Head or Cape Cod. I didn't go boating out on the ocean. So, I ended up in Orlando, Florida, and I checked into this Days Inn. They were only charging me $20 a night in Orlando, which is unheard of. I had never been to Disney World, so I figured I might as well go to Disney World. I went to Disney World, and I also went to Universal Studios.

"I don't deny it," Rundle said. "But I wasn't having any fun," he protests. "I didn't go on any rides. I walked around at Disney World, and all I did was walk around trying to be anonymous while I watched people have fun, which I couldn't do anymore. Then, after I had gone and saw everything I wanted to see in Florida, I spent almost all of my time at a TGI Friday's bar and restaurant in Orlando eating and drinking beer. I was even thinking of staying in Florida and looking for some type of work."

Bill Rundle claimed not to have had any fun at Mount Rushmore, Disney World, or Universal Studios. He said he spent most of his days at a TGI Friday's restaurant eating, drinking beer, and watching television broadcasts of sporting events he'd gambled on.

"One day, I was sitting at Friday's, and these two guys come in," Rundle said. "They were clean-cut, kind of husky, and I'd never seen them before. I'd been in Friday's every day for fifteen days, and I looked over at them, and I said to myself, 'Those are cops.' There was no question in my mind they were cops. I knew they were there for me. There was no question.'"

Rundle paid his tab and headed back to the Days Inn on foot. Were the two men in the restaurant really cops after him, or was he just being paranoid? Maybe they were cops, but had no idea who he was. His mind was racing over the possibilities, and he decided to leave Orlando soon.

"I walked back to the hotel," Rundle said. "It was a Friday night, and I had made a bet online for Saturday's games. I had Brigham Young and the University of Southern California football teams on a two-team parlay. So, I was walking back from Friday's to this Days Inn, and there is a cop car sitting in a parking lot. Then I see another cop car coming the other way and towards me. I walked even with him, and at that point I was like, 'They know. They just don't want to get me right now because they probably have some sting worked out.'"

Rundle reached his hotel room without getting arrested. He thought maybe he was just paranoid. If the cops were on to him, they surely would have nabbed him as he reached the hotel. Rundle went to sleep that night. His room phone rang at 1:30 a.m., and he was angry.

"I picked up the phone. It was the desk clerk," Rundle said. "She said, 'Mr. Rundle, there is a leak in the room above you, and we need to get in your room to see where the water is coming through. Can you come up to the lobby right now? We'll treat you to a complimentary breakfast at the Denny's that is hooked to the hotel.'"

Rundle knew immediately the end was upon him. His heart raced as he climbed out of bed and grabbed his gun.

"I was like, 'You've got to be kidding me,'" Rundle said. "I knew at that point they were outside the door. I went to get my gun, and I was going to kill myself."

Rundle grabbed the loaded handgun and debated what to do. He heard a knock at the door and an announcement:

"FBI! Open the door!"

I'm going to jail for the rest of my life. End it right now!

Rundle put his finger on the trigger of the gun, but he couldn't put the cold steel in his mouth and pull the trigger.

"I hadn't confessed my sins to anyone," Rundle said. "I hadn't been forgiven for what I did. I had the gun, and I came so close, *so close* to killing myself right before I opened the door. If I had been drunk, I would have killed myself."

Rundle opened the door and was greeted by a team of FBI agents and Orlando police officers pointing shotguns and flashlights at him.

"It was the most frightening thing I've ever seen," Rundle said. "Nine FBI agents, and all of them had shotguns. They were standing two feet from me, screaming at me. I put the gun down. I told them it has never been fired. We went inside, they handcuffed me, and I told them I have $10,600 cash in my pocket."

Orlando Police Department Officer Mike Canty would later describe the arrest to Las Vegas authorities.

"I said, 'Please get down,' at which time he started backing away from me," Canty said. "At that time, I saw a silver-colored revolver in his left hand. He dropped that to the floor, and he sat on the bed . . . [and] the FBI secured the weapon.

"After he was arrested, he complained that his right arm . . . was possibly broken," Canty said. "He complained about it. He said he had been involved in a domestic altercation about a month and a half earlier, and that was the reason why we were there."

The call was made to Las Vegas. Rundle was in custody. Tremel and Huggins boarded a flight to Orlando, Florida, that morning.

19 ... FOLLOW-UP (PROSECUTORS)

After walking out of the interview with Bill Rundle in the Florida detention center, Detective Sheila Huggins used her cell phone to call Magda Belen. The emotional phone exchange with Shirley Rundle's daughter was captured on camera by the *Dateline* camera crew.

"Hello. Magda?" Huggins said. "You've got family with you?"

"Uh-huh," Magda said.

"Okay," Huggins said. "Listen—I talked to [Bill] today. He told us that Shirley died, and he put her in the trunk, and he told us where to find her."

"Where?" Belen said.

"Umm . . . She was up in Northern California," Huggins said. "We have located her."

"You did?"

Magda sobbed over the phone.

Shirley's body had been cremated, so she had little to offer Magda for the purposes of a funeral and burial.

"It broke my heart," Huggins said afterward. "You know

what I had to offer Magda? Her mom's jaw. That's all that was left. Just her jaw for dental records. It's terrible.

"She just cried, and I cried with her. I remember talking to her on the phone, and I remember crying with her, and I remember asking her if she had somebody there with her.

"Then, she was telling me, 'Thank you for finding my mom,'" Huggins said. "I tried not to get emotional because I knew I was on TV. I said, 'I'll call you back later,' because I knew I was losing it. What stood out to me was her thanking me. Here she is, on the worst day of her life, and she said, 'Thank you for finding my mom.'"

Shirley Rundle was memorialized on October 23, 2002, at a Catholic church in Las Vegas. It was an extremely emotional ceremony, and Shirley Rundle was remembered as a loving mom, a great person, the perfect grandmother, and a victim.

"There can be a desire for vengeance, certainly for justice, but hopefully for forgiveness. There must be some attempt at forgiveness," the Reverend Kevin McAuliffe told mourners gathered at St. Elizabeth Ann Seton Catholic Church.

Mike Kalil, the *Las Vegas Review-Journal* reporter, interviewed Magda Belen prior to the service. She told Kalil she planned to attend every court hearing for her stepfather.

"After today, we'll put this behind us and concentrate on Monday," Belen said, referring to the day authorities were schedule to extradite Rundle to Las Vegas. "We're ready for them to bring him back."

Mourners offered fond memories of Shirley in the newspaper the next day.

"She was always smiling," said Annie Burch, a longtime friend of Shirley's who'd worked with her at the Luxor.

Jennifer Brandon, another friend who said she'd grown up with Shirley in the Philippines, said she had nightmares about how her friend died.

"I have trouble sleeping and have dreams that she's begging me for help to get away from someone," Brandon said.

Bill Rundle agreed to waive extradition. The detectives, still accompanied by *Dateline NBC*, arranged to fly back with Rundle to Southern Nevada to face justice. Producer Daniel Slepian was sitting in a police cruiser when the detectives brought Rundle out, and he soon found himself sitting next to Rundle in the car. The man who had seemed like a ghost for nearly a month was now right beside him.

"We'd been searching for him for weeks, and here I am sitting next to him," Slepian said. "It smelled like he hadn't showered in a couple of days."

Slepian and Detective Don Tremel made small talk with Rundle, who agreed to a future interview with *Dateline*. Detective Huggins had no interest in talking to Rundle at this point.

"I barely said a word to him the whole way," Huggins said. "He disgusts me."

Slepian said that, in talking to Rundle, he was struck by the accused killer's normalcy. The man seemed almost harmless, and the producer had a difficult time reconciling what he knew about Rundle with the seemingly docile man in front of him.

"We talked for nearly the whole flight," Slepian said. "We talked a lot about sports. [In asking for an interview], I pledged to him that in the broadcast, I would report on how important his son [Richie] was to him. He said, 'You got it. I'll do the interview.' He told me that [remembering Richie] is what was important to him.

"He's a fascinating individual," Slepian said. "If you were to see him in the family videos of him and Shirley at SeaWorld, he looks like a normal, average guy, and it's hard to wrap your mind around the fact that this same person could be so cruel, vicious, and violent. He used [his wife's] head as a baseball. Who could do that?

"The dichotomy of what he appeared to be and what he actually was is really quite remarkable," Slepian said. "He's a guy you could have a beer and watch a game with. After spending that time with him on the flight, talking to him, I said to myself, 'Is this even true? Could he really even have done that? It makes you think to yourself, 'Who else is like that?' "

Near the end of the flight, Slepian even fell asleep with his head on Rundle's shoulder.

Upon their arrival back at the police homicide office in Vegas, Rundle gave a second statement to police, and when pressed by Tremel, he acknowledged it was possible he'd hit his wife more than once. He said he'd used a "full bat swing" on Shirley.

Huggins and Tremel were thrilled at the progress of their investigation. Two months ago, all they had to work with was a bloodstain, a missing car, and a missing couple. Now their suspect was in custody. They had a murder weapon, and they had forensic evidence. The bloodstains on the chair and floor in the Rundle home and the stain in the trunk of their car all matched Shirley's blood. Rundle had confessed during his police statement to what seemed, at a minimum, a crime of manslaughter in the death of his wife. He detailed during his interview the lethal attack with his dead son's baseball bat, and police didn't believe his contention that Shirley had started the violence by swinging at him with a champagne bottle. Most important, the detectives knew where Shirley Rundle's body had been, and they were aware of the violence that had been inflicted on her. The brutality unleashed on the woman was documented in the autopsy: Shirley had been bludgeoned to death, and a rag had been shoved down her throat. She'd been struck several times, not once, as Rundle had said, and on her skull there was an odd pattern from the injuries that suggested the possibility that two weapons may have been used on her.

Most striking to the detectives, however, was how Rundle talked about his wife. He was mostly void of emotion. In his statement, he used the term "it" (rather than "she") several times when describing what he'd done with Shirley's body.

"Here's what happened in my mind," Huggins said. "[Rundle] decides he's going to do this. He has a semi-plan. He goes upstairs while she's sitting in her chair downstairs in her jammies. He gets the bat out of little Richie's cabinet, and he hits her from behind. He hits her a bunch of times. She's holding her head, her fingers get broke, and she slumps over. He gets something to wrap her up, grabs his stuff, writes the note, drives out of town, and now it's time to move on. Another life."

The job of prosecuting Rundle belonged to Clark County District Attorney Stu Bell. Bell is a colorful man and a longtime defense attorney in Las Vegas. He assigned two of his most veteran prosecutors, Chris Owens and David Schwartz, to handle the high-profile case of state versus William Rundle.

Owens, fifty-three, and Schwartz, sixty-one, are very different individuals. Owens is of moderate height. He originally hails from Phoenix, Arizona, where he was born into a family of attorneys.

"My dad is an attorney," Owens said. "I have five brothers and one sister, and four of my brothers are also lawyers. It just happened that way. My father used to take us down to work a lot, and we never talked or planned anything out as far as us all being attorneys. I guess we just figured it was a pretty good career."

Chris Owens is of the Mormon faith, and he is a man who appreciates right versus wrong. He's a tall man, with sharp features and a well-groomed mustache, is physically fit, and his hair is almost completely white. He is both kind and quiet, and he gives off the impression of being an extremely by-the-book individual. He doesn't say a lot, and it takes some time to get to know him.

Owens is as tough as they get in the courtroom, especially toward violent criminals who've obviously committed murder. His skills have earned him the position of the chief of the district attorney's Major Violators Unit, and he seems to know every Nevada criminal statute like a quarterback in the National Football League has memorized every intricate detail of the playbook. Owens is prepared in the courtroom, and you get the sense watching him that prosecuting violent felons is what he was meant to do.

"There is a lot of power in the job," Owens said. "There is a tremendous amount of power because you are dealing with people's lives. So, it's very important as a prosecutor to exercise that power with extreme caution. Don't be reactionary. Be measured, and do the right thing.

"I'm real facetious sometimes when people ask me what I do," Owens said. "I say, 'I put people in jail.' But the reality is, if I felt that was the only thing I did, I wouldn't feel very good about myself. Not every crime is the same, and each one has a lot of different circumstances. You look at the whole situation, and you do justice. I'm interested in the cases themselves, the myriad of facts, and organizing them in a way juries will grab ahold of and understand them."

David Schwartz differs from Chris Owens both in appearance and courtroom style. He was born and raised in Brooklyn, and was fed a steady diet of baseball as a kid. When asked if he is a Yankees or Mets fan, he says his favorite team is the "Brooklyn Dodgers."

"My mom worked into her eighties, and my dad would have worked that long, too, but he passed away," Schwartz said. "You had to have an education in my family, and you had to work hard. Money was tight because we didn't have any."

Schwartz is not your stereotypical, ultraconservative prosecutor born and raised in a conservative Republican family. He protested against the Vietnam War as a young man. He taught school out of philanthropy in a low-income neighborhood in Brooklyn for several years while pursuing an education in the law.

"I was anything but conservative," Schwartz said. "I marched against the war, and I was very liberal. I hung out with defense lawyers a lot."

After law school, a friend urged him to apply for a job as a prosecutor with the Brooklyn District Attorney's Office, and he got the job. Schwartz has family in Southern Nevada, and after a few years in the Brooklyn DA's office, he got a job at the Clark County District Attorney's Office in Las Vegas and moved west.

"I moved here, and I grew to like Las Vegas a lot," Schwartz said. "There is another side to the city. It's not just the Strip."

Schwartz said he still has a liberal streak in him even after three decades of prosecuting criminals, but he acknowledges that his experience in prosecuting hundreds of murder cases has left him very conservative when it comes to the criminal justice system.

He is a supporter of the death penalty, and says he has no tolerance for violence.

"When you see what you see every day in the criminal justice system, it makes you conservative," Schwartz said.

David Schwartz is truly unique among prosecutors. Watching prosecutors day in and day out, one might often sense that many appear to operate from a script, for fear of making a mistake that sets a criminal free. Even veteran prosecutors can get overly cautious, but not Schwartz. He is flamboyant, aggressive, and colorful in court. He is willing to take chances. In a world of laptops and high-tech presentations for juries, Schwartz takes notes by hand on a yellow notepad. He outlines his openings and closings on the pad, but he's not afraid to veer from the script in his remarks. His most defining characteristics are his booming, powerful voice, his moral indignation, and his willingness to use pieces of physical evidence as props. He uses the emotion of a trial to drive home a verdict, and when Schwartz is on, he offers some of the most powerful courtroom drama one may ever have an opportunity to witness.

The perfect example of Schwartz's courtroom power was on display during the veteran prosecutor's stellar performance in the trial of what is perhaps Las Vegas's most savage murder case. In 2004, a pair of Utah siblings, Beau and Monique Maestas, stabbed two little girls in a trailer park in Mesquite, Nevada, over a bogus methamphetamine deal. They butchered three-year-old Kristyanna Cowan and left her half-sister, Brittney Bergeron, twelve, paralyzed from the waist down. The crime was horrific by any standard. The Maestas siblings were arrested on murder charges, and Beau Maestas wrote from jail he was glad he'd carried out the attack on the children, whom he referred to as "little piggies."

Schwartz put on quite the show as he asked jurors to order death for Beau Maestas. He stood in front of them holding a photo of the murdered baby and the huge butcher knife used to slay the child, and he screamed for justice.

"If not this case, which case?" the prosecutor asked. "You are sitting in judgment of a brutal, uncaring, violent, remorseless killer.

"Don't forget Brittney Bergeron," Schwartz said. "Don't forget about what he did to Brittney Bergeron.

"Don't forget about Kristyanna Cowan," the prosecutor said. "Don't forget about what this defendant did to Kristyanna Cowan.

"Kristyanna Cowan will never see another sunrise, never

get to go to school, go to a dance, go on a date, marry, have children," Schwartz said. "And she'll never ever see her best friend in the world, Brittney."

One juror cried with grief at the display. Beau Maestas is now on death row.

One of the first things Owens and Schwartz did with the police in the Rundle case was help obtain warrants during the investigation. They gave the police advice during the manhunt, and following Rundle's arrest, Owens and Schwartz crafted a complete timeline of the events surrounding Shirley's death to analyze what facts they had.

The following are the contents of the prosecutors' timeline:

8/17/02—Magda Belen's last contact with Shirley Rundle.

8/20/02—Note found in garage at Poppywood Drive. "Alarm is set! Be Home 9/06. Emergency Trip to the Phillipines." Body of female found dumped off Highway 44 in Susanville.

8/21/02—Missing persons report filed by Magda Belen. Autopsy of Unknown Female by Dr. Clark. Brain injuries and blunt force trauma. Fingerprint from Jane Doe. Dental records.

8/22/02—Search warrant for Poppywood home. Blood recovered.

9/8/02—Bill Rundle goes to Seattle for X-rays. Storage of car. Opens bank account.

9/12/02—Search warrant for Poppywood home. Chair recovered, empty gun case, etc.

10/2/02—Bill Rundle's car located in Seattle storage.

10/4/02—Las Vegas police process car.

10/11/02—Bill Rundle arrested in Orlando, Florida.

10/12/02—Bill Rundle's first statement to Las Vegas police.

10/12/02—Search warrant for motel. Search warrant for rental car.

10/15/02—Dental records of Jane Doe match those of Shirley Rundle.

10/16/02—Search warrant for Poppywood home. Bat—murder weapon—recovered.

10/30/02—Bill Rundle's second statement.

11/26/02—Search warrant for Poppywood home.

One thing Owens knew for sure in analyzing the evidence and statements was that Rundle was lying about a lot of things. Several facts stood out to the veteran prosecutors. Owens and Schwartz, like the police, did not believe Rundle's claim that the baseball bat just happened to be in the closet, and that the bludgeoning death was a spontaneous act. "Everything here points to a planned attack," Schwartz said. "The money withdrawals from the bank accounts show some thought went into this."

Rundle told detectives during the interview that Shirley had broken his arm with a champagne bottle during a domestic dispute prior to the killing of Shirley. Rundle told police that he then went to see a doctor in Seattle on September 8, 2002, for treatment of the broken arm. The district attorney's office contacted the doctor, and they legally obtained Rundle's medical records from the emergency room visit. Rundle had visited the Virginia Mason

Medical Center's Department of Radiology on September 8, 2002, complaining of a sore elbow. He was greeted by Dr. Chris Moore, who briefly discussed with Rundle the pain and Rundle's medical history.

"The patient is a fifty-six-year-old gentleman who tripped on the sidewalk, breaking the fall with his outstretched right upper extremity . . . He is a well-developed, well-nourished, middle-aged gentleman in no acute distress but favoring right extremity," Moore wrote in medical reports. "Shoulder has full range of motion with no discomfort . . . He complains of some very mild wrist pain, and is mostly concerned about some elbow pain and swelling. There was no loss of consciousness, and he denies any other injuries."

Rundle reported he had a "significant medical history for hypertension," and when asked why he was in Seattle, Rundle said, "He just moved to the Seattle area approximately two weeks ago and was widowed approximately one month ago."

Dr. Moore ordered two X-rays of the elbow and saw a break. The full diagnosis? A right radial head fracture of the elbow.

The prosecutors then contacted a respected local orthopedic surgeon in Las Vegas, Dr. Gary Steven Marrone. Marrone was asked to examine Rundle's X-rays and medical report. The medical records showed "there was a break close to the elbow of the radius, which is the upper bone of the two-bone system in the forearm," Marrone said.

Marrone then offered a very significant observation to the prosecutors. He said Rundle's arm was likely broken from some type of fall, and not from a beating with a champagne bottle.

"This is not a blocking injury," Marrone said. "This is a compression injury. The only way you can get this . . . would be from a falling type of injury."

The doctor's conclusion was huge to prosecutors because it was proof that Rundle was lying about the details of the domestic dispute. Rundle had broken his arm in a fall. It was not broken by Shirley attacking him with a champagne bottle. Owens and Schwartz concluded they had Rundle dead to rights in the murder of Shirley. In addition to all the forensic evidence, the police had evidence of flight, and they had a bogus letter talking of an emergency trip to the Philippines. Rundle admitted that he'd written the letter and that it was a lie. The FBI found books about how to change one's identity in Rundle's car in Orlando. The autopsy showed Shirley had been brutally slain, and Rundle admitted he'd beaten her to death. Prosecutors put little stock in the prospect that Rundle could convince a jury the crime was a "heat of passion"-type moment, warranting a manslaughter verdict. But what was particularly interesting about the case to the prosecutors was the question of what had happened to Willa. She, like Shirley, had gone missing, and like Shirley, she'd been close to Rundle. Rundle, they believed, was lying about not knowing his mother's whereabouts.

"I found it intriguing—like a puzzle," Owens said. "The novelty of the case isn't so much that it's a murder or it's gory. In this case, it was very offensive what happened to the victim, but there were twists to it. We had him on the wife, but the mother disappearing was a mystery, and any time a district attorney can step into an investigation, it gets interesting."

Rundle had told police Willa Rundle was dead. Perhaps she'd been murdered for her money. The problem was, they didn't have Willa's body, and Rundle was blaming his missing mother's demise on the woman whom he'd beaten to death. Shirley certainly couldn't tell her side of the story, and prosecuting a murder case without a body is difficult. But when Schwartz and Owens analyzed Rundle's statements about his missing mother, they were convinced he was lying, and that Willa was dead at his hands—not his wife's.

"He said his wife poisons his mother, and then she hires two Filipinos to dispose of the body, and that he went to work that day," Schwartz said. "Does that sound believable? That your wife is in the process of disposing of your mother's body, and you head off to work?"

Owens and Schwartz convened a grand jury of Las Vegas Valley citizens to serve two purposes: to investigate the circumstances of Willa's disappearance, and to seek an indictment against Rundle in the murder of his wife. The grand jury is a powerful investigative tool, and the prosecutors wanted to use the grand jury's full powers granted to it by Nevada law to find out what happened to Willa.

"The mother disappeared about five years earlier," Owens said. "Rundle kept telling everyone she was touring Europe, and she was kind of disabled, so that gets your interest. Very intriguing. Is there some foul play associated with that?"

The grand jury heard about Shirley's disappearance, the note on the door, the confession in Florida, and the details of the autopsy on the victim. The grand jury performed an extensive investigation of the Rundles' finances in late 2002, and they did it with a sense of urgency. Bank tellers were called to testify in front of the grand jury, and video stills from the banks showed Bill Rundle, in shorts, T-shirt, and baseball cap, standing at bank counters draining his family's bank accounts in the two months prior to Shirley's slaying. The grand jury paid close attention to the spending of Willa Rundle's money in the years prior. Bill and Shirley Rundle had burned through more than $300,000 of Willa's money, and the evidence showed that someone—presumably a female—had arranged for the direct deposit of Willa's Social Security checks into Bill Rundle's checking account.

"Somebody called into the Social Security Administration and said, 'I'd like to receive my checks on automatic deposit,' and they represented themselves as Willa Rundle," Owens said. "At that same time, Bill began transferring large sums from the joint bank account into his and Shirley's bank account and spending it."

The grand jury heard witness testimony from the Rundles' friends, family, and neighbors. Willa Rundle's doctor, Dr. J. Corey Brown, testified that he'd treated Willa in 1996 and 1997. The doctor indicated that at that time, Willa was "an elderly lady who had a number of medical problems."

Willa had been diagnosed in California with severe pain in her extremities. She was on narcotics for this pain. Willa also had an "anxiety and panic condition, [for] which she took antianxiety medication," Brown said. He had prescribed two drugs, Endocet/Roxicet, which are generic forms of Percocet, and MS Contin.

The grand jury heard in Rundle's confession his claim that Shirley had killed his mother by upping her medication, and then disposed of the body while he was at work. A toxicologist, James Bourland, opined that in order for Willa Rundle's medication to reach a lethal level, she would have to have ingested "three to ten tablets at the time she would normally take one."

Rundle's first son, Justin, was a crucial witness for the grand jury because he told how Willa went to live with his father, and then disappeared a short time later.

"The last time I saw my grandmother she was actually very, very weak and feeble, and I did notice," Justin said on the stand.

Justin recounted for the grand jury how his dad had announced Willa's absence, and how Shirley had seemed like she'd wanted to tell him something.

"We were eating dinner, and he looked over at me while he was sitting at the head of the table, and he asked me if I'd heard anything from my grandmother," Justin recalled. "He asked me in just a very matter-of-fact way. 'Hey, have you heard from your grandmother? Has she contacted you?'

"And, you know, I thought it was a very strange question for me because I thought she was living there," Justin said, adding that later Shirley told him, "Justin, your grandmother was real tired."

On January 24, 2003, the grand jury charged Rundle with five felonies. The following are excerpts from the charging document issued by the grand jury.

Count 1: Murder with use of a Deadly Weapon/Open Murder.

[The defendant] did, about or between April and July of 1997, then and there willfully, feloniously and without authority of law, and with premeditation and deliberation, and with malice aforethought, kill Willa Rundle, a human being, with use of a deadly weapon, by to wit: by medications or drugs and or by manner and means otherwise unknown.

Count 2: Theft.

[The defendant] did, on or between May 1997 and August 2002 . . . obtain in excess of $2,500 or more, lawful money of the United States, belonging to Willa Rundle, following her untimely death by homicide.

Count 3: Theft.

[The defendant] did, on or between May 1997 and August 2002, convert property having a value of $2,500 or more . . . belonging to Willa Rundle. [The indictment charges William Rundle with making] a material misrepresentation . . . to come into control of mislaid or misdelivered property [from] the Social Security Administration.

Count 4: Murder with use of a Deadly Weapon/Open Murder.

[The defendant] did, on or between August 16, 2002, and August 20, 2002, then and there willfully, feloniously and without authority of law, and with premeditation and deliberation, and with malice aforethought, kill Shirley Rundle, a human being, by repeatedly striking said victim in the head and body with a deadly weapon, to wit: a baseball bat.

Count 5: Robbery with use of a Deadly Weapon.

[The defendant] did, on or between August 16, 2002, and August 20, 2002, then and there willfully, unlawfully, and feloniously take money and personal property including a ring, watches, and other jewelry from Shirley Rundle.

One of the charges was for Shirley's death, and the other was for Willa's. The grand jury, based on the financial records and Rundle's statements, believed there was evidence to indicate Rundle murdered his mother. It was a significant event in Las Vegas, and it made an already juicy story even more interesting for the Vegas papers. "The man who became known to Las Vegans for his anguish upon losing his son in a tragic accident 16 years ago now faces charges that he murdered both his wife and his mother," wrote *Review-Journal* reporter Mike Kalil in the January 25 edition of the paper.

Owens and Schwartz were proud of the indictment. They never doubted the decision to indict Rundle in his mother's death, even without Willa's body or knowing exactly how she'd been killed.

"Prosecutors and the police don't tend to believe in coincidences," Owens said. "When you have disappearances in the same family—Shirley and Willa—you start to wonder if they are related. In this case, we determined they were related. The money from the mother had run out, and I believe Shirley was threatening to go to the police with what happened to Willa."

20 . . . DEFENSE

Curtis Brown and Nancy Lemcke play critical roles in the Las Vegas justice system. They are defense attorneys with the Clark County Public Defender's Office's homicide team, and they regularly find themselves saving clients from Nevada's death penalty.

"Defense lawyers really are the gatekeepers of justice," Brown said. "Not everyone looks at it that way, but they are. The [police and prosecutors] get all the advantages. The system is built for advantages for the police and prosecutors. People think defendants have all the rights, but those rights are only invoked after everyone else has their advantage first."

Curtis Brown is a good guy in the Las Vegas Valley courts. The forty-four-year-old chief deputy district attorney for the public defender's office is clean-cut, athletic, and has a movie star face. He's always in a suit in court, and he is very good at what he does.

Juries like him.

"In all honesty, if every police officer went to work and

never made a mistake or never did something wrong, and every prosecutor only prosecuted cases that were reliable and necessary, then we wouldn't have a job," Brown said.

Brown is the son of well-known Las Vegas attorney Jim Brown, but he didn't set out to be a lawyer. He originally thought he was going to be a biologist.

"I lived in the Virgin Islands on a field studies program through college for a while," Brown said. "I did a lot of fisheries biology lake systems, and a lot of ocean systems biology. I did a lot of coral reef ecology stuff. My interest was in the behavior of dolphins and mammals. But I learned early on it is a really tough existence because it takes a long time before you get to do the stuff [in biology that] you really want to do. You're an associate. You are working for someone else doing other projects, and I was a little impatient."

Brown tried law school at the urging of his mother, and nearly two decades later, it was obviously the right decision. Brown is a very skilled attorney. He fights, he's honest, and he's polished, and these skills give him credibility in front of skeptical juries.

Fellow defense attorney Nancy Lemcke grew up in Mesa, Arizona, in a conservative family, and is just as talented as Brown in court. She is a tall, strikingly attractive woman with long, straight blond hair, and she, too, is very impressive in front of a jury. She is a sleek, very smart fighter who is always prepared.

"I always knew I wanted to go to law school," Lemcke said. "It was something I naturally aspired to do."

The case was originally assigned to Lemcke, and she asked for Brown's assistance. The two are friends, and they work well together; more significantly, Lemcke said Brown has a way with the press in high-profile cases, and she knew that his ability to deal with the media would be a major asset to Bill Rundle's legal defense. Reporters were all over the story, and it was guaranteed that Rundle's murder trial was going to get gavel-to-gavel coverage.

"I have a lot of respect for Curtis," Lemcke said. "Curtis is wonderful in dealing with the media. Dealing with the media makes me uncomfortable for a lot of reasons, and Curtis is very at ease doing that. It takes a lot of pressure off me."

Bill Rundle liked the two attorneys assigned to his defense. He recognized that he could die in the execution chamber if his trial went badly. Luckily for Rundle, he couldn't have done any better for a defense team if he had hired an attorney in the private sector.

Lemcke and Brown, in assessing the case against Rundle, found themselves in a familiar situation. The most glaring asset of the state's case was Rundle's own words. He did a lot of talking to the cops before his defense attorneys were able to meet with him. He talked to the Las Vegas cops, the FBI, and he even granted a taped interview to the *Dateline* camera crew. In each interview, he claimed that his wife had attacked him with a champagne bottle, and that he'd beaten Shirley to death with a baseball bat. There were plenty of taped statements out there, and the defense attorneys knew the statements to the cops were going to be something they'd have to reckon with. Rundle was consistent in his statements, but he was definitely pinned in now on what he said had happened the night Shirley was killed.

"We started off by telling him, 'This is a high-profile case, and you are going to get a lot of requests from the media to talk,'" Brown recalled. "We said, 'Don't talk to anyone,' and then he proceeded to let us know he'd spent the evening in the detention center with the guys from *Dateline* [giving a full interview].

"This was after he'd already talked to the police twice," Brown said. "If I had my choice, and I knew early on [about his situation], I'd tell him not to give a statement. But the reality of it is in almost every case we have . . . they all talk. It requires a client to know enough to say, 'I'm not talking to you.' But for the most part, all of our cases come with some level of a statement. All you can do is ask them at the jail, 'What did you tell them?' Then, the best you can do is wait and see what the statement says."

Like nearly everyone else who met Bill Rundle, Lemcke and Brown were struck by how he seemed to be a genuinely nice guy.

"From the moment I met him until today, the nice guy thing has never changed," Brown said. "A nice guy who did a very bad thing. He has never been anything less than polite, appreciative, gracious, and cooperative from the very first moment. Bill had a full appreciation for the situation, and he knew he couldn't get out of it on his own. He was willing to rely on people who know what they are doing."

The defense attorneys talked extensively with Rundle over the following weeks and months. They learned he had quite a story to tell. He hadn't accomplished much in life, and he certainly had some skeletons in his closet as far as the women in his life were concerned. The defense attorneys, however, saw good things in Bill Rundle, too.

"There is a part of this that can't be denied," Brown said. "Richie was a diabetic, he needed constant personal care, and Bill really did dedicate himself to that kid. There was a bond between those two. When you formulate a picture of Bill Rundle, the state wants to paint it entirely black to personify [a] monster. But when you look at that picture, realize there is actually a lot of white in it. It shows this person's existence shouldn't be discounted."

The defense attorneys determined they'd shoot for a second-degree murder or manslaughter verdict. There was no way they could argue that Bill Rundle didn't beat his wife to death, but they could argue that he had been provoked by Shirley's actions. (As for Willa's disappearance, they believed that if Rundle was charged in his mother's death, the charges wouldn't stick, due to a lack of evidence.) They figured a manslaughter verdict in the death of Shirley was also a possibility, and if their scenario played out, Rundle could feasibly get out of prison in a decade or less.

"[Shirley's homicide] did seem like a reasonable provocation, and Bill snapped," Brown said. "After that, he clearly panicked. It was a very poor strategy [for running]. He did everything possible to get caught. He left a trail of where he was the whole way."

Curtis Brown said Rundle's actions on the run were of a man who knew he was going to get caught.

"Bill was a visionary," Brown said drily. "He bought Seahawks tickets when they sucked."

The defense attorneys and their private investigators spent a great deal of time documenting the money problems the couple had. They documented the financial pressures the Rundles were under, and they prepared to argue that Rundle's decision to beat his wife to death was a momentary, instantaneous loss of control.

"You learn about all these little dirty secrets that are going on [in the family]," Brown said. "The pressure, the money, the bills, and you could see it building."

"Be wary of the fury of a patient man," Nancy Lemcke said.

It seemed to the defense attorneys that there was very little information out there in regards to what really happened to Willa. Rundle was blaming his mother's death on his dead wife, and it didn't seem like there was much else out there to go on. The defense attorneys noted that Shirley was clearly involved in spending Willa's money, and this seemed to raise legitimate questions about what Shirley had known about Willa's death.

"Is she [Shirley] involved in something: either the death

or the cover-up?" Brown said. "Likely. If Willa died naturally, Shirley is as bought in to this as Bill regarding the money, and that's probably a secret she keeps."

Lemcke performed a thorough analysis of the money spent by the Rundles. It was clear to her that Willa's money was repeatedly transferred from a bank account in the name of Bill and Willa Rundle to an account in the name of Bill and Shirley Rundle. If Rundle was the only one spending his mother's money, then why would they have needed to even transfer the money to an account with Shirley's name on it?

"The flow of the money—it was going from Bill and Willa's account to Bill and Shirley's account," Lemcke said. "It was the only way Shirley could get her hands on that money. There was something funky going on there."

The defense attorneys believed prosecutors would be forced to speculate if they were going to charge Rundle in the death of his mom. But after Rundle's defense team came to this conclusion, the grand jury indicted Rundle on charges of first-degree murder in the deaths of his wife and mother.

"We thought, 'Well, they've got that [Willa's disappearance] out there," Brown said. "Then boom, the grand jury indicted. It was another thing we had to deal with."

Rundle's pretrial hearings would be heard in the courtroom of longtime Chief District Judge Kathy Hardcastle—a disciplined, no-nonsense judge widely respected by her peers. The Texas Tech graduate was formerly a Washoe County, Nevada, deputy district attorney and a lawyer for the State Bar of Nevada before moving to Las Vegas in 1983 as a deputy prosecutor with the state Attorney General's Office. While in the Attorney General's Office, Hardcastle headed the Insurance Fraud Unit. From 1991 to 1997, she represented the criminally accused as a deputy public defender.

Judge Hardcastle is an attractive, classy woman who, off

the bench, is charming. On November 27, 2002, William Rundle was formally arraigned in district court and entered a plea of not guilty in front of the judge and news cameras.

Afterward, prosecutor David Schwartz told reporters that the death penalty was clearly on the table.

"There is a chance the state will file a notice of intent to seek the death penalty," Schwartz said. "We are going to meet on it within a week or so."

Clark County Assistant District Attorney J. Charles Thompson confirmed the pursuit of the death penalty for Rundle in an interview with the *Las Vegas Review-Journal* newspaper. The prosecutor said the death penalty was appropriate for Rundle because authorities believed Shirley's murder was motivated by money and an attempt to conceal a previous crime.

"It was committed for financial gain and/or to prevent a lawful arrest for financial gain," Thompson said. "It may be one of our theories that his wife was killed to avoid her notifying the authorities that he was taking money that did not belong to him. The murder was forceful and violent . . . and committed to receive money.

"The defendant's own statement to Detective Huggins will be used to establish the death of Willa Rundle by homicide, establishing the criminal liability of the defendant, for more than one offense of murder in the first or second degree," prosecutors wrote in related court records.

The stakes couldn't get any higher for Bill Rundle. His life was literally on the line. If the state of Nevada got its way, he was going to be strapped to a gurney and injected with a lethal dose of chemicals for killing the two women closest to him.

Judge Hardcastle's bailiff, Al Fitzgerald, said there was little difference in Rundle's demeanor after the death penalty declaration. Fitzgerald is the longest serving bailiff working in Southern Nevada, and his view of the court-room carries with it nearly three decades of experience. Fitzgerald said Rundle was always calm in court, and he even came to like Rundle as he escorted the suspected killer in and out of Hardcastle's courtroom.

By chance, Fitzgerald and Rundle had something in common: Fitzgerald, too, was once named Father of the Year in Las Vegas by a civic organization in the Las Vegas Valley.

"My daughter nominated me in '88-'89," Fitzgerald said.

Fitzgerald is not the physical specimen usually found performing a bailiff's tasks in other courtrooms these days. He is aging and balding and a little bit more frail each year, but time has shown Fitzgerald doesn't need muscle. He uses his smarts, his people skills, and his law enforcement train-ing to make sure Hardcastle's courtroom in Las Vegas's Regional Justice Center is safe.

Fitzgerald served as bailiff in hearings for Rick Tabish and Sandy Murphy—the Vegas lovers accused of killing millionaire gaming mogul Ted Binion. Murphy and Tabish ended up acquitted of murder but implicated in the theft of Binion's silver, and the story was as high-profile as it gets. Fitzgerald was also lead bailiff in court hearings for infa-mous Vegas gangster Jose Vigoa and his gang, which was widely considered one of the most dangerous groups of men ever known to the city of Sin. Vigoa's crew, carrying high-powered assault rifles, made a career of storming ar-mored car vehicles that shuttled cash to and from Vegas casinos and businesses in the late 1990s. Anyone who got in the way of the Vigoa crew was murdered point-blank: in their most notorious crime, the Vigoa crew slew two ar-mored security guards in cold blood in front of a Ross Dress for Less store. The take was a few thousand dollars in profits. And during court hearings for Vigoa, there were constant rumors of a planned escape by Mexican gangsters from the Clark County Detention Center. Vigoa was regularly brought into court in restraints that bore a slight resemblance to the ones worn by fictional *Silence of the Lambs* cannibal Hannibal Lecter.

"I remember when they brought [into court] all the high-powered automatics that [the Vigoa crew] were using," Fitzgerald said. "We certainly made sure that the ammo wasn't there."

Fitzgerald said he knew Rundle wasn't going to be much of a challenge security-wise.

"He was very respectful of the uniform, and he never gave us any problems," Fitzgerald said. "I was just doing my job—I'm not a judge or jury, and Rundle respected the judge. No outbursts or anything like that. He was an older fellow in court with a suit and tie—a brown suit usually—and he was always respectful. He always called me Mr. Fitzgerald."

During Rundle's pretrial hearings, the media was attracted to the Rundle case like moths to a flame. All of the local television stations and newspapers wanted photos of Rundle, and reporters came and went from Hardcastle's courtroom with each witness. One photo snapped of Rundle and Fitzgerald during a pretrial hearing eventually made it onto a wall in Fitzgerald's office that he refers to as the "wall of shame." The photo was autographed by Rundle, and it serves as a reminder of Fitzgerald's time on the case.

Curtis Brown and Nancy Lemcke spent the next three months litigating the case in pretrial motions in front of Hardcastle. One of their first steps was to make an attempt at limiting further pretrial publicity.

"The defendant is before the court charged with a well-publicized murder," Brown said. "As a result of the underlying offense, there has been massive, highly prejudicial publicity regarding this case. Both the television and print media are reporting on this case extensively. Coverage of the proceedings has resulted in the dissemination of highly prejudicial information regarding the defendant and this case, at least some of which will not be relevant at the upcoming trial of this matter."

Lemcke and Brown asked the judge to exclude print and electronic media cameras from all pretrial hearings. The attorneys also wanted what amounted to a gag order on all "parties, witnesses, law enforcement personnel and court personnel," and they called for an impaneled jury.

Brown said his intentions were simple: "to control the publicity to the point where it won't affect the client."

During a January 13, 2003, hearing on the matter, Prosecutors Chris Owens and David Schwartz opposed any gag order.

"There was no objection previously to the presence of the media in the case," Owens said. "And the court should be aware that there has been national media; NBC's *Dateline* has been following this case since its inception. They're doing it with the understanding that nothing that they film is going to be released publicly until after all the events in this case are totally over."

Judge Hardcastle quickly dispatched the request to control the media as unnecessary. "There's been coverage already about this case," Hardcastle said. "I don't find that it's undue coverage. We've had a number of cases over the last several years in the Eighth Judicial District Court where we've had a lot of media coverage, as well as television coverage. We've actually had televisions in the courtroom, and there's been no showing of any type of prejudice having been created by that."

Hardcastle also noted that the media, using grand jury transcripts, had already reported on much of the contents of Rundle's statements to authorities.

"I see no reason [to] justify kicking the press out at this point," Hardcastle said.

The defense attorneys knew going into the Rundle case that it would be a long and difficult battle. Their strategy was to litigate the issues they felt they had the strongest chance of winning, and one of those issues was whether Rundle's statement was admissible in court. Lemcke and Brown focused on the detectives' interview with Rundle at the Seminole County Jail in Florida.

"According to the taped statement, at some point after meeting Mr. Rundle, Detective Huggins indicated that 'I'm gonna advise you your rights just like I said because you are in custody and under arrest,'" Lemcke said. "'You understand you're under arrest for a warrant?'

"With respect to Mr. Rundle's Miranda rights, Detective Huggins then stated, 'I'm gonna read 'em off a little card,'" Lemcke said.

But instead of reading a Miranda rights card verbatim, she paraphrased the rights card, saying to Rundle, "It's basically that you have the right to remain silent. That anything you say can be used against you in a court of law. You have the right to speak to an attorney. And, if you can't afford an attorney, one will be appointed to you. Do you understand these rights?'"

Rundle responded in the affirmative. Detective Huggins then continued by indicating that "once I start talking to you, if you decide that you don't want to talk to us anymore, you can say, 'Hey, I'm done. I don't want to talk to you.' And the questioning will stop. Do you understand that?'"

Again, Rundle responded in the affirmative.

Detective Huggins then instructed Rundle to sign a Miranda rights card. At this moment, the defense attorneys noted, Rundle made clear he was having "a lot of trouble breathing . . . [and that] it's affecting me."

He told the detectives he was on heart medication and that he had not had a chance to take the appropriate medication prior to the interrogation. Additionally, Rundle requested a four-way nasal spray to help with his breathing problems. Rundle again indicated that he "can't breathe." Detective Don Tremel, according to transcripts of the interview, said he would try to get the medication.

The defense attorneys said Huggins then began questioning Mr. Rundle without providing him with medication. The defense attorneys argued that the statement was therefore inadmissible for two reasons: that Miranda was not fully read from the Miranda rights card, and that Rundle was in the middle of a medical condition and was under duress to give his statement as a result.

Hardcastle took up the issue in a January 2003 hearing. Detective Sheila Huggins took the witness stand and described how she and Detective Tremel had obtained the statement from Rundle.

"He didn't seem to be in any distress, except for that he was sniffing his nose," Huggins said. "And he did mention right away that he needed his nasal spray. While I stayed with Mr. Rundle, my partner did go up right away and check with the nurse to make sure she had given him his medicine and to see if he could, in fact, get another dose of nasal spray."

The detective then made the acknowledgment that she paraphrased Rundle's Miranda notice.

"You didn't read them verbatim off of the card?" Prosecutor Chris Owens asked.

"No," Huggins said.

Huggins said that despite her paraphrasing, she managed to cover all of the tenets of Miranda: that he didn't have to talk and that he had a right to an attorney.

Huggins said Rundle signed a copy of a Miranda rights card.

"He was actually reading a copy of the Miranda card," Huggins said.

Hardcastle again sided with prosecutors and ruled the statement admissible, saying Rundle's Miranda advisement was adequate.

The next motion filed by the defense was one they felt they had a great chance of winning: that the search of the Rundle home on Poppywood was illegal, and that, as a result, all evidence gathered from the inside of the home was inadmissible. Among the evidence that could feasibly be suppressed under the defense motion was Shirley Rundle's blood from the carpet and chair, and the Louisville Slugger baseball bat.

Lemcke and Brown said that when Magda Belen found the blood underneath the chair on August 22, and summoned Missing Persons Detective Thomas Marin into the home, Marin's entry into the home to look at the bloodstain was illegal. Law required him, they said, to get a warrant.

Lemcke and Brown outlined the entire argument and the circumstances in their pretrial motion:

> At approximately 4:30 p.m. that afternoon, Detective Marin met Belen at the residence Shirley and William Rundle shared. When he arrived at the Poppywood address, Marin noticed that Belen had broken into the residence with the help of two friends. Detective Marin went and interviewed some of the Rundles' neighbors while Belen searched the Rundle home. After searching the home, Belen reported to Detective Marin that she noticed a suitcase, a cordless phone, a portable

stereo, and a laptop computer missing from the Run-
dles' home. She then returned to the residence and
conducted a second search.

She then reported to Marin that she noticed some
throw rugs and a large flowered armchair that were
out of place. According to Belen, when she moved the
rugs and the large flowered armchair, she observed a
large dark stain on the floor. Belen then returned to
Marin and notified him of her observations.

At that point, without obtaining a search warrant,
Marin entered the Poppywood residence. He observed
the stain identified by Ms. Belen; he then secured the
home and applied for a telephonic search warrant to
search the residence. A search warrant was ultimately
approved . . . Crime scene analysts then responded
and the Poppywood residence was searched and pro-
cessed for evidence.

Brown noted in the motion that Nevada and federal law
has made clear that warrantless searches and seizures in a
home are presumed unreasonable, and that warrantless
searches are only permitted when both probable cause and
exigent circumstances exist. Exigent circumstances, as de-
fined by the Nevada Supreme Court, are "circumstances
that would cause a reasonable person to believe that entry
was necessary to prevent physical harm to the officers or
other persons, the destruction of relevant evidence, the escape of a suspect, or some other action that would improp-
erly frustrate legitimate law enforcement efforts."

Brown and Lemcke said that standard was clearly not
met when Marin entered the home.

"At the time Marin entered [the] Rundle residence, there
was no one present other than Belen and two of her
friends . . . In as much as the residence was empty and
locked, Belen, with help from [her friends], had to break in
to gain entry," Brown said. "Belen searched the home

twice. She never found anyone inside the home. She reported her findings to Marin.

"Despite the clear lack of any exigent circumstances, Marin entered . . . before obtaining a search warrant," Brown said. The warrantless search, he said, "violates Mr. Rundle's right to be free from unlawful searches and seizures."

The argument seemed compelling, and Judge Hardcastle took the matter seriously enough to hear witness testimony about the search during a January 2003 court proceeding. Prosecutor David Schwartz was asked to call witnesses to document exactly what happened in the moments leading up to the search, and the first witness was the victim's daughter, Magda Belen. Belen recounted Detective Marin's warning to her, before the discovery of the blood, that he could not enter the house without a warrant.

"He asked me if I had full access to the house first," Magda said, adding that Marin told her he could not enter the home.

"He said he needs a search warrant to do that," Belen said.

Belen recounted the discovery of the blood and how Marin "followed me inside the house" without a warrant.

Detective Thomas Marin testified next.

"She [Magda] explain[ed] to me where she found it and how she found it, and she made mention about the throw rugs . . . and she noticed the blood," Marin said. "At that point, she took me and showed me the bloodstain inside the family room . . . I had everyone leave . . . the residence and contacted Dispatch.

"We made a sweep of the residence and then came back out," Marin said. "[I] secured the residence until we got a telephonic search warrant."

Schwartz and Owens argued to Hardcastle that Marin had every right to go into the home given what he'd been told by Belen. Two people were missing, there was a report of blood in the home, and Marin couldn't have known ahead of time what he had on his hands.

Hardcastle agreed. The blood evidence, the bat, and everything else culled from the searches of the home would be presented to a jury at Rundle's murder trial. The defense attorneys were frustrated, but they still had one huge pretrial motion left: the argument that there was not enough evidence to prosecute Rundle in the death of his mother.

The insufficient evidence argument was Defense Attorney Nancy Lemcke's ace. There was no body and no cause of death for Willa Rundle. Pretty much all prosecutors had to go on was Justin Rundle's statements about Willa's disappearance and the spending of her money by Bill and Shirley Rundle. Lemcke knew that wasn't enough even to take a murder charge to trial, much less get a conviction.

Prosecutor Chris Owens felt otherwise, and he believed the murder charge in Willa's death would stand even though authorities didn't know exactly how she was killed or where her body was. Owens argued that a possible motive for Shirley's death could have been that she knew what had happened to Willa, and Bill wanted to keep his wife quiet.

"[The defendant engaged in] a seamless pattern of theft, cover-up, and blackmail leading to the death of the defendant's wife, Shirley Rundle," Owens said. "The previously undiscovered murder of the defendant's mother, Willa, the looting of her bank accounts to perpetuate an addictive gambling and spending lifestyle, and the fraudulent acquisition of her Social Security funds for four years were the motivating factors in the murder of Shirley Rundle. As the last of the mother's $390,000 in assets dwindled in the summer of 2001, Shirley's threats to blow the whistle on the defendant's activities resulted in her death. The defendant himself makes this clear in his statements to the police that interweave these events into a comprehensive fabric that cannot be unwound or separated."

Owens seized on Rundle's own words in his 108-page statement to police from the interview at the Seminole County Jail as evidence that Shirley was murdered because she knew too much about what happened to Willa.

"Did you ever think of calling the cops?" Huggins had asked.

"Uh, I didn't," Rundle said. "I'll tell you something, she told me that if I had done that, she would tell the police and everybody else that I had given her the idea, uh, about my mother."

In a January 2003 hearing, Lemcke reminded the judge that prior case law in Nevada supported her argument. In one case, "the victim had been burned by a defendant. I mean, he basically lit the body on fire to dispose of the body by way of burning, [yet] the Supreme Court still held that even under those circumstances, there was not sufficient [evidence] of death by criminal agency."

Lemcke said the murder charge against Rundle in the death of his mother didn't even meet the most basic standards for evidentiary proof. The indictment, she said, proved only three things:

"One, Willa Rundle quit communicating with friends and family sometime in 1997," Lemcke said. "Two, that at this time, although [Willa was] eighty-seven and barely able to walk, she was in frail but stable health, and three, that according to Bill Rundle, Shirley Rundle increased his mother's morphine dose, thereby killing her."

Lemcke said there simply wasn't enough evidence to support the murder charge.

"The prosecution must show that Willa Rundle is, in fact, dead, and that her death was the result of a criminal agency," Lemcke said.

Those standards seemed hard to meet given that Willa's body had never been found and any presumed cause of death was unknown. On April 22, 2003, the defense attorneys' diligence paid off. Judge Hardcastle ruled that there was not enough evidence to try Rundle on a murder charge in the death of his mother.

"All right, having reviewed this and looking at it fairly closely, this is a case where the court feels compelled to grant the [defense motion]," Hardcastle said. "I've previously indicated, I think, to the state, that there was sufficient evidence presented to support a probable cause finding of death of the mother by criminal means, [but] there was insufficient evidence to establish a murder charge against Mr. Rundle as having been the one who caused the death or committed the act. There may have been enough evidence to support an accessory after the fact, but not enough to support a murder charge. For that reason, the petition is granted."

"Your Honor, just for some clarification, are we just talking about the case of the mother?"

"Just the murder of the mother," the judge said.

The ruling was a huge victory for the defense, and it was a sweet one, too. Without a jury hearing specifically that Rundle was charged with murdering his mother for money, the death penalty now seemed like a long shot.

"It was the right decision," Lemcke said.

21 ... JUSTICE (TRIAL)

Longtime Nevada Judge Michael Cherry is widely regarded as one of the best judges in the state. He sits on Nevada's highest court—the state Supreme Court—after a long and distinguished judicial career. He is a tall man with dark hair and full beard, and he has an exceedingly kind and affable demeanor.

But there is also another side to Judge Cherry: a tough side. He can be brutal if an attorney crosses him, and he uses his tough side to keep order in his courtroom.

"I try to do justice and put aside whether someone is rich or poor or whether the defendant is someone who is high-profile or not," Cherry said. "I give everyone the same breaks I would want as a litigant or a defendant. I'm as fair as possible, and I try to keep control of the courtroom."

Michael Cherry was born in St. Louis, Missouri, and his parents divorced when he was ten years old. Cherry credits his mother, Naomi Cherry, as the greatest influence in his life. She worked as a single mom in the retail field to support her family, and all the while, Cherry's mother was encouraging her son to dream big.

"My mother taught me that if you want to get something done, give it to the busiest person you know," Cherry said. "My mother also taught me to never give up."

There are two reasons Cherry is one of the most respected judges in the state. First, he was blessed with talent: His people skills are remarkable, and with words alone, he can calm even the most violent killers who've appeared in his courtroom. The other reason Cherry is so good is his experience: The guy knows the law, and he knows how to administer it.

Cherry started his career as a deputy public defender in the Clark County Public Defender's Office. He represented multiple killers and rose to assistant public defender, where he ended up training a flock of attorneys. Many of those Cherry trained are now recognized as the best attorneys in Las Vegas.

"Our legal system could use some changes," Cherry said. "Someday, there has got to be a civil forum where people who can't afford it are given an attorney. . . . If you don't have an attorney, you just don't have a chance, because there are so many rules."

When Cherry was a state judge, he oversaw huge cases in Vegas. He was the judge in the 311 Boyz case—a high-profile media event that centered around accusations that a group of affluent Las Vegas teens had maimed a boy in a spree of violence. Cherry also served on three-judge panels that decided whether to sentence convicted killers to death. In one case, convicted killer Terry Dennis begged for execution, and he eventually got his wish.

"We fought with him [and begged him] to accept a lawyer, but he wouldn't do it, and unfortunately his wish was accommodated," Cherry said.

But when the murder trial of Bill Rundle was assigned to Cherry's courtroom, he knew that this would end up being his most high-profile murder case of all. As he readied to take the bench in May, the veteran lawyer and judge conceded he was nervous.

"I always get butterflies," Cherry said, "but in a case like this, you make sure you don't do anything stupid. Nervousness is typical [when you are in the] public spotlight, so when you go on the bench, you make sure you don't make any major mistakes. Being televised makes you want to be even better—not as much for yourself but for the judiciary."

Cherry understood why the Rundle trial was so high-profile, and why multiple media requests for permission to videotape and photograph the proceedings had been filed with the Clark County, Nevada, District Court. Simply put, the facts of the case were remarkable. A Las Vegas Father of the Year, who had lost a child to tragedy, was now accused of killing his wife, and he was suspected—but no longer charged—in the disappearance of his mother.

"This was a very, very unique situation," the judge said. "He's married to her, she's running up the credit cards, he got pissed and supposedly killed her. He supposedly killed her with the dead child's bat. What does he do then? He buys season tickets to a football team. He left her body on the side of the road, and then, Bill Rundle, what are you going to do? 'I'm going to Disney World!'

"A really unusual fact pattern," Cherry said. "His actions afterward were very strange, and then you [also] have him suspected in the mother's death. You don't hear about stuff like that very often."

Beyond the facts, Cherry said there was something else that struck him about the case. The defendant, Cherry said, seemed from a distance, at least, to be exceedingly normal when compared to most murder suspects.

"He didn't look like your typical criminal," Cherry said. "He was very different than the average murderer. This wasn't for robbery or drugs."

Cherry launched Bill Rundle's murder trial on May 12, 2003, by thanking jurors selected to sit in judgment of Rundle and determine whether he was guilty of murdering his wife. Those same jurors, if they convicted Rundle, could also be asked to sentence him to death. Cherry told jurors their job was not an easy one, and he truly appreciated their service to the community of Las Vegas.

"Now, what I'd like to do at this point is I'd like to have Lee Greenwood, the singer, come out here and sing, 'I'm Proud to Be an American.'" Cherry told jurors. "Then I would like, first, the district attorney's office, then the public defender's office, then the judge, and Danny the bailiff to stand up and tell you how important your function is in this case. All kidding aside, we can't conduct business without jurors."

Sitting in the gallery of Cherry's district seventeen courtroom gallery at the aging Clark County Courthouse in downtown Las Vegas were five reporters and a flock of high school kids from a Las Vegas High School business class who were at the courthouse for a tour on the opening day of Rundle's trial. The teens had been invited into the courtroom by the judge so they could witness the criminal justice machine at work, and they saw Rundle sitting at the defense table in a suit and tie. He looked like a businessman, who occasionally sniffled into a tissue, not a suspected murderer.

A clerk read the charges of first-degree murder, and Cherry read the jury pages of instructions.

Prosecutor Chris Owens gave his opening statement in front of television cameras and the jury. He stood next to a large flat-screen television, and he used a PowerPoint presentation on the screen to accompany his words. Owens gave jurors a complete outline of the state's case against Bill Rundle as photos of the home on Poppywood and the crime scene flashed on the television.

"'No man, for any considerable period, can wear one

face to himself and another to the multitudes without finally getting bewildered as to which may be the truth,' " Owens recited to jurors. "[That's from] *The Scarlet Letter* by Nathaniel Hawthorne.

"A lot of what we are going to hear in the evidence in this case is going to deal with the faces of Bill Rundle," Owens said. "There was the face that he had to himself, and other evidence will show the face he wanted the multitudes to see. At the end of this case, and after you've heard all of the evidence, you're going to be able to make a determination as to what is the true face of Bill Rundle."

Owens quoted Rundle's own words from his second statement to police.

" 'I grabbed a bat,' " Owens quoted the defendant as saying. " 'Like I said, I hit her, and then I hit her again, and I hit her again, and I hit her again. When she hit the chair, she uttered nothing more.' "

The prosecutor relayed the details of Richie Rundle's tragic death. He told jurors that Rundle was once named Father of the Year in Vegas, and now he stood accused of murder. He told jurors that Rundle beat his wife to death, ran off to Seattle, and then lied about it. The prosecutor also mentioned Willa Rundle's death, and how the Rundles had spent all of her money. He painted a portrait of a man consumed by money and a desire to control the women around him.

"An ancient proverb says that, 'If you want to know what a man is really like, make notice of how he acts when he loses money,' " Owens said. "The evidence will show that at some point in time, the crunch period came, and on August 17, Bill Rundle found himself out of money. He squirreled away enough money to run. And, when he found out the person he needed to keep quiet wasn't going to go with him, he beat Shirley to death with a bat.

"He stole from her, and he fled the jurisdiction, dumping her body like garbage on the side of the road," Owens said. "The evidence in this case will show you the true face of Bill Rundle. It will, ladies and gentlemen, not be the face Bill Rundle wants to offer to the multitudes. He couldn't remember what he told one person over another, and he couldn't remember his misstatements compared to what statements were true. But you are going to be able to tell the difference. And then we'll be back in front of you asking for justice in this case. We'll be asking for a balancing of the scales, to find the defendant, Bill Rundle, guilty of murder in the first degree. That will be the true face of Bill Rundle in light of all the evidence."

Chief Public Defender Curtis Brown was next. Opening and closing statements are where Brown is at his best. He is the clean-cut, All-American kid complete with sophistication, and he doesn't look like your stereotypical liberal defense lawyer. This makes Brown very convincing with juries even when his client appears to be a violent felon.

"This case is about a tragedy," Brown told jurors. "A real-life human tragedy. This is about a patient man who became a broken man. Simply put, this was about a fight between a married couple that resulted in the death of a spouse. Accusations aren't evidence. Opening statements are not proof, and nobody would even be here if there weren't two sides to this story."

Brown gave the jury background about the relationship between the Rundles and the Belens in his opening statement. It was clear from Brown's opening statement that he and Lemcke were trolling for a manslaughter verdict. Brown focused his statement on all of the financial stresses the Rundles were under, and the defense attorney sought to humanize Rundle in the eyes of the jury.

"Richie Rundle was the reason Bill got up every morning," Brown said. "Richie was Bill's entire world. In 1986, Bill received a pleasant surprise in Shirley. Shirley expanded Bill's world, and she was terrific with Richie. She raised him as if he was one of her own, and Bill opened up his life to Shirley's daughter, Magda. Magda, at first, was a little resistant to accepting this new man in . . . her life, but over time, she would grow to love the man who she would refer to as Dad."

Brown told the jury of Richie's death, and Rundle sniffled at the reference to his dead son. Brown also portrayed the relationship between Bill and Shirley Rundle as a tense one filled with financial stresses and Shirley's uncontrollable jealousy. Shirley, Brown said, had constantly checked up on Bill to see if he was having affairs.

"The accusations would fly frequently, but particularly when Shirley would consume alcohol," the defense attorney told the jury. "She didn't drink very much, but when she did, she would get into these moods with Bill."

The defense attorney talked about the thorniest topic of the day, which was Willa Rundle's death. In doing so, Brown dropped a courtroom bombshell: that Shirley was once arrested for stealing while working as a change clerk at the Luxor. The information was a shock to those sitting in the courtroom. The detail that Shirley had an arrest record amid allegations she stole a little bit of money had never been publicly known until now.

"Shirley lost her job at the Luxor," Brown said. "She received a conviction for doing some stealing. She was at home [after she lost her job,] and her duties at this point became being the primary caretaker of Willa.

"Shirley made sure that Willa got her medications," Brown said. "She made sure Willa was fed. She took Willa to places she needed to go. She was the primary caretaker of this elderly woman, and on May 4, 1997, Bill Rundle found his mother had passed away in the night."

Brown told jurors no one really knew how and why Willa died. He hinted that perhaps Shirley poisoned her with morphine.

"Shirley indicated to Bill that she had been slowly increasing the morphine amounts in the [morphine] tablets,"

Brown said. "Bill assumed that it was done on purpose, but the reality is nobody is on trial for the disappearance of Willa Rundle. Not Shirley Rundle and certainly not Bill Rundle. There is no evidence either way Shirley or Bill was involved. It is just as possible that Willa Rundle died of natural causes, and that Shirley merely believed she and her actions contributed to Willa's passing."

Brown acknowledged to jurors that Bill and Shirley spent a lot of Willa's money, and perhaps this was why everyone decided to keep Willa's death a secret.

"What we do know is that Shirley and Bill absolutely took advantage of Willa's death," Brown said. "They continued to cash Social Security checks. They each spent it. They spent the money, and they participated jointly in the cover-up with regard to explaining to family members where Willa was.

"Shirley was just as much involved in telling family members that Willa was gone and they didn't know when she would be back," Brown said. "Regardless, the Rundles now had a big secret. This dimension, this secret, added a strain to their relationship. Reasonable people can only imagine the stress. It was the big, giant, pink elephant in the middle of the living room, and it was heavy."

The defense attorney told jurors Shirley liked to spend money, and her spending habits caused a lot of stress in the Rundle household.

"Although it appeared that there was plenty of money and it would last forever, Shirley had a thirst for spending," Brown said. "It couldn't be quenched, and it was large. In addition, Shirley spent thousands of dollars sending money to her relatives in the Philippines to support them. Care packages and food packages and things of that nature. The phone bills with respect to Shirley and her conversations with family members in the Philippines would average 250 to 300 dollars a month, and it seemed Rodel and Magda were always in need of some financial help. These consistent siphons eventually dried it up, and they were running out of money."

Brown documented for the jury the immense amount of credit card debt the Rundles were drowning in at the time of Shirley's killing.

"Nearly [all of the credit cards] were maxed out," Brown said. "They had an Avanta card, $2,229 balance. Visa. $6,475. Another Visa, $12,485, Dillard's, $2,671. Home Depot $1,522. Visa, $9,748. JCPenney $3,363. Macy's $4,689. Wells Fargo MasterCard, $4,500. A Sears card, $5,331. Target, $940. First USA Visa, general use, no balance. Master-Card AT&T, $956, and another Wells Fargo Visa, $5,170."

"The debt is stacking," the defense attorney said. "The stress associated with paying the debt is rising. Bill recognizes that they owe over $90,000 to twenty different credit card companies. They owe a monthly house payment that they didn't have a couple of years ago. They have a monthly car payment they didn't have six months ago. They're still sending money to the Philippines, and they still have to bail Magda and Rodel out of financial trouble.

"Last year was also a very difficult time for Bill personally," Brown said. "It was the fifteen-year anniversary of the death of his son Richie. Every year is hard, but this particular year . . . all of those feelings of loss were brought straight up to the surface one more time."

Brown then outlined for the jury Rundle's version of his wife's killing.

"Shirley is angry that night after consuming some champagne," Brown said. "She is angry at the prospect of having to leave her family for the Philippines. She is angry at being so far away. 'How dare you take me from my daughter and my granddaughter? It's all your fault!' Those are the feelings that she's bringing.

"Shirley begins to berate Bill," Brown said. "She reminds him of his disappointments and his failures in life. The stress is instantly building. It's coming back. The stress

that was put aside is back in a flash. Shirley becomes a little violent. She begins whacking him with the champagne
bottle. Bill reaches into the closet, which is less than a few
feet away, and he grabs a baseball bat. He holds it [to] defend himself.

"He's not afraid of her," Brown said. "He knows she's
not a threat. She's not gonna hurt him. But he holds up this
bat. He's frustrated and he's angry that she's backing out of
this solution they've created to go to the Philippines.

"Shirley's not afraid, either," the defense attorney said.
"She's not. She has nothing to worry about with Bill. She
knows he's not gonna hurt her. In their sixteen years of marriage, he had never laid a violent hand on her, so she has no
fear, and no reason to fear. She continues at him with the
champagne bottle. She hits him on the arm. Bill feels instant
pain, and he would later learn that his elbow is broken. This
pain flash, in combination with the stress that had just been
dumped immediately upon him, resulted in Bill breaking.
He broke. And, at that moment, he struck."

Brown described in detail the lethal moment for Shirley.

"The strike comes down with great leverage. He struck
her on the head," Brown said. "Shirley stumbled and fell
into her chair, and he hit her again, and again, and again,
until the rage he was feeling inside had subsided," Brown
said. "He was out of breath, and he realized what had happened. He realized what he had just done. He confirms
what he feared: that Shirley, his wife, is dead. Bill is confused and scared, and he decides to run."

After two very dramatic opening statements, the Bill Rundle trial proceeded at a rapid pace over the next four days.
The jury heard from a string of witnesses, including Senior
Crime Scene Analyst Daniel Holstein and the deputies
from Lassen County who had discovered Shirley's body.

"I observed what appeared to be two human feet point-ing down towards the ground," Lassen County Deputy Benny Wayne Wallace said. "I backed away, secured the scene, and awaiting for my investigators to arrive . . . a fe-male wrapped in a blanket and also wrapped in a very bloody blue and white sheet."

The jurors learned that Shirley had been badly beaten with a blunt object. She'd had a towel shoved deep into her throat. She wore no jewelry or identification. The jurors learned about the bloodstains, the forensics, the car in the garage in Seattle, Rundle's life on the run and the fake trip to the Philippines that bought Rundle time. Shirley's fam-ily testified next, and Rodel Belen told the jurors that he, his wife, and their child had loved Shirley dearly. She was a cherished woman.

"My mother-in-law is a great person," Rodel Belen said. "Bill would just sit and watch television, and my mother-in-law would clean the house, and cook, and he would watch sports."

Magda Belen was next on the witness stand. She re-counted the terrible series of events that started with the disappearance of her mother, the note in the garage, and the discovery of the bloodstains under the throw rugs.

"I was in shock," Magda Belen said of the stains. "I was crying, and my friend Christine had to pull me out of the family room."

She told jurors about Willa coming to the Rundle home and then suddenly disappearing to the hills of Austria.

"Bill Rundle and my mother told me [the home on Pop-pywood] was a gift from Bill Rundle's father," Magda Belen said. "Most of the time, [Willa] would be using a walker. She moved in with them because Bill Rundle's fa-ther died, and she [was] all by herself. Bill Rundle told me she went to Austria; that she wants to spend the rest of her life there, and she wants to tour with her friends."

Magda confirmed for jurors that her mother and step-father had been good to her. They'd helped her and Rodel out when they had some financial difficulties.

Magda confirmed on the witness stand that her mother sent money to the Philippines, and she also confirmed she'd received $15,000 from the Rundles for a down payment on a house.

"As a gift, yes they did," Magda said. "Bill Rundle and my mother agreed to do that because they were going to get their house and they wanted to do the same thing for us. As far as what I can remember, they helped us. They offered to help us to pay for our credit cards, and that was when my daughter was like a few years old . . . [They] gave us [money] one time because [they] knew that we had car problems, so [they] told us that it's a gift," Magda said.

Magda told jurors Shirley was not a big drinker, and she said everyone in the family seemed to get along, though she portrayed Bill Rundle as lazy.

"He would just be sitting on his recliner watching television," Magda said. "He would get up to go to the restroom or go to the kitchen, get something to eat, [then] go back to the couch and watch television. That's all he's doing every single day. The only other thing that I noticed him doing would be just going out to the mailbox and getting his mail, and then going back to his recliner and watching television again."

The cross-examination of Magda Belen by Defense Attorney Nancy Lemke was tense. Lemke was tough on the victim's daughter as she chronicled the amount of money the Rundles had spent, and Lemcke reinforced the premise that her client was generous to the Belens. Magda confirmed the defense attorney's questions about Bill Rundle taking the family to Disneyland and Universal Studios, and Lemcke showed the witness family snapshots from the trips the Rundles had taken together.

"They were always together," Magda said of her mother and the defendant.

Prosecutors spent the next day in court documenting an obvious fact: that Rundle was a forger. The proof of the forgery came in the form of two pieces of evidence. The first was the note found on the garage door of the Rundle home, and the second was a form filled out at the U.S. Post Office that put a hold on Rundle's mail. The latter document was filed before Shirley Rundle went missing, and it seemingly had her signature on it.

Witness Paul Loney investigates fraud involving mail, identity theft, and bombs sent through the mail. He described for jurors the authorization form for holding mail.

"It's something the postal customer fills out and provides to the post office that authorizes them to hold your mail for a certain period of time," Loney said. "You can get it from your post office, or you can get it from your local letter carrier. You can mail them in, you can give them to your letter carrier, you can place them in your mailbox, or you can drop them off at the post office."

Loney said the hold mail form in question had been filled out at the Spring Valley Post Office on Desert Inn and Rainbow Boulevards in Las Vegas.

It read, he said, "Going to the Philippines. Be back 9-7. Name, Rundle. Begin holding mail 8-17. And [there was] a checked off box which states, 'I will pick up all accumulated mail when I return,' and it's signed 'Shirley N. Rundle,'" Loney said.

The next witness was Jan Seaman Kelly, a questioned document examiner with the Las Vegas Police Department, who was also asked to examine the mail hold authorization form, as well as the note from the garage

door. Kelly knows his stuff: He previously worked at the
Oklahoma County District Attorney's Office as a document examiner and trained with the U.S. Postal Crime Lab
in San Bernardino, California. He wrote a book on the forensic examination of rubber stamps and their markings,
and he's currently the president of the American Board of
Forensic Document Examiners.

Kelly explained to the jury the process of how he traces
handwriting to a particular source. A "questioned document," he said, is a document where the source of the writing is unknown. A "known document" is a document
containing writing from a known source. The comparison
of writings, or marks, on "known" versus "unknown" documents can confirm whether the source of writings on the
unknown document is the same as the author of writings
on a known document.

"Handwriting and hand printing is identified or elimi-
nated based on a combination of habits or characteristics
within your writing," Kelly said. "It's not based on one
letter—it's that combination. Once I determine the combination of habits and characteristics in the set of the questioned and the known [documents], I will then do a
comparison between the two [documents] to see if they are
in agreement.

"In this case, [the comparison] dealt with two documents that contained hand printing and a signature," Kelly
said.

With writing samples from both Bill and Shirley Rundle in his possession, Kelly examined the note from the
garage door.

It was written by Bill Rundle, Kelly stated.

The second document was the note left at the post office. Kelly said he "identified William Rundle as the author of the hand printing," and that he also signed the
name "Shirley M. Rundle" on the hold mail form, showing

that Rundle had forged his wife's signature on the mail form filed prior to her death.

The next mission for prosecutors was to prove that Rundle was a thief; an easy task, given the evidence previously gathered by police. While Rundle wasn't charged with the murder of his mother, he *was* charged with stealing the missing woman's money, and prosecutors made sure jurors knew all about the swindle. Bank investigators testified about the emptying of Willa Rundle's financial fortune while she was missing. Bill and Shirley Rundle burned through more than $300,000 of Willa's money, the bank witnesses said, after someone posing as Willa Rundle called up her stockbroker and ordered the sale of her stocks.

A detective with the Social Security Administration was called to the witness stand to testify how federal law was broken to access Willa's monthly Social Security checks.

"She was getting $1,082 a month," Investigator Theron Hanes said. "In 1997 the total was $12,984. And then in 1998 it would have been $13,272."

The payments continued for the next three years. More than $79,000 was overpaid to Willa Rundle, Hanes concluded, using January 1997 as the approximate date on which Willa had gone missing.

"My understanding of this is she was missing since sometime in that period of time," Hanes said.

Even more interesting was the fact that, in 1997, shortly after Willa's disappearance, there was a change on Willa's account from check format to direct deposit. Someone called to make the change after Willa went missing, but the records with the Social Security Administration did not specify who made the call.

Again, it was presumed the caller was a woman.

"It's pretty easy [to do]," Hanes said. "You can call an 800 number, identify yourself, answer a few questions such as your mother's maiden name . . . date of birth, and make the change."

The bank routing number given to the Social Security Administration was Shirley's Social Security check routing number.

"Any person could call in if they knew the answers to those certain questions?" Owens asked.

"Unfortunately, yes," Hanes said.

"Why do you say unfortunate?" Owens asked.

"Because I have a lot of cases where people are cheating other people's accounts like that," Hanes said.

The next witness was Nathan Eaton, a branch manager for a Wells Fargo bank branch on Rainbow Boulevard in northwest Las Vegas. Eaton offered more testimony showing that the Rundles were desperate financially in the months leading up to their disappearance. Eaton's testimony also gave a few details about a life insurance policy taken out on the Rundles in March 2002. That same month, the Rundles took out a personal loan against their car—the Buick with the HONYBUN license plate.

"Principal amount of the loan, $15,293.50," Eaton said. "[Collateral was] a 2001 Buick."

When the loan was secured, the Rundles signed up for life insurance policies. The details of the policies were not disclosed in court, but shortly after signing up for them, Bill Rundle abruptly canceled the coverage a month later.

"Both [Bill and Shirley] Rundle were covered [by] the life insurance," Eaton said. "Just Mr. Rundle was covered for the accident and health insurance, and Mr. Rundle canceled both."

For prosecutors, this seemed to indicate that Rundle might have been planning to take out life insurance on his wife, then make a subsequent death of Shirley look like an accident. But with nothing other than suspicions, all the jury would ever hear about was that there was, at one point, some life insurance out there. An amount of the policy was not revealed in court.

Eaton said that on May 21, 2002, Wells Fargo mailed the Rundles a standard marketing mailer that offered a "draft check" worth $2,065. The Rundles cashed it.

Eaton was asked about the status of the Buick that Bill Rundle had used to flee Las Vegas. Given that Wells Fargo had an outstanding lien on the vehicle, Eaton knew exactly where the vehicle was.

"As of yesterday, it was in the possession of the state of Washington at Lincoln Towing in Seattle," Eaton said.

Detective Sheila Huggins was next on the witness stand. In Huggins's testimony, prosecutors used her account of the investigation into Willa Rundle's disappearance to raise suspicion that Willa had been murdered. Prosecutors would make sure, through Huggins and other witness testimony, that the jury would know as much as possible about Willa's disappearance, even though the jury would not learn that Bill Rundle was once charged with his mother's murder.

"We did a lot of investigation on this case," Huggins told the jury. "We actually were trying to contact Willa Rundle, hoping to find any information on where Bill and Shirley might be or if anybody in California had seen them. Obviously, we did some records checks and found that Willa Rundle actually had an address on Lawrence Welk Drive in Escondido.

"So I had a contact there . . . with the San Diego Police Department," Huggins said. "He actually drove out there to see if we could locate her. We were looking for any family members of William . . . [and] the cop called me back and said that Willa no longer lived there. He was told that Willa had moved back to Las Vegas with her son Bill.

"I asked Magda about it," Huggins recalled. "I said, 'You know, where's Willa?', and she told me that she was in Austria traveling, and that she had lived with Shirley and Bill, but now she was traveling."

Prosecutor Owens asked the detective what other steps she'd taken to locate Willa.

"[We] contacted the FBI and the State Department," Huggins said. "We were looking for passport information. I felt she needed a passport to go to Austria. There was absolutely no passport information. We were at a dead end trying to find her. We had no idea where she was. I even talked to some neighbors about [Rundle's] mother, wondering if they knew where she was and where she could be located."

"Did you look to see if there was a death certificate?" Owens asked.

"I never found a death certificate," Huggins said.

"Did you find anybody that had seen or talked to Willa Rundle after, say, May of 1997?" the prosecutor asked.

"No," Huggins responded.

With Owens's help, Huggins marked out what the prosecutor called "the odyssey of Mr. Rundle" by having the detective mark on a map the places where Rundle had traveled after the death of his wife. They included Reno, Seattle, Mount Rushmore, and Disney World. Huggins told the jury about seeking the media's help in tracking Rundle down.

"There was quite a large [media] following here locally because of the tragedy that had happened to Bill and Shirley Rundle earlier," Huggins said. "I'm speaking of the death of Richie Rundle. So, there was quite a lot of coverage here. I actually wanted to get the media to help me as far as, like, the car, and the plate, and the description of Bill Rundle.

"After I obtained a warrant for him, I wanted anybody that had seen him to notify police no matter where he was, so I actually let the national media cover it as well, hoping that someone would see him and call," Huggins said.

Huggins then talked to the jury about Rundle's apprehension in Orlando and the taped statement he gave to detectives at the Seminole County Jail. She warned the jury that if she sounded friendly to Rundle during the interview, it was because she wanted him to relax and talk.

"You try to use a little bit of sympathy or [em]pathy at least," Huggins said. "I want him to talk to me, and not block me out. If I'm mean to him, or act like I'm disgusted, or that what he's telling me is shocking me, he's not going to tell me the story. He's not going to open up like I want him to."

Rundle's taped statement was played for the jury, and it was a damning moment for Bill Rundle. Rundle spoke clearly on the recordings about beating his wife to death. He at first said he only hit his wife once, but in his second statement, he admitted to taking a "full bat swing" on Shirley.

"*She hit me everywhere,*" Rundle said on the tape. "*As many places as she possibly could. And then, she would threaten me that she would kill me during my sleep and this and that. So, I couldn't get her to stop.*

"*I went into the closet,*" Rundle said." *I took out a baseball bat and I hit her once.*"

"With the baseball bat?" Huggins's voice asks.

"*Yes,*" Rundle said. "*With the baseball bat . . . She fell into the chair when I hit her. Blood was coming out of her . . .*"

During Magda Belen and Detective Huggins's testimonies, defense attorneys entered into evidence a staggering number of credit card purchase receipts and billing statements that showed Shirley Rundle was charging a lot of money onto credit cards. There were at least fifty different receipts alone from high-end department stores like Dillard's. Also entered into evidence by prosecutors were Bill

Rundle's gambling statements, and copies of all the checks Bill Rundle had cashed while spending his mother's money.

The profligate spending didn't look good for either Bill or Shirley Rundle. But Defense Attorney Chris Brown sensed the momentum in the courtroom changing when Rundle's statements to detectives were played. He figured it likely that the jury found Rundle's comments to be uncaring and callous.

"It got worse for us when the statements were played," Brown said. "Some of the points he makes in the statements are accurate and true, but there is a matter-of-factness and callousness about the way he is talking. He's constantly sniveling through the whole thing, and the jury was probably like, 'Where's his remorse?' He was still angry."

Rundle's prospects for a manslaughter verdict in Judge Cherry's courtroom became even slimmer when prosecutors called Dr. Gary Steven Marrone to the witness stand, and the doctor offered his opinion about the circumstances in which Rundle had broken his arm. There was no way his arm had been broken by Shirley Rundle wielding a champagne bottle, and it seemed Rundle was caught in another lie.

The prosecutors suspected it was possible that Rundle broke his arm while carrying Shirley's body, and following the doctor's testimony, the defense attorneys and prosecutors started talking about a plea deal. Owens offered a unique plea deal: He would drop the death penalty, but Rundle had to plead guilty to first-degree murder in Shirley's death. He also had to enter a no contest plea to the death of his mother, Willa. A no contest plea is not a formal admission of guilt. It involves, instead, the defendant acknowledging that a guilty verdict is likely.

Finally, Owens demanded that Rundle agree to a life sentence without parole. Bill Rundle could take the plea deal and agree to die in prison, or he could take his chances with the jury and risk getting a death sentence. With the evidence mounting against him and one of the most powerful prosecutors in Nevada, David Schwartz, waiting in the bullpen for closing arguments and a death penalty hearing, Rundle took the deal. He pleaded guilty to his wife's murder, he pleaded no contest to his mother's murder, and he accepted the sentence of life in prison without parole.

"I deserve to go to prison," Rundle said. "I deserve what I get."

At a September 12, 2003, sentencing hearing, Rundle apologized to the Belens and the court, but he refused to tell Judge Cherry where his mother's body was.

"I came clean, Your Honor," Rundle said.

The whereabouts of Willa Rundle's body and the details of what really happened to her are a mystery to this day.

During the September hearing, Cherry sentenced Rundle to life in prison without the possibility of parole. Cherry had no reservations about levying the sentence given the cruelty unleashed by the defendant upon his wife. The judge also recognized that at Rundle's age, fifty-eight, there would have been little difference between a sentence of life with parole versus life without.

"He's going to die in prison," Cherry said.

Sitting in the back of Cherry's courtroom and listening to the judge's remarks was Bill Rundle's second wife, Sherri Grayson, whom Rundle had abandoned while she was pregnant nearly three decades earlier. He'd walked all over her, and he'd caused her immense pain. She said she was glad, in retrospect, that Rundle did not remain in her life, and that her daughter never knew her father.

"At least Las Vegas knows now that he was not Father of the Year," Grayson told the author in an interview after the sentencing. "He was never Father of the Year.

"For thirty years, I wanted something bad to happen to this guy," she told the *Las Vegas Review-Journal*. "Supposedly, he can't gamble or drink [in prison.] Those are the two things he loved to do."

For Sarah Reitig, Rundle's first wife, the news that her ex-husband was a convicted murderer was both disturbing and heartbreaking.

"When I first heard about it, I just shut it off, and I was cold," Reitig said. "But now I think it is so sad. It's just so horrible because he had so many advantages. Willa and [Richard] were really good to him, yet he had this vein of not telling the truth. What a waste of somebody's life. I think it's tragic. I do feel sorry for him, because he was good at what he did, which was lying. You really thought you were talking to the most charming person on the face of the Earth."

22 ... PRISON

Bill Rundle currently has a pretty miserable existence. He's locked in prison for the rest of his life, and he knows he'll never get out. He was sent to the maximum security Nevada State Prison in Ely, a dismal place of concrete and bars with the occasional view of the harsh plains of the Nevada desert out of a small vertical slit of a window.

Rundle will never walk as a free man again. He'll never see the little girl he still thinks of as his granddaughter, he'll never get to place a bet in a sports book, and he'll never drink another ice-cold beer. He acknowledges that his wife Shirley, whom he beat to death with a baseball bat, was a good person who never deserved what he did to her.

"The best memory I have of Shirley was her kindness to Richie," Rundle said. "Lots of people told me it was just an act to get me to marry her. I know different. You can't fake the type of love that she showed my son. She was truly a great mom to Magda and Richie, and a super-good grandmother to Gretchen.

"She just wasn't a good wife," he rationalized. "But, again, that was my fault for not leaving the marriage shortly after Richie died."

In prison, Rundle is surrounded by some of the most violent criminals in the state, and he's handcuffed at the hands and feet if he goes anywhere.

"It's like being in solitary on death row," Rundle said.

Rundle does have some things to look forward to. Sometimes, he receives magazine subscriptions or other gifts from people on the outside. Al Fitzgerald, the bailiff during Rundle's pretrial hearings, once sent a magazine subscription to Rundle, but it came back in the mail.

"I wrote to him after the trial, and we kept in touch," Fitzgerald said. "I got him a subscription to a magazine or something—*ESPN The Magazine*—which I do for a number of [convicts]. For some reason it came back in the mail. I'm assuming he was trying to cut all ties and move forward."

Rundle listens to baseball games on the radio at night. He sometimes gets to watch sports on television with other inmates, but the *Dateline* special on his murder case was broadcast in the prison, and it was not a big hit with the other prisoners.

"It was not that I killed my wife—it was that I was a security guard," Rundle said. "That was the big issue with the inmates—that I was an officer for as long as I was, and the inmates thought that I would turn them in if I heard anything. Several guys told me, 'Watch your back when you go to chow. Be careful.' But I had another friend who went to the guy in charge, and he asked him to leave me alone. He told the guy that everybody has to have a job, and he told him I wasn't a cop. I was a security guard in the [casino], protecting the clientele.

"You can't be touched unless somebody says so," Rundle said. "I never knew what prison politics were about, but I know you don't get involved in them. There are people who run this prison, and they are inmates. If they want someone killed, they kill them. They get some of these kids to do it for them."

In a July 2008 letter to the author, Rundle revealed he'd been transferred to the Nevada State Prison in Carson City. The prison, commonly referred to as NSP, is a little more forgiving than the maximum security prison at Ely, but he'll still serve hard time. He wrote about his daily existence in the letter:

"I received my transfer to Nevada State Prison . . . [and] the only bad [thing] about NSP is that the prison is not air-conditioned, and it is hell here during the summer," Rundle wrote. "I have been in the prison system since January 2004 and I have never had a write-up for anything. I can't work because of my health, I can't take classes because I already have an education.

"Prison life . . . has changed my life," Rundle wrote. "Ely was a terrible place for anyone to have to go. All of the friends I had from my years in Las Vegas deserted me except for two. I still keep in touch with them. Prison is tough on any 56-year-old first timer, but Ely was really tough. They did not need to send me there, but [the prosecutor] Owens insisted on it.

"If you don't have money [here], you are fucked," Rundle wrote. "I have never been approached by a homosexual, and although it does exist, to some extent it is way over exaggerated.

"The two worst things you can be in prison are a child molester, known as a chomo, or a rat," Rundle stated. "In prison, you don't tell on anyone. If you witness a beating or even a murder, you say nothing to no one—no exceptions. Once the other inmates know that you will keep quiet, you are relatively safe. Chomos and rats are not safe anywhere."

Rundle said he regrets killing Shirley. He thinks about it every day, and he said he feels incredible guilt over the pain he's caused Magda, Rodel, and their daughter.

But he still maintained his version of the fateful events. "Every day, I think back to that terrible night in August of 2002 when Shirley and I had that horrible fight. I was guilty of killing her, but not of what [the prosecutor] Chris Owens tried me for. I never denied I did it, and confessed I did it, and I should have been sentenced for second-degree murder at the most."

He doesn't regret taking his plea deal because he said he deserved to go to prison, but he continues to insist that he doesn't know where his mother is.

"No one knows how much I've done," Rundle said. "How many lies I told. How many lives I've ruined. If people forgive me, that's fine. If they don't forgive me, that's fine, too."

Rundle said he's become devoutly religious since his incarceration, and he's confessed his sins to Jesus. But although Rundle writes that "I know I've been forgiven for my sins by God," he also says that his "conscience will never be clear."

"I'm going to die in prison," Rundle said. "There is no question about it. There is no reason to fight to get the sentence overturned. I pray for Shirley every night. I have a twenty-five-minute prayer every night for everyone I've hurt.

"I pray every day that Gretchen will someday forgive me for taking the life of her grandmother. They were close.

"So many inmates wait to find religion until they are in prison, and pray to God that he will watch over them, and keep them safe," Rundle said. "I do believe in Jesus Christ, and I do believe that God has forgiven me for my sins, and that my soul will rest in eternal peace. This belief keeps me going. Currently, I am living in hell, but one day I will graduate.

"My religion is my own," Rundle said. "I have salvation."

ABOUT THE AUTHOR

Glenn Puit is an investigative journalist and policy specialist for the Michigan Land Use Institute in Traverse City, Michigan. He performs investigative journalism that seeks to protect Michigan's natural environment.

Puit was born and raised in Lansing, in Upstate New York, and he graduated from Indiana State University with a bachelor's degree in journalism communications. He covered the Las Vegas criminal justice system and violent crime in Las Vegas for twelve years in his work as an investigative reporter for the *Las Vegas Review-Journal* newspaper. While at the *Florence Morning News* newspaper in Florence, South Carolina, Puit was the first reporter in the nation to document the identity of John Doe #2 in the Oklahoma City bombing. The accomplishment was featured in *American Journalism Review*.

His first book, *Witch: The True Story of Las Vegas's Most Notorious Female Killer*, about the bizarre and gruesome case of matriarchal Vegas killer Brookey Lee West, was released by Berkley Books to national acclaim in

2005. The book was recently the subject of a literary section cover feature story in the *San Jose Mercury News*. His second book, *Fire in the Desert* (Stephens Press, 2007), is considered the evidentiary handbook for the Las Vegas homicide case of national bodybuilder Craig Titus and his fitness champion wife, Kelly Ryan.

Puit lives on the shoreline of Lake Superior in Michigan's Upper Peninsula with his wife and three children.

He maintains a webpage where he chats regularly with fans about his books: www.myspace.com/kingoftruecrime.